POCAHONTAS AND THE ENGLISH BOYS

POCAHONTAS

and the

ENGLISH BOYS

CAUGHT BETWEEN CULTURES

in

EARLY VIRGINIA

KAREN ORDAHL KUPPERMAN

NEW YORK UNIVERSITY PRESS
New York

NEW YORK UNIVERSITY PRESS
New York
www.nyupress.org
© 2019 by New York University
All rights reserved

Library of Congress Cataloging-in-Publication Data
Names: Kupperman, Karen Ordahl, 1939– author.
Title: Pocahontas and the English Boys :
Caught between Cultures in Early Virginia / Karen Ordahl Kupperman.
Description: New York : New York University Press, 2019. |
Includes bibliographical references and index.
Identifiers: LCCN 2018037666 | ISBN 9781479825820 (cl : alk. paper)
Subjects: LCSH: Pocahontas, –1617. | Savage, Thomas, –1635. |
Spelman, Henry, 1595–1623. | Poole, Robert, active 17th century. |
Virginia—History—Colonial period, ca. 1600–1775—Biography. |
Powhatan Indians—History.
Classification: LCC F229 .K88 2019 | DDC 975.501092/2 [B] —dc23
LC record available at https://lccn.loc.gov/2018037666

CONTENTS

[v]

NOTES ON SOURCES AND ON TERMINOLOGY

NOTE ON SOURCES

THE STORY OF POCAHONTAS, THOMAS SAVAGE, HENRY SPELMAN, AND ROBERT POOLE has to be pieced together from many disparate, and spotty, sources. For one thing, we have no Native of the Americas speaking or writing in her or his own voice. Sometimes the English sources quote Powhatans, Patawomecks, or Accomacs, but we have to assume those renditions may have been poorly understood and were often tailored to suit the impression that the English author wanted to create.

Henry Spelman, one of this book's subjects, was the only person who wrote out of his own extensive personal experience of life among the Chesapeake Algonquians and who had knowledge of at least two American languages. His memoir was not published until the nineteenth century; but many people interested in America had seen it, and some quoted from it.[1]

The English sources consist broadly of the following general categories. One is Englishmen who made a business of collecting travel accounts. The first, a clergyman named Richard Hakluyt the younger, was inspired by his cousin, also named Richard Hakluyt. Hakluyt the elder was a lawyer with many friends among London scholars who were interested in cosmology. The younger Hakluyt began collecting notes from sailors and other adventurers while he was a student at Oxford in the 1570s. His first work about exploration, *Divers Voyages Touching the Discoverie of America, and the Ilands Adiacent*, was published in 1582. Hakluyt went on to publish massive collections of travel narratives: *The Principall Navigations, Voiages, Traffiques, and Discoveries of the English Nation* in 1589 and updated as *The Principal Navigations Voyages, Traffiques, and Discoveries of the English Nation* in 1598–1600. Hakluyt sometimes interviewed returning voyagers in order to get the most complete accounts.

Richard Hakluyt died in 1616, while Pocahontas was in London, but early in the seventeenth century, he quit publishing travel accounts and turned his manuscripts over to the man who is considered his successor, Samuel Purchas. Purchas was the minister at St. Martin's Ludgate, which was a near neighbor to the Belle Sauvage Inn, where Pocahontas and her entourage were lodged. Purchas continued Hakluyt's methods of thoroughness in searching out accounts, and his volumes included pieces from sources, including Spelman's, that were not published until the nineteenth century. His first collection, published in 1613, was titled *Purchas His Pilgrimage*, and several more editions followed. Then, in 1625, he published his major collection, *Hakluytus Posthumus, or, Purchas His Pilgrimes*, which extends to twenty volumes in its modern edition, and it includes all the reports he could gather from the Jamestown colony.

Two men who spent time in Virginia also created collections of experiences in the colony. Capt. John Smith went with the original ships and stayed in the colony just over two years. From 1610 forward, with the exception of a brief reconnoitering trip to New England, he carved out a career as a writer and theorist of colonization. As he reminded his readers, "I am no Compiler by hearsay, but have been a real Actor."[2] Unlike Hakluyt and Purchas, he wove the reports he collected into a coherent narrative, and he named his sources, usually people still in America, at the end of each section. His first several books were about Virginia, and he then turned his attention to New England. He invented the name "New England" to support his argument that that region was more suitable to English bodies than Virginia was. In 1624, he published his grand history of all the colonies, and he argued strongly for a plan in which ordinary English men and women could have land of their own and a degree of self-government. During his decades as a literary man in London, he formed connections with many people who were influential in cultural and colonization circles.

William Strachey also formed the fruits of his own observations and the reports of others into a coherent description of Virginia. He was in the flagship wrecked on Bermuda in 1609, so he spent his first year in America there. He arrived with the others from Bermuda in spring 1610 and returned to England in late 1611. Although his *Historie of Travell into Virginia Britania* was not published until the nineteenth century, many people had access to the manuscript, and it offers an unparalleled compilation for modern readers.

Another important source is letters written by colonists, many of which were published by the Virginia Company once they had arrived in London. Those that were not published presented views or information that the company did not want to get around.

The final important source of information is official reports and records of meetings of the governor and council in Virginia. These, of course, present a version of the facts that the colonial government wanted the sponsoring company in London to believe, but the testimony presented by individuals gives modern readers insights into where people were, what they were doing, and how they related to other colonists. Susan Myra Kingsbury spent countless hours transcribing the records, and her transcriptions were published by the U.S. Government Printing Office in four volumes between 1906 and 1933. More recently, David Ransome has discovered and transcribed many other papers that are part of the Virginia Company archive, and these are available online as *Virginia Company Archives: The Ferrar Papers FP 1–FP 2314, Ferrar Print 1-562, 1590–1790*, published by Adam Matthew Digital.

Recent archaeology is a new source of understanding about early seventeenth-century Virginia. The team led by William M. Kelso has uncovered the original settlement and much about the life of the people within it, and the Werowocomoco Research Group, under the direction of Martin Gallivan, has revealed the homes and lifeways of the Powhatans in their capital city. Archaeological findings can change the way we read the colonists' accounts. One simple example concerns a statement that the paramount chief Powhatan made to Capt.

John Smith: "Captain Smith, you may understand that I have seen the death of all my people thrice." Once scholars understood the impact of European diseases in the early colonies, we assumed that Powhatan was talking about three huge epidemics. But archaeologists have not found the kinds of mass burials common after such epidemics, so we now think Powhatan was saying that he was an old man and that he had seen three generations pass away. In many ways, archaeology has made us reread the early documents with new understanding.[3]

Finally, it is important to say that none of the engravings reproduced in this book were created by artists who had actually been to America and had seen the scenes they depicted at first hand. The only images we have from early English colonization were paintings made by John White of the first Roanoke colony. Sir Walter Ralegh, the colony's sponsor, sent him and the young scientist Thomas Harriot to create a natural history of the region's land and people. White's paintings were rendered as engravings in the workshop of the German publisher Theodor de Bry, and they were reused many times to illustrate works on Virginia and other places.

Spellings in quotations have been modernized, but punctuation has been preserved as in the original.

NOTE ON TERMINOLOGY

One of the problems facing everyone who writes about the time of first contact and European settlement in North America is what name to use for America's Native people. Both "Native American" and "Indian" are European impositions, and we need to use terms that the people would have used themselves. Using tribal names where possible is the best practice. But how do we write about Native people in general?

Before the Europeans came, Natives referred to themselves as "The People." When the need to distinguish between Europeans and Natives became pressing, many began to adopt the imported term "Indian." The

National Museum of the American Indian answers the question "What is the correct terminology: American Indian, Indian, Native American, or Native?" in this way: "All of these terms are acceptable. The consensus, however, is that whenever possible, Native people prefer to be called by their specific tribal name. In the United States, *Native American* has been widely used but is falling out of favor with some groups, and the terms *American Indian* or *indigenous American* are preferred by many Native people."[4]

The Virginia Council on Indians created *A Guide to Writing about Virginia Indians and Virginia Indian History* in 2006. This guide contains wide-ranging information on how to describe the civic culture of the various Virginia tribes and the people within those populations.[5]

Another category that writers use is language groupings. Just as French, Italian, and Spanish are all Romance languages, meaning that they share a root language in Roman Latin, so the people along North America's east coast spoke languages belonging to the Algonquian family, with some Iroquoian speakers in eastern North Carolina and slightly to the north and west of Jamestown. Beyond the fall line in Virginia, there were tribes who spoke languages of the Siouan group. The people in New England and in the Chesapeake whom the English first met all spoke Algonquian languages. But when we refer to Algonquians, we do not mean a political group, only a degree of shared culture.

INTRODUCTION

THIRTEEN-YEAR-OLD THOMAS SAVAGE arrived in Jamestown in January 1608. Before Thomas had even had a chance to settle in, the fleet's admiral, Capt. Christopher Newport, gave him to Wahunsenaca, who ruled over most of the tribes in the English colony's vicinity. In turn, Newport received a boy named Namontack. Living in Werowocomoco, Wahunsenaca's capital, Thomas met Pocahontas, who was ten or eleven, and she could help Thomas adjust to life with her people. Pocahontas had participated in a ceremony involving Capt. John Smith, who had been brought to Werowocomoco as a captive not long after the colony's founding in 1607, and she came to Jamestown accompanying official embassies.[1] Smith wrote that she was "a child of ten years old" and that not only was she the most beautiful of Powhatan's people "but for wit, and spirit the only Nonpareil of his Country." Smith demonstrated his sophistication in using a word borrowed from French, and he meant that no one equaled Pocahontas for her intelligence and personality.[2] She was certainly curious about the English and their lives and apparently liked coming to Jamestown, but she was not just a casual visitor. She actually played a very significant role. Pocahontas always came with a small party of her father's men, and her presence signaled their peaceful designs. A female presence was a well-established sign of benign intentions in Native missions.[3]

As the paramount chief in the region, Wahunsenaca ruled over and protected more than thirty client tribes along the rivers that feed into Chesapeake Bay. The name of the land that the English called Virginia was Tsenacomoca. Jamestown was on the James River,

A cheiff Ladye of Pomeiooc. VIII.

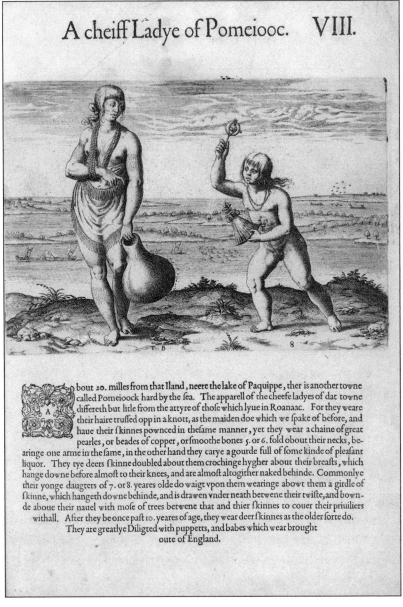

About 20. milles from that Iland, neere the lake of Paquippe, ther is another towne called Pomeioock hard by the sea. The apparell of the cheefe ladyes of dat towne differeth but litle from the attyre of thofe which lyue in Roanaac. For they weare their haire truffed opp in a knott, as the maiden doe which we fpake of before, and haue their fkinnes pownced in thefame manner, yet they wear a chaine of great pearles, or beades of copper, or fmoothe bones 5. or 6. fold obout their necks, bearinge one arme in the fame, in the other hand they carye a gourde full of fome kinde of pleafant liquor. They tye deers fkinne doubled about them crochinge hygher about their breafts, which hange downe before almoft to their knees, and are almoft altogither naked behinde. Commonlye their yonge daugters of 7. or 8. yeares olde do waigt vpon them wearinge abowt them a girdle of fkinne, which hangeth downe behinde, and is drawen vnder neath betwene their twifte, and bownde aboue their nauel with mofe of trees betwene that and thier fkinnes to couer their priuiliers withall. After they be once paft 10. yeares of age, they wear deer fkinnes as the older forte do. They are greatlye Diligted with puppetts, and babes which wear brought oute of England.

A ten-year-old Roanoke girl and her mother. Engraving by the workshop of Theodor de Bry from a painting by John White. Courtesy of the John Carter Brown Library at Brown University.

and Werowocomoco was on the York River just north of the James. Wahunsenaca was a Pamunkey. Because he ruled over many tribes, the English referred to him as "king" or "emperor," and "The Powhatan" was his title. All the people over whom he ruled were known collectively as "the Powhatans," and the English called him "Powhatan." All the tribes that he ruled spoke Algonquian languages.

Youths, both Native and English, were absolutely essential in these new transatlantic relationships. Four boys, including one named Samuel Collier, sailed in the very first fleet.[4] One of the four ran away early on, and the chief of the Paspaheghs, who lived just northwest of Jamestown, returned him.[5] But later in 1608, the same year Newport left Thomas with Powhatan, Capt. John Smith left Samuel with the chief of the Weraskoyacks, who lived east of Jamestown on the same river.[6] Fourteen-year-old Henry Spelman came the next year, and Smith gave Henry to Parahunt, the Powhatan's son, a few weeks after his arrival. Parahunt ruled over the town of Powhatan, the paramount chief's birthplace, farther inland on the James River near modern Richmond.

The records tell us nothing about Samuel's or Thomas's origins or about who decided that they should go to America. Richard Savage sailed on the same ship as Thomas Savage, so Thomas may have traveled with his father or brother. We do know about Henry Spelman's family, partly because he wrote about his experiences but also because he had very prominent relatives. His uncle Sir Henry Spelman had been a member of Parliament and was the sheriff of Norfolk and a founder of the Society of Antiquaries, an elite group of historians. Robert Poole arrived in Jamestown in May 1611, and he traveled with his father, also named Robert, and brother John. They were on the *Starr* with the new governor, Sir Thomas Dale, and the Reverend Alexander Whitaker. Robert was sent to live with Opechancanough, the Powhatan's kinsman, in 1614.[7]

Why were so many boys on the ships, and why did colonial leaders just dump them with Native people they hardly knew? Part of the answer lies in English theories of child rearing. As English kids entered their teens, they entered a transitional stage of life. Most writers termed this stage "youth," but it was also called "nonage" and sometimes "adolescence." Youth lasted until girls and boys reached adulthood, which some writers put well into their twenties.

English parents relinquished control over their children as they entered nonage, perhaps because parents did not consider themselves able to exert the strict discipline required to shape their sons and daughters in this "dark and dangerous" stage of life.[8] The solution for most families was putting sons and daughters into servitude, where good masters or mistresses would exercise a kind of parental control but without the sentimental attachments a true parent might feel. In seventeenth-century England, most boys and girls were servants in another family's home by the time they were thirteen or fourteen. Even families that could afford servants sent their own children into servitude. Fortunate children would have learned some basic skills—reading, writing, maybe arithmetic—at their village school. Many remained illiterate.[9]

For a few youths, servitude meant going abroad. Some signed on as soldiers in the European wars. All of Jamestown's leaders had been educated in what the colonial official John Pory called the "university of war" in the conflicts between Roman Catholics and Protestants in Europe.[10] Others went to sea. Ship's boys were a standard part of the crew in this new ocean world, so no one would have been surprised to see boys aboard. After all, there were four boys in the first Jamestown fleet. Most of the Virginia-bound youths remained within the fort or its environs and worked as servants; relatively few were placed with Native leaders. All the boys on the ships had experienced the pain of separation from their families, and they lived with the knowledge that they might never see friends and family again.

The Powhatans had very different ways of incorporating young teenagers into their societies as they emerged from childhood. Powhatan boys of thirteen or fourteen went through a long and elaborate ritual called the Huskenaw, which marked the end of their childhood and prepared them to take up adult roles. Early English accounts described the Huskenaw as human sacrifice. Henry reported that the Powhatans' gods demanded a sacrifice of children in this religious ceremony, which was held deep in the forest. The men gathered in a circle around a fire built by the priests. As the ceremony progressed, a voice came out of the fire indicating the sacrifice that the gods required. Henry made a mistake when he wrote that the boys were ritually sacrificed. Reports such as Henry's fed the notion that the Chesapeake Algonquians were savage, but later English observers corrected the early reports when they found out that those who were supposedly sacrificed were alive years later.[11]

The true story was that boys who were ready for adulthood went into the woods for a long ordeal that marked the transition. As part of the ceremony, they consumed a drink, probably Jimsonweed, that made them appear temporarily insane. The English had been misled by the mothers weeping as the children were taken away. They wept, it turned out, for the loss of close ties with their children, who were now becoming men and would no longer stay with their mothers.[12] Girls also took up adult roles as they entered their teen years. Girls joined the women as the agriculturalists of their society, and boys joined the men as hunters, fishermen, and warriors.

Powhatan youths entered adult life, but English adolescents were neither children nor adults. Because people in their nonage were not yet fully formed, they were flexible and full of possibilities. As Lafeu in Shakespeare's play *Alls Well That Ends Well* remarked, youths are "unbaked and doughy." Sir William Vaughan put it this way: "youth is like unto moist and soft clay."[13] The boys' doughiness made them more capable of adjusting to new circumstances and more able to learn new languages, and their youth made them less threatening. Therefore, they were the ideal colonists to be placed with Natives throughout Tsenacomacah.

Most of the boys on the ships quickly disappeared from the records; some died, but most were not doing anything that officials saw as important enough to record. But Thomas, Henry, and Robert played crucial roles. The boys soon came to understand how important their knowledge was and what a strong position it gave them. And because of the way they were treated, they came to like and respect the Native people they lived with.

Pocahontas, Thomas, Henry, and Robert spent the rest of their lives caught between cultures. They were the only people who could understand the goals of the Chesapeake Algonquians as well as the English, and they often faced hard choices. They knew they were being used by both sides, but they also cared about the outcomes. As tensions between the colonists and the people on whom they had intruded erupted into conflict, the go-betweens' very lives were sometimes at risk. Because they were so young, they had little control over what happened to them and to everyone involved, but they understood the stakes better than anyone.

The conflicted loyalties faced by Pocahontas, Thomas, Henry, and Robert are exemplified by the experiences of a Paspahegh boy named Paquiquineo, who was taken by a Spanish vessel on the Carolina coast in 1561. Paquiquineo lived with the Spanish for a decade—he lived in Havana, in Mexico City, and in Spain—and they treated him as a prince. He was baptized in Mexico City, and the Spanish named him Don Luís de Velasco after the viceroy of New Spain, who became his godfather.

In 1571, Paquiquineo was finally brought back to Virginia. He accompanied a small party of Jesuits who intended to found a mission on the York River, Werowocomoco's river. The Jesuits' goal was to begin the great work of converting all the American Natives to Christianity. They were so certain that Don Luís was completely converted to their faith that they refused to take any soldiers for protection. Their convert was all the protection they needed. But once Paquiquineo was back in his home territory, he was torn between his two loyalties. He returned to his own people, but he did come back and ask the priests to baptize his young brother, who was very sick, showing how much he valued Christianity. The priests, frustrated in their efforts to begin the mission, kept sending messengers to Paspahegh to urge Paquiquineo to come back to them. Ultimately he dealt with the intolerable pressure to make a choice by leading a war party that wiped out the mission. Only one of the Spanish was left alive: a boy named Alonso de Olmos. Paquiquineo asked Alonso to show the Paspaheghs how to bury the priests properly in their own chapel, so he continued to honor their religious commitment even though he felt compelled to shun them and stay with his own traditions. Alonso lived with the Paspaheghs for two years until a Spanish war party rescued him.[14]

A surprising number of boys and girls were forced to live in multiple cultures as Europeans, Americans, and Africans turned their attention toward the Atlantic in the sixteenth and seventeenth centuries. Leaving youths, usually boys, with Native communities was standard practice for Europeans. Pedro Álvarez Cabral's fleet, which landed on the coast of Brazil in 1500, carried twenty young men who had been released from prison with the expectation that they would be left with Native people wherever the ships landed. The Portuguese left two of these *degredados* behind when the fleet departed from Brazil, despite the Brazilians' clear indication that they did not welcome the newcomers. A second expedition to Brazil two years later, including Amerigo Vespucci, found at least one of the youths. The recovered *degredado* translated for the Portuguese and returned with them to Portugal, where his knowledge was a precious commodity.[15]

A few decades later, in 1554, English venturers left fifteen-year-old Martin Frobisher as a hostage as they attempted to initiate trade with an African king at Shamma on Africa's west coast. When Portuguese ships threatened the English, they fled, leaving Frobisher behind. He was held by the Portuguese in their fort at Mina and later in Portugal but was allowed to return to England after about four years. Two decades later, in the 1570s, he led three major expeditions seeking a sea passage through northern North America to Asia; his ships brought back what they considered to be rich gold ore, but it turned out to be worthless rock. His expeditions also brought several Inuit people to England, including a mother and her baby.[16]

In the 1560s, when a French Protestant colony on the Carolina coast departed in a hurry under threat from a Spanish fleet, fifteen-year-old Guillaume Rouffin elected to stay behind because he thought the colonial leaders lacked the skill to cross the ocean. Guillaume then lived with the Guales for two years before he was discovered by Spanish agents and taken to Florida. As Guillermo, he became the principal interpreter for the Spanish in Florida.[17]

Around the world, children were employed in different types of exchanges. Portuguese Jesuits working in Asia arranged to send four Japanese boys, all thirteen or fourteen years old, on an embassy to Europe, where they were received by the Spanish king Philip II and two popes. They set out in 1582, and their voyage spanned more than eight years.[18]

As the Atlantic opened to myriad enterprises, it became a scene of self-invention. All kinds of actors were thrust into situations in which they had to make up new kinds of roles for themselves because their expectations were thwarted and survival required adaptation. Guillaume Rouffin began his American experience as a French boy who became a Guale and then a Spaniard. If someone had woken him up in the middle of the night and asked him who he was, how would he have replied? Would it depend on who was asking? Loyalty and identity were fluid, not absolute, in this new Atlantic world. If you did not adapt to whatever conditions you faced, you did not survive.

Some of the most dramatic cases of forced fluidity in the early English Atlantic are ones we know the least about: the various sets of lost Roanoke colonists. And these involve English, Native, and African characters. Sir Walter Ralegh, who had been given a patent to colonize North America's east coast by Queen Elizabeth, sent a reconnoitering voyage in 1584 to look at the land and select a good site. That party returned with a site, Roanoke Island within the North Carolina Outer

Banks, and two young coastal Carolina Algonquians, Manteo and Wanchese. Over the winter of 1584–85, the two Americans worked with Thomas Harriot, a young recent Oxford grad. Manteo and Wanchese taught Harriot their language, and he taught them English.[19]

All three were with the first colony that went in 1585; Manteo stayed with the English, but Wanchese, like Paquiquineo before him, immediately left them to return to his own people. This colony, like Jamestown, consisted of young men in a military regime. When Sir Francis Drake arrived with reinforcements that his fleet had collected in attacks around the Caribbean and on the coast of Florida in 1586, he found the colony in very bad shape and frightened of the Native Roanokes, whose chief they had killed, cutting off his head and mounting it on a pole. According to the reports, Drake had collected some three hundred Caribbean Natives and enslaved Africans, including Muslims from North Africa. Drake promised the colony's leader, Capt. Ralph Lane, one of his ships for exploration in search of a better site for his people, but all plans were scuttled by a massive storm that sank many of Drake's ships. Everyone who survived the storm, including the colonists, piled onto the remaining ships and returned to England, and Manteo elected to accompany them back to England. No one mentioned the people Drake had seized in the Caribbean; some probably died in the sunken ships, but the rest presumably were left behind and joined the Carolina Algonquians. Had Drake taken them to England, their arrival would have made a great stir, and no one mentioned it.[20] Sir Richard Grenville arrived soon after the colonists departed with Drake, bringing new supplies from England. When he found the site deserted, he left fifteen men to hold the site.

Ralegh did not give up. The next year, he completely revamped his plan and decided to send families that were promised land, the kind of plan that would eventually be seen as the successful model. Manteo returned with this colony, but Harriot did not; and the new colonists did not see any of the people left behind in 1586. Ralegh left the colonists on their own for three years because events in England, including the threat of the Spanish Armada in 1588, had made it impossible or inconvenient to send supply ships. When a ship finally did get through, the sailors found the site abandoned, and no English person ever saw the colonists again.

What had happened to these all these Roanoke colonists? The best guess is that they split up and joined Native communities that would accept them. Manteo's role in helping the English families gain acceptance and make the transition must have been crucial. If this scenario is correct, they lived out the rest of their lives as American Natives and adopted wholly new identities.[21] On the Jamestown colonists' very first exploration "up the river," George Percy saw "a Savage Boy about the age of ten years, which had a head of hair of a perfect yellow and a reasonable white skin."[22] How much better Jamestown's early years would have been if they had been able to learn from surviving Roanoke colonists, but the colonists did not then have the linguistic skills to question the boy and his companions. This was the deficiency that Thomas, Henry, and Robert were supposed to rectify.

Ralegh soon turned his attention to what he considered better prospects, and this time he took personal charge. Ralegh conducted an expedition to Guiana on the South American mainland bordering on the Caribbean in search of the fabled golden city of El Dorado in 1595. Ralegh and the Native leaders exchanged boys. Topiawari, "the lord of Aromaia . . . freely gave me his only son to take with me into England . . . and I left with him one Francis Sparrow . . . (who was willing to tarry and could describe a country with his pen) and a boy of mine called Hugh Goodwyn to learn the language."[23]

Many young actors benefited from their own self-invention and their flexible identities. Several were in Jamestown from the beginning. William White, identified in the records as a laborer who was said to have "lived with the Natives," gave testimony about the daily life and religious observances of his hosts. He was among the first to describe the Huskenaw as an actual sacrifice. George Percy, an "honorable gentleman" among the original colonists, conveyed some of White's knowledge in his *Observations Gathered out of a Discourse of the Plantation of the Southerne Colonie in Virginia by the English, 1606.* In the margin next to White's name, it says, "He was a made man," which meant that his success was assured.[24]

A young Irish sailor, Francis Magnel or Maguel, came in the first ships and was in Jamestown for much of the first year. By 1610, he was in Spain and was interviewed by the archbishop of Tuam, who forwarded his information to the royal court. Magnel described Virginia in the most glowing terms: precious metals, pearls, wine, furs, and the promise of silk and diamonds just to the west. He mentioned the boys who had been sent to live with the Natives and said that many of them already knew the language "perfectly." Most important, he said that the English aimed to be "lords of the South Sea" (the Pacific Ocean), which the Powhatans assured them could be reached easily by a series of rivers. He certainly was now a made man, as he received a grant from the Spanish king Phillip III in September of that year.[25]

Capt. John Smith, early Jamestown's most important leader, is an example of highly successful self-invention. Smith went to fight in the religious wars between Roman Catholics and Protestants in Europe at the age of sixteen, but, as he put it, he quickly tired of seeing Christians slaughter each other. So he decided to serve in the wars in eastern Europe, where Hapsburg armies tried to push back the advance of the Islamic Ottoman Empire. He gave a long account of how he prepared himself for his goal of becoming an officer, a status he achieved under the Hapsburgs. He was knighted on the field of battle, but after many heroic exploits he was captured and taken to Istanbul, where he served a highborn young woman. He escaped from captivity and traveled through Europe, finally reaching England again as the Virginia Company was making its plans.[26]

§

Thomas Savage, Henry Spelman, and Robert Poole were supposed to learn the culture of the other from the inside and especially to learn the language so that they could interpret. But this assignment involved a huge amount of innovation. Each language involves a different way of looking at the world. Translation never involves a one-for-one rendering of a concept from one language into another, because the two languages will inevitably not have words that convey exactly the same meaning. This can be true of closely related languages such as French and Italian. How much more true would it have been with languages and cultures so very different as English and Chesapeake Algonquian?

These youths must have been acutely aware that they were constantly changing meanings as they passed messages back and forth, but they had no choice. In that time, the word *traduce* meant both "to translate" and "to betray."[27] Betrayal was an integral part of translation, however hard the boys tried to be accurate.

For example, the English language has multiple meanings for the word *lord*. It could refer to a high-ranking man, such as Lord de la Warr, who later became governor of Virginia. So Henry, Thomas, or Robert might translate it as *werowance*, the Chesapeake Algonquian word for a leader. But *lord* was also a religious term, referring to Jesus as a spiritual figure. So how would the boys make clear which meaning pertained in any given exchange? And would they translate the spiritual meaning of *lord* by using the name of the Native God? That might imply a kind of equality between the Native religious figure and the Christian God, a terrible heresy. It was a minefield.

As the boys worked to convey the meanings of one group—their own original culture or their newly acquired one—to the other group, they had to improvise and try to make both sides understand. And they were so young themselves that they might not necessarily understand everything about their own culture and the deeper meanings attached to words and concepts.

The more successful among these intermediaries ended up feeling really trapped between cultures. The more they came to understand the viewpoint of the people they had been forced to live with, the harder it was just to disregard their interests. No one had foreseen these fluid loyalties. Colonial leaders had assumed that youths who lived with the Natives would remain wholly English and completely committed to the English way of thinking. But that is not how it worked.

English and Chesapeake Algonquian leaders made use of this ambiguity. Sometimes they sent the boys with false messages that put them in serious danger. No wonder the boys' own sense of loyalty was ambiguous. And English leaders saw youths as more expendable than full-grown adults were. Smith casually mentioned that he had left his "page" Samuel Collier with the Weraskoyacks "to learn the language" in 1608. The records never referred to Samuel again until Smith recorded his death in the early 1620s. He wrote that Samuel was "one of the most ancientest Planters, and very well acquainted with their language and habitation, humors and conditions, and Governor of a Town."[28]

Samuel Collier's story shows how limited the flow of information was. He was governor of an English town but does not appear in the records except at the beginning and the end of his life in Virginia. Youths such as Pocahontas, Thomas, Henry, and Robert were mentioned in the records only when they were doing something official for the colony or when their activities were seen as somehow threatening to Jamestown's well-being. Everyone who wrote was trying to push his own viewpoint about what was going on or, especially in the case of official communications, to reassure investors that everything was fine and success was just around the corner.

Everyone wanted to claim friendship with Pocahontas, so we are not surprised to see her mentioned again and again. But it is amazing that Thomas's, Henry's, and Robert's names appear as often as they do in records and letters. The boys spent extended times in Native towns; and although Pocahontas did not stay with the English until she was captured and forced to live in the colony, her role was similar to the boys'. Their job was to understand the other from the inside and interpret the other's culture and language for their own people. And they carried messages from their own leaders to the other side. Leaders on both sides could accept what the go-betweens said and act on it, or they might reject the messages. How leaders would react was always up in the air. Duplicity and double-dealing were always part of all these relationships, and the go-betweens themselves did not necessarily know whether the messages they carried were genuine. Sometimes they suspected that they were being asked to carry false information, and they had to decide where their true loyalties lay. They could easily be caught in the middle of developing hostilities. Often they were.

SETTLING IN

JAMESTOWN WAS FOUNDED in an effort to catch up with other European countries that had established strong and permanent ties with America. English leaders knew that Spain and Portugal had become wealthy beyond imagination through their American colonies, but coming in so late, a century after the first Iberian colonies, meant that the English took the part of America that no other Europeans wanted. Ships from many countries had looked at North America's east coast and found no products for immediate development into rich commodities. Colonization was expensive, and no one wanted to lay out a fortune without any returns; so planting colonies on North America's east coast would require commitment and willingness to experiment.

Although England lagged behind in founding colonies, its seamen had been engaged in Atlantic pursuits for a long time. English fishermen were involved in annual trips to the rich fishing grounds off the Newfoundland coast, which did not require expensive year-round bases. Fishermen from all over western Europe came in the spring and went home with their dried and salted fish in the fall—no need to maintain settlements and no need to intrude too much on the Native people.[1]

Other English sailors and merchants, including Captain Newport, were involved in the Atlantic as privateers attacking Spanish ships in the Caribbean and nearby Atlantic and seizing their cargoes. England and Spain were at war from 1585 until the accession of James I in 1603. England thought of itself as the leader of the Protestant nations in Europe, and Spain was the undisputed leader of the Roman Catholics. So the conflict had religious overtones.

England did not have a royal navy large enough to carry on this war, so the admiralty issued letters of marque to merchants and elite men who could establish a claim that their ships had been attacked by Spaniards. The letters of marque gave them the right to recoup their losses, but in reality the privateers attacked whenever and wherever they saw an opportunity. The English government took 20 percent of the loot, and some wealthy men built huge privateering fleets. Martin Frobisher capitalized on his experience on the coast of West Africa and with the Portuguese by becoming a privateer.[2]

The fishing and privateering enterprises had built English mariners' navigational skills, but founding and maintaining a colony was different. Ireland was England's only colony; it was close by, and the strategy there was tight control over the Irish, who could be forced to work for colonial masters.[3] Ventures in America, much farther away, had foundered on poor planning, lack of resources, and a persistent assumption that everything would turn out fine.

Everyone in Jamestown realized how contingent their situation was as a small settlement three thousand miles from home. They all knew about the Roanoke colony's abandonment by Ralegh twenty years earlier. Many colonial ventures from Guiana on the South American mainland to Sagadahoc, founded at the same time as Jamestown in Maine, were quickly given up, and no one thought that was abnormal.

The English lacked the resources to make colonization a royal project as the Spanish had done, so they privatized overseas ventures as they had their war against Spain. The government issued charters to companies of private investors, and the wealthy bought shares, partly out of patriotism but also to make money. The Virginia Company was formed by a small group of aristocrats and leading merchants who were absolutely convinced that England must have a permanent presence in North America if it was to compete with the great nations of Europe, especially as King James had shut down privateering and the war with Spain when he came to the throne in 1603. Previous colonial failures had pointed the way forward for this new venture. In particular, an expedition from Roanoke in 1585–86 had decided that Chesapeake Bay was the best place for a true settlement.

Unfortunately, Jamestown's planners had little knowledge about designing new societies in unfamiliar environments. The investors named the men who were to rule as governor and council in a secret document that was kept sealed until the colonists had safely arrived in Virginia. The designated government comprised men whose main experience was fighting in the cruel wars between Roman Catholics and Protestants in Europe. The first group of colonists famously included a large number of gentlemen, and gentlemen did not do manual labor. The ships carried a few skilled workers, a number of men listed as laborers, and the four boys, including Samuel Collier.

From the beginning, Virginia Company planners clearly did not have a good idea of what the colonists would actually do. The instructions sent with the first ships made it clear that exploration westward in search of a way to the Pacific was a top priority. The riches to be found in trade with Asia were secure, but the planners also hoped the colonists would find precious metals or other rich commodities such as pearls or silk in America if they just looked hard enough.

Backers in London sent food along with the colonists but not nearly enough to sustain them until new supplies arrived. Planners expected that local people would feed the colonists. After all, military expeditions in Europe always "lived off the land." But living on handouts was going to be very problematic. This was true partly because the Powhatans were in control—they supplied what food the colonists got and had no intention of allowing the newcomers to push them around. Also, Virginia was in the grip of a devastating drought. The drought, which had begun the year before the first colonists landed, continued for several years more and was the worst in the past 770 years.[4] Tsenacomacoh's food supplies were under intolerable pressure, and feeding a hundred demanding Englishmen was going to be difficult.

The colony left England in late December 1606 and landed at its chosen site in mid-May 1607. The leaders picked a small peninsula miles up the James River, the southernmost of the rivers that flow into Chesapeake Bay, because they believed it offered the best defense. A peninsula was harder for the Powhatans to attack, but the main concern was the possibility of a Spanish fleet discovering their whereabouts and wiping them out. What they sacrificed for this sense of security was a good water supply and fields for planting. In fact, the site was swampy and quite unhealthy. A lot of the colony's problems in the first years stemmed from its choice of location.

Another huge problem was the colonists themselves. Some, such as George Percy, were probably sent to get them off their relatives' hands. Percy was the brother of the Earl of Northumberland. He had been a sickly child, and his "fits" continued into adulthood. Percy was the highest ranking person in the colony, but he was not on the colony's original governing council, a sure sign that officials in London thought he was incompetent.[5]

Capt. John Smith represented the other end of the spectrum among the colony's elite. He was the only leader who was not of high birth; his father had been a prosperous farmer. He was the one person put on the council for what he knew about dealing with other cultures, and he always made it clear that he thought his supposed superiors in Jamestown were weak and ignorant.

The colonists could have tried to plant some food crops for the coming winter, but they were not prepared to do that. The fleet that brought them departed in late June, leaving the men "very bare and scanty of victuals." In early August, George Percy began to record the daily deaths, saying that most died of "mere famine." He wrote, "There were never Englishmen left in a foreign Country in such misery as we were in this newly discovered Virginia." Capt. Christopher Newport had promised to return with new supplies within twenty weeks, but two-thirds of the original colonists were dead by the time his fleet actually did come back more than six months later.[6]

Why did the Powhatans not just starve out the colonists and be done with it? One reason was that leaders knew the English had some products that they wanted. Many ships had been in Chesapeake Bay over the preceding decades, and the Powhatans had sophisticated knowledge of what they had to offer. In particular, they wanted tools made of metal: axes, knives, swords, hoes, and kettles. These were all tools that made their own lives smoother and more productive. It was easier to cut down a tree with an axe made of iron or steel than with one made of stone, and a metal hoe made farming faster and better. Powhatan realized he could control the hapless colonists and get what he wanted from them. Giving them just enough to keep them going was a smart strategy.

Uncertainty was a fundamental reality in all colonial ventures. Everything from political change in England to the depredations of pirates or storms at sea could wreck what looked like the best laid plans. No one in Virginia could have any illusions about where that venture stood in the total scale of English priorities, especially as the colony was costing a fortune and not making any money. If Jamestown's colonists did not get their act together, they could be dropped as so many others had been.

The colonists tried to make up for their poor record in the early years by sending home reports telling of the wonderful resources to be found in Virginia. Henry Spelman reported walnuts "growing in every place," and many of the trees in Virginia produced edible nuts. Smith described Chenchinquamens, "a small fruit growing on little trees," which was "husked like a Chestnut, but the fruit most like a very small acorn." The Powhatans "esteeme these a great dainty." William Strachey, who arrived in 1610, drew on his extensive travel in the Mediterranean in saying that Virginia had peas that were the same as fagioli in Italy and beans like those the Turks call *garnances* (garbanzos). The grapes were as "luscious . . . as those found in the villages between Paris and Amiens." And the chestnuts, he said, "equalize the best in France, Spain, Germany, or Italy or those so commended in the black-sea, by Constantinople, of all which I have eaten."[7]

One early colonist wrote that the soil was "altogether aromatical, giving a spicy taste to the roots of all trees, plants, and herbs." Smith wrote that there were two or three kinds of oaks, and the acorns of one with whiter bark produced oil, for which the Powhatans had many uses. Acorns are nutritious but are high in tannic acid, so they can be dangerous to eat. The women boiled the acorns "half a day in several waters," which made them safe to eat, and then made bread of them.

The colonists found many herbs in the spring woods for "broths and salads." Virginia also produced many kinds of fruit. Henry said the Chesapeake Algonquians had no orchards but two kinds of plums, one "sweet and luscious" and the other similar to the English medlar, which was not eaten until it was "rotten, as ours are." Smith agreed that the medlar-like plums should not be eaten too early, saying, "if it be not ripe it will draw a man's mouth awry, with much torment, but when it is ripe, it is as delicious as an Apricot." They also had a fruit that tasted like cherries, and berries like English gooseberries. The country was draped by vines, and where the sun hit, they produced grapes. Some grapes, as big as a cherry, had thick juice. In the summer, there were "beautiful strawberries, four times bigger and better than ours in England," mulberries, and raspberries. They also had a fruit called Maracocks, "which is a pleasant wholesome fruit much like a lemon." Another fruit was like capers, which they dried and then boiled half a day before eating, "for otherwise they differ not much from poison."

The Powhatans preserved many of these foods for the winter. The medlars, or plums, were dried on racks and turned into prunes. The walnuts, acorns, chestnuts, and chenchinquamens were dried in the sun. When they needed nuts, the women broke the shells between two stones. Because some of the shells stuck to the nuts, they dried them again on racks. Then they ground them in a mortar and put in water so the shells would sink to the bottom. Once everything was removed, the women stored the milk-colored water, called *Pawcohiscora*, for later use.

Knowing how to prepare food meant knowing how to survive, so even Jamestown's highest officials wrote about it. Strachey described two ways of making bread. In one, the women boiled chestnuts and chenchinquamens for four hours and made them into "bread for their chief men, or at their greatest feasts." He also described a grass whose seeds were like rye, only smaller. The women made these into "a dainty bread buttered with deer suet." George Percy also described how Native women made bread. He said the women pounded the corn into flour, then mixed it with hot water to make a paste, of which they made round balls or cakes. These were simmered in boiling water and finally put onto stones, where they "harden it as well as in an Oven."

Roots formed a big part of the Virginia diet, which helped the Powhatans live through the terrible drought. One, which grew in the swamps, was tuckahoe, which Smith said tasted like potatoes. Local knowledge really mattered in preparing these roots. The Powhatans covered a large pile of tuckahoe with leaves and ferns and then put dirt over the top. On the sides, they built fires, which they kept going for twenty-four hours. This treatment made the roots safe to eat. "Raw it is no better than poison, and being roasted, except it be tender and the heat abated, or sliced and dried in the sun, mixed with sorrell and meal or such like, it will prickle and torment the throat extremely, and yet in summer they use this ordinarily for bread." Onions also grew in the swamps or marshes, but they were small, only the size of a man's thumb. Other roots had medicinal uses if you knew how to prepare them.

All these foods indeed existed in Virginia; but colonists had to know how to identify and prepare them, and they had to be able to go outside the fort without running into danger. This is where Pocahontas and Thomas Savage, Henry Spelman, and Robert Poole came in. Their job was to learn as much as they could and to try to build relationships.

Pocahontas played a starring role in her first encounter with the English, as Powhatan began to unroll his strategy. In December 1607, as the men in the newly founded colony pined for the supply ship that would end their misery, John Smith decided to do something rather than just sit and complain. He set out to explore farther up the network of rivers that flowed into the James. Unfortunately this venture ended with his capture and the deaths of the men with him.

Smith's captors were Pamunkeys, Powhatan's tribe. Opechancanough, the Pamunkey leader, took charge of his captive and paraded Smith

[21]

Engraving of Pocahontas saving Capt. John Smith. Courtesy of the John Carter Brown Library at Brown University.

around some towns in the area. At one town, Opechancanough showed Smith to a family whose son had been taken by a European intruder, but they said Smith was much too short to be the man they were looking for. Priests conducted a dramatic series of ceremonies over several days, and Smith was terrified. He was anxious about what it all meant and whether the final ceremony would be his execution.

Finally, Opechancanough marched Smith to Werowocomoco, where he was brought into the great Powhatan's presence. After feasting and more ceremonies, Smith was dragged to "two great stones," and he was forced down to lay his head on them. Men with clubs were ready, he thought, to "beat out his brains," when suddenly young Pocahontas came forward and "got his head in her arms, and laid her own upon his to save him from death." Powhatan relented; Smith said Pocahontas was his "dearest daughter," and he could not resist her pleas.

Two days later, Powhatan called for Smith and gave him a list of items he wanted the captain to get for him in Jamestown, including two "great guns," probably ship's cannons, and a grindstone. In return, Powhatan said that he would give Smith "the Country of Capahowsick, and forever esteem him as his son Nantaquoud."[8]

What had just happened here? Did Pocahontas risk her own life to save his? In reality, the long train of ceremonies and the final dramatic demonstration may have been an adoption ceremony, in which Smith was symbolically stripped of his life as an Englishman and reborn as a Powhatan man. This would fit with Powhatan's bestowal of a town to govern and his adoption of the captain as a symbolic son. Pocahontas's role, then, would have been scripted, as she acted for the Powhatan lineage. Powhatan saw Smith's capture as an opportunity to make the Englishman his client or vassal and to use him to get the manufactured goods he wanted from the colony.

Smith wrote about Pocahontas's intervention when he was back in London and out of the colony for good. The English stage was full of plays about European men who were captured by North Africans in the Mediterranean, the people the English called Moors, and the plays' climax was often the rescue of the unfortunate captive by a beautiful and highborn woman.[9] So Smith may have been trying to put his American adventures into this popular genre.

Pocahontas began coming to Jamestown accompanying official emissaries after Smith's capture and redemption, and the parties often brought badly needed food for the colonists. Smith had learned a lot during his captivity, and he included a list of Powhatan words with their English equivalents in one of his books. The list included words for various weapons and for friend and enemy. But the last entry was a sentence that showed how familiar Pocahontas's presence had become: "*Kekaten pokahontas patiaquagh ningh tanks manotyens neer mowchick rawrenock audowgh.* Bid Pocahontas bring hither two little Baskets, and I will give her white beads to make her a chain."[10]

William Strachey, who arrived in 1610, wrote a long account of colonists' experiences, *The Historie of Travell into Virginia Britania.* In it, he described Pocahontas and her visits to the English. In the grim reality of the fort, where most of the men felt like prisoners because they did not dare to go beyond its walls, Pocahontas's visits were a welcome relief from the deprivation and boredom. Strachey described her as a playful eleven- or twelve-year-old in 1610. She taught the English boys to turn cartwheels—she would "get the boys forth into the market place, and make them wheel, falling on their hands turning their heels upwards, whom she would follow, and wheel so herself naked as she was all the Fort over." She was naked because she was so young. Strachey said that when girls reached the age of twelve, they put on a leather apron and were very ashamed to be seen naked.[11]

Just after Smith's brief captivity and the ceremony in which Pocahontas played such an important role, the Virginia Company's first supply fleet finally arrived, in January 1608. Thomas Savage traveled on the flagship, which left London on October 4, 1607. On the passenger list, Thomas's name appeared among the laborers.[12] Sailing from the busy port of London, with ships departing for the East Indies as well as America, was a great adventure.

Adventure also meant great risk. Every English person had learned Psalm 107 and its warning: "They that go down to the sea in ships and occupy by the great waters, They see the works of the Lord, & his wonders in the deep. For he commandeth and raiseth the stormy wind and it lifteth up the waves thereof. They mount up to the heaven, and descend to the deep, so that their soul melteth for trouble. They are tossed to and fro, and stagger like a drunken man, and all their cunning is gone." The psalm goes on to warn that all the skill of the mariners cannot save them. Only through God's intervention would they arrive safely at their destination.[13]

Cosmic signs marked the fleet's departure. As the ship was being prepared and the passengers gathered, a brilliant comet appeared in the night sky. George Percy, who was in the first fleet, had seen a "blazing star" in February as they crossed the Atlantic, but this comet, which first appeared in the middle of September, was far greater and paraded across the sky every night for a month. The great blazing star was Halley's Comet, which appears approximately every seventy-six years. Scientists across Europe viewed and analyzed its phenomenal appearance. Comets were not just scientifically interesting and spectacular; everyone believed they foretold important events.[14]

When the fleet finally got a favorable wind and crossed the Atlantic, Thomas had a taste of America's varied environments. The ships stopped in the Caribbean, so he saw the fantastic plants and animals and experienced the ever-present mosquitos of its semitropical clime. The constant warmth and brilliant sunshine seemed both attractive and weird, because they were such a contrast to England's foggy and chilly weather. So rarely did the sun shine in England that a departing Spanish ambassador jokingly told his English friends to give his regards to "the blessed Sun of Heaven when they chanced to see him."[15]

After their Caribbean stop, the ships sailed north into Chesapeake Bay and entered the James River, and Thomas had his first view of Virginia. The river was two miles across at its mouth, with "fragrant and fertile banks." The river abounded with fish, and near the banks, the English found oysters and "many great crabs rather better in taste than ours." Not only were the crabs luscious, but they were so big that one could feed four men. The banks were "a black, fat, sandy mold [soil] somewhat slimy in touch and sweet in savor." Everyone who wrote about early Virginia went on and on about the variety and number of trees, "the fairest, yea, and best" they had ever seen. The forests of England were so depleted that the English were forced to import timber for fuel and for building, so the woods in Virginia were stunning.[16]

John Smith wrote that "the country is overgrown with trees." Most common were oaks and walnuts, and there were also elm and ash trees. Smith identified a "kind of wood we called Cypress, because both the wood, the fruit, and leaf did most resemble it." The trees he identified as cypress were huge: "some near 3 fathom about at the root, very straight, and 50, 60, or 80 foot without a branch." A fathom was the length of a man's outstretched arms from fingertip to fingertip and was supposed to be about six feet, so these trees were almost eighteen feet around.[17]

After traveling up the James through the splendid trees along the river's aromatic banks, Thomas got a view of a very different reality at Jamestown. When he and the other new colonists and supplies arrived that January 1608, the fort was a dismal sight.

The few original colonists who had survived thought their misery was at an end, but nothing ever went as planned. Three days later, a disastrous fire broke out and burned much of the fort. Despite all this, Captain Newport carried out the Virginia Company's plans to impress the Powhatans.

Newport, accompanied by Thomas, made a state visit to Werowocomoco in February. He approached Powhatan's capital with a trumpeter blaring before him and accompanied by an armed guard to exaggerate his own importance. As part of this visit, he gave Thomas to Powhatan to cement their friendship. He lied to Powhatan to enhance the significance of his gift, telling the chief that Thomas was his own son, so the Powhatans always called him Thomas Newport. Clearly, Thomas had no choice in the matter; but he knew that life in Jamestown was going to be hard for those who were stuck there, and he was embarked on a whole new adventure.

The next day, "the King having kindly entertained us with a breakfast, questioned with me in this manner. Why we came armed in that sort, seeing he was our friend, and had neither bows nor arrows, what did we doubt. I told him it was the custom of our country." Smith actually despised Newport's great show of bravado. Powhatan was clearly a very experienced bargainer, and Smith recorded his many changes of strategy. His first approach was to disdain mere trade, saying, "Captain Newport it is not agreeable with my greatness in this peddling manner to trade for trifles, and I esteem you a great werowance. Therefore lay me down all your commodities together, what I like I will take, and in recompence give you that I think fitting their value." Newport fell for it, and according to Smith, the English paid a huge price for the corn they received. Another day, Powhatan "cunningly" refused to come to meet the English for trade, and, Smith reported, Pocahontas "came to entreat me, . . . saying her Father had hurt his leg, and much sorrowed he could not see me."[18]

Soon Newport, Smith, and the other colonists returned to Jamestown, leaving Thomas behind. For the colonists, placing an English boy with the great leader of the Chesapeake was important. It was so noteworthy that both the Venetian and the Spanish ambassadors in London reported home about it. Pedro de Zúñiga had the story slightly garbled in his letter to the Spanish king, as he thought Captain Newport had told Powhatan that Thomas was the son of King James I of England. He did say that Powhatan "makes much of him." So, however apprehensive Thomas may have been, he was treated as an honored guest by his hosts and quickly settled in to the role.[19]

Powhatan gave Newport a young man named Namontack, "his trusty servant and one of a shrewd, subtle capacity," in return for Thomas. The English were sure he was supposed to spy on them and report back, but that was because they were playing the same game by placing Thomas in Werowocomoco. Namontack sailed for England with Captain

Newport's fleet. Powhatan later said that he "purposely sent" him to "King James his land, to see him and his country, and to return me the true report thereof."[20]

Thomas Harriot, who, as the scientist with the Roanoke colony, had spent a great deal of time with coastal Carolina Algonquians in 1585–86 became a principal adviser to American expeditions in England. He drew up a list of things to take along for one of Ralegh's shipmasters, Samuel Mace, who sailed in search of the lost Roanoke colonists left there fifteen years earlier, in 1602. The list began, "Copper not brass 20 or 30 pound in plates, some as thin as paper & small & great." The list also included "Hatchets. 5. doz., Knives. 50. doz., Mattockes. 20, Iron shovels. 20." A mattock is a tool like a pickaxe used for breaking up hard soil. While Namontack was in London, Harriot's current employer, the Earl of Northumberland, appealed to him for advice on how to treat Namontack, and Harriot suggested a gift of copper; the earl's account books for 1609 show a payment of three shillings for "2 rings and other pieces of copper for the Indian prince." Earlier, also at Harriot's suggestion, the earl had sent his brother in Jamestown, George Percy, six shillings worth of "blue beads" and nineteen shillings worth of "red copper."[21]

Both the Venetian and the Spanish ambassadors sent home reports about Namontack's presence in London. And he was mentioned by name in a 1609 play by Ben Jonson, *Epicoene; or, The Silent Woman*, in which one character claims to have made a sketch of him during his stay in London. Namontack went back with the next fleet.[22]

Namontack's impressions of London are lost to us, but we can have some idea of how life in Werowocomoco would have looked to Thomas, based on what Henry Spelman and others wrote. He probably did not find it very different from life in an English village. The people's houses were right along the riverbank. Chesapeake Algonquians lived in longhouses with sleeping benches along the sides and fires burning in the center. Henry described them as built like ovens "with a little hole to come in at" and "spacious within." The Powhatan's house was set back

Town of Secoton from John White's Roanoke painting. Courtesy of the John
Carter Brown Library at Brown University.

from the river across a large open space. It was larger than the others, "having many dark windings and turnings before any come where the King is."[23]

Floors in England were covered with rushes, reed-like plants that grow near water, and often the floor under the rushes was the dirt that the house or cottage was built on. And chimneys were only just coming into general use in England, so the central fire and smoke hole in the ceiling would not have looked particularly odd to Thomas. Communal sleeping arrangements were also normal at home. Only members of the highest elite would have had their own chamber, and even they would not necessarily have slept alone.[24]

Americans drank water, which was disconcerting for Thomas as he settled in to life among the Powhatans. The water in England was not safe to drink, so English people drank beer, or wine if they were rich enough, even with breakfast. Henry wrote that the men and women sat on mats in separate groups to eat. The women gave each person a dish of food, "for the better sort never eats together in one dish." When a diner finished, he did not expect a "second course" but put down the dish and "mumbles certain words to himself in manner of giving thanks." The women gathered up leftovers to be saved for the next meal or given to "the poorer sort, if any be there."[25]

This all would have sounded perfectly normal to Henry's English readers. They did not sit on mats but did sit on backless benches. Only the highest ranking person had a chair. This is why heads of committees and firms came to be called "chairmen"—they sat in the one chair. The idea that each diner had his or her own dish would have sounded very posh to people at home. In England, the "better sort" or elite people might each have their own dish; but those farther down the table would all have eaten out of a common pot, and they would dig in with their unwashed hands. You could tell the status of all people by where they sat. The salt cellar separated the gentry from the commoners; if you were below the salt, you were at the low end of the social order but still high enough to get to the table. After great feasts, the servants would distribute leftover food at the gates of the big house to the assembled poor, who waited for sustenance. Henry's description of Powhatan mealtimes told his English readers that they had much in common.[26]

Thomas must have been stunned by the American habit of beginning the day by bathing in streams. The boy who had run away to the Paspaheghs during Jamestown's first year told the governor that every morning the women brought all the little children to the riverside, "but what they did there he did not know." English people did not bathe.[27]

And for Thomas, giving up his English clothes was a big change. Did he find it liberating to switch to Powhatan clothing, which was so much freer than English? Or did he find it hard to adjust to being so exposed? As a boy in England, Thomas wore a long linen shirt day and night, which he changed for a clean one once in a while. The linen shirt was supposed to absorb dirt, which made bathing unnecessary; it also replaced underpants, as men and boys just pulled the shirt's tails between their legs. For warmth, boys and men wore a waistcoat, which they pulled on over their heads or tied down the front. Over the waistcoat, they wore a doublet or jacket that opened in the front. Some just hung open, but most were laced together. They wore long stockings, which were either knitted or made of heavy woolen fabric, cut on the bias for stretchability. The stockings were held by a garter above the knee, and their breeches just covered the tops of the stockings. Thomas's boots or shoes would have had a very hard sole.[28]

As a Powhatan boy, Thomas wore a deerskin loincloth. He wore a belt tied around his waist, and the loincloth went between his legs, with the ends pulled through the belt in front and behind. In the 1680s, William Byrd sent "an Indian habit" for the son of a friend in England. It consisted of "a flap or belly clout, 1 pair stockings & 1 pair moccasins or Indian shoes, also some shells to put about his neck & a cap of wampum." Wearing only a loincloth and moccasins took some getting used to.[29]

In England, your clothes indicated your status, and the law actually dictated what people could wear. You were supposed to be able to tell at a glance how high a person stood in the pecking order and what

[31]

kind of occupation that person followed just by their clothes. Women's appearance showed whether they were married or single. Among the Powhatans, by contrast, the king did not dress differently from any other leading men. Henry wrote that Powhatan was distinguished by his dignity and the reverence and gifts the people gave him when he visited them.

Chesapeake Algonquian priests sometimes had beards, but the "common people" did not have them; Henry thought they pulled out the hair on their chin. In England, the reverse was true. Ministers were clean shaven, and other men wore beards. Powhatan men cut the hair on the right side of their head "that it might not hinder them by flapping about their bow string, when they draw it to shoot." They allowed their hair to grow to shoulder length on the left side.[30] Fashionable Englishmen about town in London, having read accounts such as Henry's, began to grow their hair long on the left side in what came to be called "lovelocks."

As Thomas settled into life with the Powhatans, did he meet and talk with Paquiquineo? Paquiquineo's experience of Europe and Europeans gave him an angle that no one else among his people could possibly have had. The Paspahegh territory was on the James River just beyond where Jamestown was founded, and they were part of the Powhatan chiefdom. Paquiquineo was a youth at the time the Spanish took him and therefore would have understood what Thomas was going through in a way that no one else could. And he knew what it was like for someone so young to be thrust suddenly into a wholly different culture. He might even have talked with Thomas about Europe and his experiences there. Even if Paquiquineo was not present or even not still alive, the Powhatans who now dealt with Thomas Savage recalled his stories of Europeans and his experiences with them.

Thomas Savage continued at Werowocomoco as Thomas Newport until Powhatan suddenly sent him away, back to Jamestown, in May 1608. The English were holding some of Powhatan's men in the fort, and he was angry; he may have even suspected Thomas of conspiring with other tribes. Then, almost as soon as Thomas returned to the fort,

Pocahontas came after him. Pocahontas asked, on her father's behalf, "that the boy might come again, which he loved exceedingly."[31]

One of the most interesting aspects of these relationships is how often they were expressed in kinship and adoption terms. Although they were diplomatic exchanges, both the English and the Powhatans characterized them as parent-child relationships. Powhatan adopted John Smith after the elaborate ceremonies he had undergone and gave Smith a town to govern, as his other sons did. Before Captain Newport had visited Werowocomoco, Smith told Powhatan that Newport was his father as a way of indicating that he was Smith's superior. Newport presented Thomas Savage as his son, and later Powhatan addressed Thomas as "my child." And Powhatan's best emissary was his "dearest daughter." In the cases that we know about, American leaders all spoke of their love for the boys who lived with them and thought of them as sons.

William Strachey wrote of how "very dearly" Powhatan women loved their children. They made their children "hardy" by washing them in the rivers, even on the coldest mornings, and tanned their skins with "paintings and ointments," which made them impervious to harsh weather. They taught their boys to shoot bows and arrows from a very young age. Boys had to earn their breakfast, by shooting "a piece of moss or some such light thing" that his mother threw up into the air. Only after the boys had successfully hit their mark did they get their morning meal.[32]

Sir Thomas Dale, who held several high offices in Virginia, answered the Virginia Company's demand that the colonists get some Powhatan children and convert them to Christianity and European life by saying it was impossible because "the children are so tenderly beloved of their parents that neither copper nor love can draw any from them," and the parents said "their little children will cry and be sick." English writers saw the affection that Natives poured on their children as extraordinary, which gives us some insight into their own parent-child relationships.[33]

Captain Newport came to the colony again in October 1608 bringing the second round of supplies and more colonists, including fourteen-year-old Anne Burras, who came as maid for "Mistress Forrest"; they were the first English women in the colony. John Forrest was listed among the gentlemen on the same voyage, and John Burras was on the list of tradesmen. Very soon after their arrival, Anne married John Laydon, who had been in the colony from its beginning, and Smith recorded this as "the first marriage we had in Virginia." That voyage also brought eight "Poles and Dutchmen [Germans] to make pitch, tar, glass mills, and soap ashes."[34]

Newport also carried a commission to crown the Powhatan, thereby incorporating him into the English system as a vassal of King James. The Virginia Company was using exactly the same strategy as Powhatan had when he ritually adopted John Smith and made him a vassal. In neither case did it work as planned.

The company had sent various presents including a crown and red jacket and, most surprisingly, a bedstead. When John Smith was first brought into Powhatan's presence as a captive, the "Emperor" had received him "proudly lying upon a Bedstead a foot high," so the English bedstead was supposed to be his new throne.[35] Newport sent Smith to invite Powhatan to come to Jamestown, where he would receive the crown and other trappings sent by King James from England. In contrast to Newport with his armed guard and blaring trumpets, Smith went with four men, including young Samuel Collier and Namontack, and they went overland. Samuel presumably met up with Thomas while they were both in Werowocomoco, so Samuel had a chance to find out what Thomas's life was like and to learn about the pitfalls.

While the emissaries were with the Powhatans, they were entertained by what Smith called a Virginia Masque. Masques were lavish entertainments held at the royal court in England. Smith and his men heard what Smith called "hideous noise and shrieking," and they were alarmed, thinking an attack was coming. But Pocahontas approached Smith, "willing him to kill her if any hurt were intended." The English relaxed, and soon thirty young women approached the English camp from the woods. All were painted with designs, and each had a different costume and props. When Smith was back in England, he described his experiences to Samuel Purchas, who wrote that the leader of these young women made him think of the story of Diana and Actaeon from ancient Greek mythology, because she had stag's horns on her head and a quiver of arrows on her back. The beginning of Queen Elizabeth's reign had been marked by a lavish masque of Diana and her nymphs combined with Actaeon and his hunters, and Purchas may have known of that famous spectacle. For an hour, Pocahontas's companions sang and danced around the fire "with most excellent ill variety." After the masque was ended, the dancers invited the English to a feast. Smith complained that he was pestered by the young "Nymphs" crowding around him saying, "Love you not me?"[36]

The next day, Powhatan came, and Smith "redelivered him Namontack." Powhatan then responded to Newport's invitation, saying that he was the sovereign here and that if Newport wanted to give him presents, he should come to Werowocomoco. Henry wrote that the Powhatan never traveled outside his own lands, and clearly he wanted the English to understand that he had no intention of becoming another king's vassal. With a great deal of trouble, the English did bring all the presents to Werowocomoco, and the coronation went ahead, although with some comic touches. Protocol required that Powhatan kneel to receive the crown, and he refused. Finally, Newport's men pushed down on his shoulders so that "he a little stooped," and they put the crown on his head.[37]

Powhatan did not even come close to being a vassal of King James. In fact, he and his people were growing more and more impatient with the English presence. During all this time, the unprecedented drought continued, and its effects were felt more and more. In times of bad harvests, people need to eat the seed corn they usually reserve for planting, so future harvests are less and less good. In the fall of 1608, the English demands for food grew increasingly troublesome, and relationships were strained. Smith and his men went up and down the river seeking corn. Smith wrote about one case in which, after the people "imparted that little they had," the English saw the women and children weeping on the riverbank as the loaded boats pulled away. His comment was that anyone would have "been too cruel to have been a Christian, that would not have been satisfied and moved with compassion." Nonetheless, they took the people's food.[38]

Smith set out on another journey to Werowocomoco at the very end of December 1608; Powhatan had sent Thomas with a message saying that if Smith came with "a grindstone, fifty swords, some pieces [muskets], a cock and a hen, with much copper and beads, he would load his Ship with Corn." He also requested "men to build him a house." Smith sent the house builders first, and they went overland. They included four Germans and two English, one of whom was Richard Savage. Smith and his party went by water and took two boats and a large number of men. Their first overnight stop was at Werascoyack, which was near the mouth of the James. There the chief warned Smith that he would not be welcome at Powhatan's capital: "Captain Smith, you shall find Powhatan to use you kindly, but trust him not, and be sure he hath no opportunity to seize on your arms, for he hath sent for you only to cut your throats." Smith thanked him for the advice, but he was determined to continue. As he and his men departed, he left Samuel Collier with the Werascoyacks. Samuel was fortunate that he had been able to talk with Thomas at Werowocomoco, because now that he was living in the Werascoyack town, he had a good idea of how to behave and what to expect.[39]

When Smith and his men arrived at Werowocomoco in January 1609, they soon understood clearly that the Powhatans no longer welcomed them. As before, Powhatan asked Smith to tell his men to leave their weapons in their boats and said, "some doubt I have of your coming hither, that makes me not so kindly seek to relieve you as I would: for many do inform me, your coming hither is not for trade, but to invade my people and possess my country." After an extremely tense set of discussions, the newcomers prepared to spend a very nervous night. Smith believed that Powhatan, with the assistance of the Germans, who had defected, had made plans to kill the party, and this was confirmed for him when Pocahontas, Powhatan's "dearest jewel and daughter, in that dark night came through the irksome woods" to warn him of the plot. She advised him to leave immediately. Smith tried to reward her with "such things as she delighted in," but she refused. With "tears running down her cheeks," she said that she did not dare to take any. If she were seen with English presents, "she were but dead," so she ran away empty-handed. Smith and his men made it through the night and got away as quickly as possible.[40]

Smith and his party continued upriver, so Powhatan sent two of the Germans, Adam and Francis, to Jamestown with a message purporting to come from Smith, saying that he needed more weapons. Powhatan kept the third German, Samuel, as a hostage to make sure the envoys would return. Apparently the Germans had confederates among the discontented colonists within the fort at Jamestown, so they gathered a huge number of weapons and brought them to Powhatan. Richard Savage and the other Englishman were appalled by this treachery, so they attempted to get back to Jamestown to inform the authorities, "but they were apprehended, and expected ever when to be put to death." Richard and the other English carpenter were never mentioned again, so their fate is unknown.[41]

That same month, Powhatan moved his people away from Werowocomoco to the town of Orapax. Werowocomoco was in a ter-rific location. It was where the York River was widest and therefore easily accessible by water, and the fishing was excellent. It was a short distance inland from Chesapeake Bay and in the middle of all the peo-ple over whom Powhatan governed, roughly the same distance inland as Jamestown was on the James, the river to the south. Orapax, by contrast, was not a great place to be. It was on the Chickahominy River, which flowed into the James, but so far inland that the river could not accom-modate much water traffic. It was a long trek overland from most of his territories.[42]

The one great advantage of Orapax was that the English could reach it only with the greatest difficulty, and the voyage took a long time. As William Strachey wrote, Powhatan decided to move when he realized

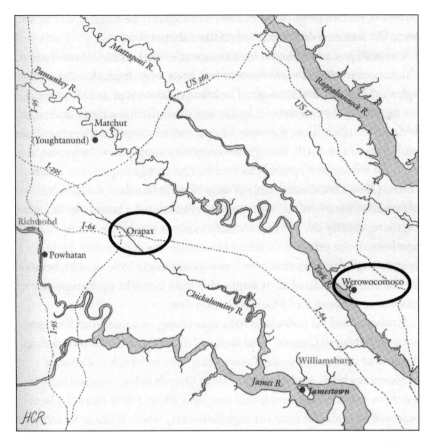

Map of Powhatan's capitals showing Werowocomoco and Orapax. Courtesy of Helen Rountree.

the English settlement provided such easy access to Werowocomoco because he did not like "to neighbor so near us."[43] The colonists knew that Powhatan had deliberately broken his ties with them. He had had enough, and Pocahontas stopped visiting Jamestown.

Thomas moved with Powhatan's people when they went to Orapax, but his life was now extremely frightening and very uncomfortable. Not only had he been used to carry a false invitation to Jamestown, but the fate of Richard Savage and the other English carpenter must have been deeply disturbing. Even if Richard was not his brother or father, the two had been together on the long Atlantic voyage, a serious bonding experience. As the desperate colonists tried to extort food from Powhatan's client tribes up and down the river, violence and retribution grew with every confrontation. The English believed firmly in the doctrine of preemptive war. Put another way, because they were so afraid, their response always was to strike first and ask questions later. As the level of violence increased, Thomas faced two questions about his status: Did Powhatan still value him? And would the leaders in Jamestown ever believe him again?

NEW REALITIES

Virginia company backers in London were only dimly aware of conditions in the colony. For one thing, voyages took several months each way, and the ships usually stayed in Virginia for at least a few weeks; so their information was always out of date. And they always assumed that, however bad things had been when the last ships had departed Virginia for the return trip, they must have improved as time went on. Moreover, the official reports carried by the London-bound ships always tried to minimize the negative and accentuate the positive. All those glowing reports about the abundance of food available were meant to make prospects look really good. The one thing colonists feared most was the Virginia Company just giving up and abandoning them as the Roanoke colonists had been, so they always tried to make it sound as if everything was just about to get better.

It is amazing that the Virginia Company investors did not throw up their hands and quit. The leaders were aristocrats and big merchants who could have transferred their money to much more promising ventures on the coast of Africa or in the eastern Mediterranean. And many other colonial ventures had been given up after faltering starts, so that is what everyone expected them to do. But in 1609, instead of quitting, the Virginia Company completely reorganized itself and its mission.

Company members thought they knew the three errors that had made the first two years go wrong. For one thing, they had sent the wrong kind of people, weak and feckless; some company members called the colonists currently in Jamestown the "scum of the earth." But as the Reverend Richard Crashaw argued in a sermon preached before the Virginia Company, good government could make "the scum and scouring of the streets," people who were "the very excrements of a full and swelling state," into good citizens. And secondly, new and better government would force the Powhatans to respect the colonists. The company warned in their instructions for the newly appointed governor, Sir Thomas Gates, the Natives "will never feed you but for fear." The third defect needing attention was the company's and colony's funding. All company members had to do was fix these things and everything would be fine. Thomas Harriot, who had written about the resources found by the Roanoke colony, was called to testify to the Virginia Company, and he provided information about the Roanokes' smelting of "red metal," which reinforced expectations that valuable minerals would soon be found.[1]

So complete was the transformation that the company asked for and received a new charter from King James. Whereas the original company had been composed of a few stockholders, now it opened membership to the great British public. Each share of stock would cost twelve pounds and ten shillings, and every stockholder was promised land in Virginia. Now, with hundreds of stockholders, Virginia became a subject of national interest, and, at least in theory, the company had the funds to support the colony properly.

The Virginia Company's plan to reorganize the colony and its finances in 1609 assumed that sending a large-enough number of colonists and supplies would make it all run well. But the plan depended on everything going just right. And members always underestimated the potential problems and drawbacks. When things went wrong, they blamed the colonists for being lazy, stupid, and weak.

The new Virginia Company, as its initial move, organized a large fleet to carry several hundred settlers to the reinvigorated colony. The company considered critical mass essential to the project's success. The *Unity*, with fourteen-year-old Henry Spelman aboard, was part of that fleet. His father, Erasmus Spelman, had died in 1605, and Henry, as the oldest of his eight children, was expected to help the family cope, even though

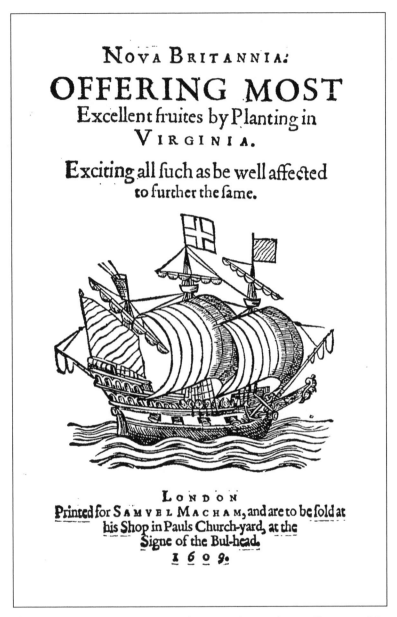

NOVA BRITANNIA:

OFFERING MOST

Excellent fruites by Planting in
VIRGINIA.

Exciting all such as be well affected
to further the same.

LONDON
Printed for SAMVEL MACHAM, and are to be sold at
his Shop in Pauls Church-yard, at the
Signe of the Bul-head.
1 6 0 9.

Title page of *Nova Britannia*, 1609, showing a ship on the sea. Courtesy of the Rare Books Division, The New York Public Library, Astor, Lennox, and Tilden Foundations.

he was then only nine or ten. At the beginning of his memoir, he said that he left home, "being in displeasure of my friends." At the time, the word "friends" meant family or patrons, people who could do you good or help you.[2]

Henry's uncle Sir Henry Spelman was an eminent man, and he was Henry's most important friend. Sir Henry had influential contacts through his government service as well as among the London intellectuals with whom he worked and socialized in the Society of Antiquaries. If Henry had committed some kind of offense—stealing, arson, or a sexual transgression, for example—Sir Henry may have used his connections to get him a place in this ambitious new Virginia venture.[3]

Henry's misstep may have been fairly serious, and one entry in the Surrey County records supports this idea. In 1613, Henry's great-uncle Francis Saunders died and left three pounds each to the seven youngest children of his nephew Erasmus Spelman. He stipulated that his nephew Sir Henry Spelman, "and not their Mother," should be in charge of distributing the money to Erasmus's children, and he added cryptically, "whereof Henry Spelman in Virginia to be exempted." Clearly the family did not trust Henry's mother to act responsibly, and Henry's being deprived of a legacy seems to indicate that his "friends" still viewed him with "displeasure" four years later.[4]

Henry never mentioned his nearby cousins, Sir Henry's sons, but they were far more fortunate. As Henry was shipped off to Virginia, his fifteen-year-old cousin John departed for Cambridge. He had already spent a year in London studying law at the Inns of Court and was clearly destined for high position in England. Henry had already experienced the death of his father, and now he was sent away from his mother and siblings; so his pain must have been very real. Henry's early experience mirrors that of Josiah Langdale, an English boy who kept a spiritual diary. He was pulled out of school when he was nine; his father had died, and his mother needed his labor. When she remarried and no longer needed him, he was sent into servitude at the age of fifteen.[5]

Henry also wrote that he was "desirous to see other countries." What better opportunity for a young man at the beginning of his life than getting involved in the new Virginia project? Unfortunately, the ships were delayed in their departure, so they did not leave until June 2. That late date meant that the fleet was in the Atlantic during the dangerous summer hurricane season, and the ships encountered a massive storm whose "winds and seas were as mad as fury and rage could make them." The hurricane scattered the fleet and damaged or ruined the supplies in the holds as seawater flooded them. Henry said the storm lasted seven or eight days, and it was a terrifying experience.[6] There were no cabins for passengers in ships of this period. Everyone was crowded into the hold, and each person had a blanket, called a rug, to wrap around himself while he slept. Shipboard life was bad enough at the best of times, but in a storm with the hold filling with water and everyone vomiting with seasickness, it was truly horrible.[7]

In sending this fleet, as always before, planners in England had been careless because they still did not take the problems seriously. All the leaders in the new redesigned government were on the flagship, the *Sea Venture*, and that one vessel was wrecked in the storm. The passengers were extraordinarily lucky. Bermuda is ringed by dangerous underground reefs that had destroyed many other ships in the past, but somehow the storm pushed the *Sea Venture* through one of the only two gaps in the reef. The passengers were able to disembark on the uninhabited islands, and they salvaged some of their stuff from the ship. There were no people on Bermuda, but the islands did have huge numbers of pigs, descended from a breeding pair that was left by a Spanish ship some time in the past. So the wrecked colonists lived high on the hog as they built two new pinnaces out of Bermuda cedar and the remains of their ship. Luckily they had shipwrights with them who knew how to build a ship; but they lacked pitch and tar to caulk the seams and make them waterproof, so they burned shells to make lime and mixed that with oil from turtles.

William Strachey wrote an account of the storm and the colonists' time on Bermuda. Because so many ships had been wrecked on the reefs in the centuries before, it was known as the Isle of Devils, but Strachey wrote that "Truth is the daughter of Time" and that people should not speculate about things they did not know through experience. There were pigs and delicious birds but no devils.[8]

While the *Sea Venture*'s company ate pork and seabirds on Bermuda and worked to get to Virginia, the *Unity* and most of the fleet did eventually make it to Jamestown in late summer of 1609. The fleet's arrival was not what it might have been if the passengers and cargo had been as they were when they left England. Seawater had ruined the food sent with the newcomers, so, once again, many new colonists arrived without the supplies needed to get them through the coming winter—and summer and the time to plant crops to feed them were mostly gone. No one welcomed the prospect of sustaining several hundred raw colonists through cold times with the supplies available. Not only did the ships arrive late and with a fraction of the intended supplies, but the unprecedented drought conditions continued, with their effects becoming worse with each passing month. This, the worst winter, became known as the "starving time," with widespread deaths punctuated by stories of cannibalism. Charges of cannibalism have recently been corroborated by archaeologists' discovery of a skeleton with marks of having been butchered for meat. The colonists were desperate.[9]

Conditions had been going from bad to worse among the English already in Virginia. In the summer of 1609, even before the arrival of all these new colonists, John Smith, who had become governor by default, tried the strategy of dispersing the colonists nearer to potential sources of food. Governor Smith sent George Percy and Capt. John Martin with sixty men to live near the Nansemonds, whose capital was close to where the James River empties into Chesapeake Bay. After their arrival, Martin and Percy sent two messengers to the Nansemond chief to trade copper, hatchets, and other desirable goods for land on which they could settle. They were puzzled when the two men did not return, until passing Natives told them that the messengers had been "sacrificed," their skulls hacked open and their brains scraped out with seashells.

Percy and Martin decided that they had to meet violence with even greater violence, or else the Nansemonds would think they were weak. They burned down the Nansemonds' houses and "ransacked their Temples, took down the Corpses of their dead kings from their Tombs, And carried away their pearls, Copper, and bracelets" from the royal tombs. They also took the chief's son prisoner, but he escaped after a boy on the ship shot him accidentally and the prisoner dove into the water and swam away. Percy returned to Jamestown, and Martin followed soon after, "pretending some occasions of business," but really because they were afraid. The men they left behind were besieged by the Nansemonds. When Smith sent a force to rescue them, they found them dead with their mouths stuffed full of bread as a gesture of "contempt and scorn." The Nansemonds' message was clear: they were tired of supplying the hapless colonists with food, and the violence was just going to escalate. As the ships from the hurricane-scattered fleet landed one by one, the new arrivals were shocked by the condition of the colony and extremely fearful for their own future.[10]

Henry Spelman actually had a chance to escape Jamestown's horrible time. In his own account, he says that after he had spent a week or two "in viewing of the country," he accompanied Captain Smith on a trip up the James River as far as the falls. They came to a town governed by a man whom Henry called the Tanx or Little Powhatan, which meant that he was subordinate to the Great Powhatan. The man's actual name was Parahunt, and he was Powhatan's son. As Henry understood it, Smith sold him to Parahunt in exchange for a site on which the English could settle. A settlement there would position them to look for the waterways they hoped would give them access to the Pacific.[11]

Henry wrote that Parahunt treated him extremely well: "he made very much of me giving me such things as he had to win me to live with him." But Henry was not sure what was going to happen to him; after all, he had been in America less than a month, and he "desired to see our English." So, after a week with Parahunt, he told the chief, using gestures, that he wanted to go to an English ship that was still anchored nearby and get some of his possessions. Parahunt agreed but let Henry know that he really wanted the boy to stay with him: "setting himself down, he clapped his hand on the ground in token he would stay there till I returned." Henry did not return as promised. He wrote that he stayed away "somewhat too long." When he finally went back, he found that Parahunt had given up and left. So he went back to the ship that was still anchored at the falls of the James "and sailed with them to Jamestown."[12]

Jamestown was in complete disarray when Henry arrived back at the fort. Captain Smith had returned to England after being seriously injured by a gunpowder explosion on the trip back down the James after his negotiations with Parahunt. Smith knew from men on the ships that survived the hurricane that the Virginia Company had replaced him as governor. Unfortunately, the governor-designate, Sir Thomas Gates, was nowhere to be seen. No one in Jamestown or in England knew that the flagship's company had survived in Bermuda and would resurface the following year. So there was no consensus on who was actually in charge in Jamestown. Smith's injury caused him to leave, but he was probably glad of the excuse. No one was able to step forward and carry out a coherent plan, and the governorship fell by default to George Percy, who was "very sick"; so poor leadership contributed to the suffering during the winter of 1609–10.[13]

Hostilities up and down the James continued to escalate. Upriver, in the town site acquired in exchange for Henry, the colonists, under the command of Capt. Francis West, behaved so badly that Parahunt's men repeatedly harassed them, killing several during that autumn. West and Smith had argued over where the outpost should be located, and Henry later recorded rumors that Smith had conspired with Powhatan to kill West.[14]

Colonists' violent reactions to every suspected threat up and down the river meant that all the people who might have helped them over the horrible winter to come were now so alienated that they wanted nothing to do with the English. And because these tribes were part of the Powhatan chiefdom, the colonists were attacking the Powhatan himself each time they tried to exact revenge on people along the James.

Shortly after Henry arrived back in Jamestown from his first trip upriver and his desertion of Parahunt, Thomas Savage came to the settlement carrying venison and accompanied by several Powhatan men. Thomas said that he was "loath" to return to Powhatan's capital alone, presumably because life at Orapax was not so comfortable, and he had good reason to be afraid. Henry "was appointed to go, which I the more willingly did, by Reason that vitals [victuals, food] were scarce with us carrying with me some copper and a hatchet which I had gotten." Obviously Henry had learned something about how relationships were constructed in America. He offered the copper and hatchet to Powhatan, who accepted them and treated Henry and Thomas well. They certainly ate better than they would have back in the fort.[15]

Thomas and Henry were at the age when Powhatan boys moved from childhood to adult roles, so, like their Powhatan counterparts who had passed through the Huskenaw, they did men's work, which meant helping clear the fields for planting in the spring and providing food by hunting and fishing. Men also made and repaired the equipment for all these jobs. Hunting and fishing were group activities. Henry described how several communities joined in the annual deer hunt; everyone contributed to the joint effort. Two or three hundred men, carrying bows and arrows and fire sticks, encircled a large thicket. Each man set the dried grass in front of him on fire, so the frightened deer would run to the center of the thicket; and then the hunters closed in from all sides and shot the trapped deer. Women accompanied the hunters to erect houses of mats for their stay in the field and also to help with dressing the carcasses.[16]

Deer were valuable for their skins and their meat, and for Thomas and Henry, eating venison was really special. Only the wealthy elite in England had venison, because they had their own deer parks where they could harvest animals. Sometimes poachers took deer from the parks, but they risked severe punishment if they were caught.[17] So most English people had not tasted venison, and Thomas and Henry had a great treat.

Nets for fishing were woven of cord made from hemp or deer sinews, and women and men both participated in the weaving. Powhatan men then constructed fish traps by fixing poles in the river bottom and putting the nets across and around them. William Strachey wrote that they resembled a "labyrinth or maze . . . with divers chambers or beds," and the fish could not get out once they had entered the trap. The Powhatans also sometimes used poles, which were sticks with the same cord fixed to the end and hooks made of bone. Henry said the fish were so plentiful that they were the main food in the summer. And as another colonist said, "as for Sturgeon all the World cannot be compared to it." Deer and fish, dried and smoked over the fire, provided protein for the winter. The American diet would not have been very different from the English, except that the fare was more varied and contained more fruits and vegetables. Henry wrote of the abundance of animals and birds, "only Peacocks and common hens wanting."[18]

Henry reported on the Powhatans' "manner of setting their corn with the gathering and Dressing," which was the women's responsibility. He described how the men prepared the ground around their houses, first killing the trees by stripping the bark and sometimes setting fires around the trees' base. Once the land was sufficiently open, the women dug holes. Formerly, they had used "a crooked piece of wood," but now they used the spades and shovels the English had given them in trade. In each hole, they put four or five kernels of what Henry called "their wheat"; he was referring to what modern Americans call corn. They also put two beans in each hole. This technique allowed the beans to use the growing cornstalks for support, like "our hops on poles." The ears of corn were impressive—"a great bigness in length and compass"—and every stalk had four or five ears.[19]

English people were always impressed by the tremendous yield produced by the Natives' cornfields. What Henry did not realize was that

Fishing scene showing weirs. Engraving by the workshop of Theodor de Bry from a painting by John White. Courtesy of the John Carter Brown Library at Brown University.

the strategy of growing the corn and beans together was one of the reasons for that great productivity. Beans produce nitrogen from their roots, so the beans were actually fertilizing the corn as they grew. When the English colonists later began to grow corn, they planted it in what they considered the civilized manner—in rows, with the beans and other crops in different fields. They could never figure out why their yields were so much lower than the Natives achieved.

Planting and harvesting were at about the same time as in England, but Henry wrote that the Natives gathered the corn as English people did apples, in "hand baskets." As the baskets became full, they transferred the contents to larger baskets made of tree bark or hemp or the cornstalks. Once the corn was gathered, the women laid it out on thick mats to dry in the sun. At night, they pulled the corn cobs into piles and covered them to keep out the dew. After the corn was "sufficiently weathered," they moved it into the people's houses. Every day the women prepared some of the cobs, "wringing the ears in pieces between their hands, and so rubbing out their corn," which they then stored in large baskets in their houses, taking up a good deal of the available space.[20]

One key difference for Thomas and Henry was that the women did all the agricultural activities—planting, weeding, and harvesting. Pocahontas was right there in the fields with the other women. English writers saw Native women's work as exploitation, but they did not understand that, because of their ownership of the crops and the fields, women claimed a crucial role in the tribe's decision-making. And they had extremely valuable knowledge, so their work in the fields anchored the community. In England, by contrast, women were legally "covered" by their husbands and did not have the right to make decisions about their own property or even make their own wills, and any money they earned belonged to their husbands. They had roughly the same legal status as children and had no role in political decisions. Only widows could control their own property.[21] Powhatan women had power and authority that English women could only imagine.

The Powhatans gathered on an appointed day every year to plant corn for the Powhatan, and, Henry wrote, they worked with such diligence that they planted large fields in one day. After the planting was done, two men brought the crown sent by the king of England, and the Powhatan put it on his head for the ceremony in which he rewarded his people with special beads. The people stood in the fields facing the Powhatan; as he walked forward, they walked backward, always keeping their eyes on him. Henry expected him to throw the beads down on the ground and let the people "scramble for them," but instead he called forward several people and put the beads in their hands: "and this is the greatest courtesy he does his people." When the corn was ripe, the people returned to harvest it and prepare it for storage in specially made storehouses.[22]

Henry wrote that the people offered the Powhatan part of their own harvest, which he also stored. Having all this corn meant that during the coming winter, the Powhatan could oversee its distribution back to the people as they needed it. No one would go without as long as corn was available. The Powhatan derived his power in part from caring for his people and sharing out his wealth rather than accumulating it for himself and his own family.

Reports such as Henry's were important because knowledge of the environment was crucial for the colonists. One point that Henry and others who wrote about Virginia stressed was that you had to know what you were doing in dealing with American plants and animals. As the colonists tried to forage for food, local knowledge mattered, because it was easy to eat the wrong thing or something that had not been prepared properly, and the results could be disastrous.

One particularly dramatic episode happened to a group of soldiers sent up the James River to find a good place for a new settlement. A week before the intended expedition, Powhatan sent messengers to say that he forbade "those quarters" to the English and, with Thomas acting as interpreter, demanded the return of two of his men being held as prisoners in the fort. If his demands were not met, the English were told, Powhatan's people would "destroy us after strange manner." According to the messengers, Powhatan's men would "make us drunk and then kill us."[23]

Acting governor Sir Thomas Dale just laughed at Powhatan's warning; he was "very merry at this threat," and the expedition went ahead. One evening, while the men upriver were at prayers, they heard noises coming out of a nearby cornfield. The noises were "hup hup!" and "oho oho," and some of them thought they saw a Powhatan leap over their own fire and run into the corn shouting the same words. The English staying near the falls that evening became "confusedly amazed." In those days, the word "amazed" meant terrified or stupefied. These men were out of their minds with fear. They were unable to speak normally and said only "oho oho." In their confusion, they could not distinguish friend from enemy, so they picked up their weapons and attacked each other, beating their fellow soldiers down and trying to break their heads. Luckily they grabbed their muskets from the wrong end, so no one was killed.

After a short while, the English woke up from their "dream" and looked around for the enemies they had been fighting, but they found only each other. They were certain that the Powhatans had bewitched them by their "Sorceries and Charms."

What actually did cause this episode? It seems likely that the Englishmen had accidentally eaten some of the leaves of the Jimsonweed plant. The word "Jimson" is actually a contraction of "Jamestown." Jimsonweed is a member of the same family as deadly nightshade, and it has powerful hallucinogenic effects. This is probably the drug that young Powhatan boys took as they were initiated into adulthood in the Huskenaw. They were rendered "mad with a kind of drink" as part of the ceremony. The supernatural explanation made the best sense to the soldiers, but it was terrifying to think that Powhatan priests had such powers.

Jamestown's leaders had sent Thomas and Henry to live with the Powhatans just so they could know Virginia Algonquian culture from the inside and could help English colonists learn about the environment.

Both Powhatan and the various governors at Jamestown used them for their own purposes, and both boys knew they were on assignment. They had to soak up as much knowledge as they could while satisfying Powhatan that it was worth while keeping them around.

Pocahontas, Thomas, and Henry all lived together in Orapax during the winter of 1609–10. Powhatan had moved his capital specifically to put more distance between his people and the colonists at Jamestown, and as relations with the English worsened, Thomas and Henry felt less welcome in Powhatan's presence than before. They felt they had to compete for Powhatan's goodwill, so they became rivals rather than allies. And goodwill seemed to be in very short supply.

After Henry had been at Orapax for three weeks, in November 1609, Powhatan sent him to Jamestown carrying a message saying that if the English would send a boat upriver, Powhatan's people would freight it with corn. The colonial leaders were delighted and immediately dispatched their pinnace. Powhatan received the English party graciously, giving them a house to stay in.

Then, the next day, while the parties were trading, the English thought they were being deliberately cheated: they thought the Powhatans were pushing up the bottoms of their baskets to make them seem full when they were not. As tensions increased and accusations began to fly, men who "lay lurking in the woods and corn about" began a "oulis" (howling) and "whopubb" (hubbub). These strange noises from unknown sources were terrifying, especially for those who had lived through the episode up the river, and the English were right to be scared. Hidden warriors shot the Englishmen as they carried baskets of corn to the ship; only two escaped and made it back to Jamestown.[24]

Powhatan had sent Henry and Samuel, the German carpenter, away to another town when the English party came, so Henry heard about the disaster after the fact from Thomas. He did not know whether Powhatan's original plan had been for a friendly exchange, but Henry suspected he had been set up when Powhatan sent him to Jamestown with the invitation to come to Orapax for food, just as Thomas had earlier carried a false invitation. Henry said, "The king in show made still much of us, yet his mind was much declined from us, which made us fear the worst."[25] Relations between the Powhatans and the English had definitely turned hostile, without even a veneer of friendliness left. And the leaders and guns at Jamestown were too far away to protect Henry and Thomas even if they wanted to.

Meanwhile, Jamestown was "a world of miseries." The colonists felt like prisoners in the fort because they knew they would be picked off and shot if they ventured out. "The Indian killed as fast without, if our men stirred but beyond the bounds of the blockhouse, as famine and pestilence did within." Reports said that one man had shocked everybody by screaming that God did not exist. He argued that God would not allow his own creatures to live and die so miserably; therefore, there was no God.[26]

In May 1610, just as the winter of suffering was ending in Jamestown, the group that had been shipwrecked in Bermuda the previous summer finally arrived in two ships, aptly named *Patience* and *Deliverance*, that they had built out of the remains of their wrecked ship and local cedar.

The new arrivals from Bermuda found Jamestown in really dire straits after the starving winter, "full of misery and misgovernment," and the population dramatically reduced. Their only food was "vermin"—snakes, rats, and dogs. The Virginia Company described Jamestown's horrible winter as a "tragical comedy"—tragical because of the suffering but a comedy because of its happy ending.[27]

Thomas and Henry did not know it, but they almost got stranded in Virginia that spring. Sir Thomas Gates, the designated governor who finally assumed his office after his Bermuda sojourn, decided to give the whole thing up as a complete failure. So in early June, everyone piled onto the ships and moved down the James River toward home back in England. No one gave a thought to Henry and Thomas and how they would feel when they found themselves deserted and cut off. Like other abandoned people, they would have become Natives and lived as Powhatans for the rest of their lives. Other Europeans had been left behind in earlier colonial attempts, so it was no big deal—from the point of view of Jamestown's leaders.

By an incredible coincidence, the departing ships met the fleet of the new governor, Thomas West, Lord de la Warr, coming up the river as they moved down it. The Virginia Company back in London did not know that Gates and his company had survived in Bermuda and had finally reached Virginia, so they had sent this new governor. Luckily, Gates had prevented the disgruntled colonists from burning the settlement to the ground, because they were now forced to turn around and go back to their place of misery. With the newly arrived supplies and people, the colony was saved. And the colonists were in time to plant some crops for food for the coming year. This was not just a piece of luck; rather, the Virginia Company saw this coincidence as the direct intervention of God, who thereby demonstrated both his existence and his favor to the venture. Sir George Somers, admiral of the shipwrecked *Sea Venture*, went back to Bermuda for supplies and to get some of the pigs and seabirds that inhabited the islands. So the Jamestown colonists went from eating rats to having pork and fowl for their dinners.

And the colony's leaders and the company also had renewed hope for the future. One of the Germans who came in 1608 was a "Helvetian" named William Volday or Faldoe. Capt. John Smith had come to mistrust him as he did the other Germans, but others put faith in him. He had gone to England in 1609 and convinced merchants in London that he knew where to find silver in the mountains to the west and beyond. He returned to Jamestown with Lord de la Warr and was said to have carried a map showing the silver mines. De la Warr reportedly intended to search beyond the falls, but his chronic illness while he was in Virginia prevented that. As hostilities increased along the river, trying to reach that site was increasingly impossible, and Volday himself soon died of a "burning fever."[28] The colony was back to looking for a source of revenue to repay its investors.

As Jamestown recovered, Thomas and Henry had an opportunity to escape the fear and danger of life with Powhatan. The Patawomeck leader Iopassus visited Orapax in March 1610. The Patawomecks lived on the Potomac River, which runs into the northern part of Chesapeake Bay. Iopassus "showed such kindness" to the boys that they decided to leave Powhatan and accompany him back north. In addition to Thomas and Henry, the absconding party included the German carpenter Samuel. Samuel had been held as a hostage when Powhatan sent the other Germans to Jamestown to steal weapons for him, and he was re-moved with Henry so they would not witness Powhatan's attack on the English traders. So Henry and Samuel had found common cause over their time at Orapax.[29]

What happened next is hard to piece together from the fragmentary accounts, but competition and tension between the two English boys led to conflict and tragedy. After they had gone a mile or two, Henry wrote, Thomas "feigned some excuse of stay, and unknown to us went back to the Powhatan and acquainted him with our departing with the Patawomeck." So Thomas abandoned Henry and Samuel and gave the plan away. Henry wrote that Powhatan sent some men after Henry and Samuel "commanding our return," but they refused and continued on their journey. The men sent by Powhatan accompanied them until sud-denly one killed Samuel with an axe. Henry ran away and was pur-sued by Powhatan's men, but the Patawomecks caught and held the pursuers. So, according to Henry, "I shifted for myself and got to the Patawomeck's country."

Capt. John Smith, who was back in England and had heard every-thing at second hand, added a detail to the story. He said, "Pocahontas, the King's daughter saved a boy called Henry Spelman, that lived many years after, by her means, amongst the Patawomecks."[30] Clearly Henry did not get to the Patawomecks' country simply by "shifting" for himself. And Pocahontas had made a bold move by intervening on his behalf. She might have been carrying out her father's orders; after his show of force, Powhatan may have acted to protect Henry. If she did act on her own, she was able to do that because she had also embarked on a new phase of life.

Powhatan had decided that Pocahontas was now at an age when she should live as an adult, so he arranged a marriage for her. William Strachey mentioned that Pocahontas married a "private Captain" called Kocoum. That he was a "private Captain" meant the couple could stay with Powhatan, because Kocoum was not part of a ruling family.[31]

As Pocahontas settled into the life of a married woman, Powhatan sent Thomas back to Jamestown. He had lived with the Powhatans for three years, and that was fine as long as he was young. But now Thomas was becoming an adult. Powhatan could have held him as a hostage but instead just told him to go.[32]

In sending Thomas back to Jamestown, Powhatan severed his last tie of friendship with the colonists. William Strachey included an "angry song" mocking the English in his *Historie of Travell into Virginia Britania*:

1. Mattanerew shashashewaw crawango pechecoma
    Whe Tassantassa inoshashaw yehockan pocosack
    Whe, whe, yah, ha, ha, ne, he, wittowa, wittowa.

2. Mattanerew shashashewaw, erawango pechecoma
    Capt. Newport inoshashaw neir in hoc nantion matassan
    Whe whe, yah, ha, ha, etc.

3. Mattanerew shashashewaw erowango pechecoma
    Thom. Newport inoshashaw neir in hoc nantion monocock
    Whe whe etc.

4. Mattanerew shashashewaw, erawango pechecoma
    Pockin Simon moshasha mingon nantian Tamahuck.
    Whe whe, etc.

In the song, the Powhatans bragged about killing the English despite, as Strachey wrote, "all our Poccasacks, that is our Guns." They singled out Thomas for scorn, singing that they could hurt him "for all his Monnacock that is his bright Sword." They also could capture Simon "for all his Tamahauke, that is his Hatchet." Simon Score was a sailor, according to Strachey, and he had been taken prisoner along with "one

Cob, a boy," in a conflict up near the falls of the James the previous year. The English cried as they lay dying, "Whe whe which they mocked us for and cried again to us Yah, ha ha, Tewittaw, Tewittawa, Tewittawa."[33] And the copper that Captain Newport brought them would not protect them. However much the Powhatans had loved Thomas, he was English and on the other side. Now back in Jamestown, he became the principal translator for the colony's leadership.

While Thomas acted as Jamestown's interpreter, and Pocahontas continued at Orapax as a married woman, Henry lived in Iopassus's household in the town of Pasptanzie, almost as a member of the family. In fact, the roles he now occupied may have been pretty similar to what an English servant would have done at home. As a member of Iopassus's family, he was particularly good at caring for the chief's baby.

Henry told a story that gives us a window into his life at Pasptanzie. Iopassus went to visit another king, and Henry said "it was my hap" to be left behind with two of the king's wives. One wife decided she wanted to go and visit her father, more than a day's journey away, and she wanted Henry to go with her and carry her child the whole way. Henry refused, and she hit him hard three or four times. Henry said that he was "loath to bear too much," so he "pulled her down" and hit her in turn. Then another of Iopassus's wives joined in, and both women beat Henry so badly that he could hardly walk.[34]

When Iopassus returned, Henry told him what had happened; the king was angry, so he picked up a tool and struck his wife. Henry was terrified because she was unconscious and "in manner dead," so he fled to a neighbor's house. After Iopassus's wife regained consciousness and Iopassus's anger was "appeased," his brother told him where Henry was hiding, and Iopassus sent the baby to him. Apparently the child was extremely upset by all that had happened, and Henry was the only one who could make him stop crying. About midnight, Iopassus sent to have the baby returned.

The next morning, Iopassus was up early, and he came to the house where Henry was staying. Henry was afraid and did not want to see him, but Iopassus was not angry. Instead he was kind to Henry and wanted to know if he was all right. He also asked Henry whether "I was afraid of him last night because I ran away from him, and hid myself." Henry then asked about his queen, and Iopassus said that "all was well." He urged Henry to return with him: "telling me he loved me, and none should hurt me." Although Henry was still unsettled, he did go with Iopassus. When they got back home, the queen looked at him with pure hostility. But because the king had promised his love, Henry said, "I cared the less for others' frowns."

As Henry found contentment living among the Patawomecks, conditions within Jamestown and relationships along the James River steadily worsened. Leaders in London and in Jamestown believed that the colonists' weakness and dependency had created their own misery and made the Powhatans despise them. So the colony's leaders instituted a system of martial law, called the *Laws Divine, Moral, and Martial*, that would force every colonist to be a virtuous citizen. The code was published under the name of the colony secretary, William Strachey, but it became known as "Dale's Laws," after Sir Thomas Dale, who was acting governor as the laws were first enforced in 1610. According to the laws, a drumbeat would force all the colonists to get up and go to work together. Every part of their lives would be regulated by the drum.

Anyone committing the smallest infraction or failing in one's duty faced severe punishment. A baker who made bread seem heavier than it really was would have his or her ears cut off, and a similar punishment would be imposed on a cook who held back part of any meat or fish she or he was given to cook. Swearing an oath untruly or giving false testimony carried the death penalty. Death was the sentence for trading with the Natives without authorization, running away to the Powhatans, or informing them about conditions in the colony. If life in Jamestown could be made any more horrible, these laws would do it. The law code was based on that used in military campaigns, a system that old soldiers such as Dale were accustomed to. Strachey brought the manuscript of the code with him when he returned to England in late 1611 and registered it for publication that December.[35]

At the same time that leaders decided to call the colonists to heel, they decided to force the Natives to fear and respect English power, by carrying out a series of attacks in the summer of 1610. In early July, Sir Thomas Gates led an attack on the Kecoughtans near the mouth of the James. He tricked the Kecoughtans into believing that his was a peaceful mission by bringing a taborer, a performer who danced while simultaneously playing a small drum and a flute. The taborer's musical dance deceived the Kecoughtans, and as they came out unarmed to greet their guests, the English soldiers attacked. As the soldiers rummaged through the town after the slaughter, they picked up several "finely wrought" women's sashes, which William Strachey sent to female friends in England. With the Kecoughtan power destroyed, the English were able to place a settlement there to give early warning of any European ships entering Chesapeake Bay.[36]

In August, the colonists attacked the Paspaheghs and the Chickahominies to the west of Jamestown along the James. After burning the Paspahegh town, they captured a high-ranking woman they believed to be the Paspahegh queen and two of her children. George Percy wrote that the soldiers on the boat returning to Jamestown were angry that the queen and her children had been spared and wanted more vengeance. The soldiers held a council and decided that the Paspaheghs should die. They began by throwing the two children into the river and then "shooting out their brains in the water." Percy intervened to save the queen, but after the men returned, an emissary came to their boat to tell Percy that Lord de la Warr had ordered her death. Some of his men wanted to burn her, but Percy said that after seeing so much blood shed that day, he could not do that now that he was in his "cold blood"; so the soldiers took her into the woods and beheaded her. The colony's commanders wanted the Native leaders along the James to know that the slightest provocation would be met with maximum force.[37]

The slaughter of the Paspahegh boys was particularly shocking because Native reprisals spared children. The Paspaheghs took in young Alonso de Olmos when they destroyed the Spanish Jesuit mission in the 1570s, and they sheltered him for two years. English disregard for the welfare of children, their willingness to abandon their own children, and their bloodthirsty extermination of the Paspahegh princes exhibited true savagery, as the Chesapeake Algonquians saw it.

Henry, living among the Patawomecks, probably knew little or nothing of what the soldiers were doing on the James. He thought that Iopassus was so good to him because he hoped for copper from the English and believed Henry could get it for him, and this promise was soon "bountifully performed" by Capt. Samuel Argall. Argall came at Christmastime 1610; as usual, he was in search of corn for the colonists and also because he had heard that "a boy named Harry" was among the Patawomecks. As Capt. John Smith wrote, Henry was "by those people preserved from the fury of Powhatan," and they welcomed Argall and supplied food because of Henry.

After Argall's ship had been anchored several days, Iopassus and Henry came aboard. It was a very cold winter, and Iopassus was sitting with Argall "by the fire upon a hearth in the Hold." One of the men was reading a Bible, and Iopassus "gave a very attent ear and looked with a very wish't eye upon him as if he desired to understand what he read"; so Argall took the book and turned to the picture of the creation of the world at the front. Argall directed Henry, "a boy . . . who had lived a whole year with this Indian-King and spake his language, to show it unto him, and to interpret it in his language, . . . which the king seemed to like well of."[38]

The Bible they had may have been the one published by Robert Barker in 1603. Queen Elizabeth died that year and was succeeded by King James VI of Scotland, who became James I of England, so Barker actually published two editions in 1603. One identified him on the title page as "printer to the Queen's Most Excellent Majesty," and the second had him as "printer to the King's Most Excellent Majesty." It was always important to be ahead of the curve. Henry described the illustration at the beginning of the book of Genesis, which showed Adam and Eve at the fateful moment of sin. They are standing on either side of an apple tree, and Eve is holding out an apple to Adam, who reaches out his hand to take it. The huge snake is wrapped around the tree trunk. They are surrounded by animals of every description: leopards, elephants, and camels are among the most exotic, but the scene also includes sheep, deer, and prancing horses. The sky, where the sun shines brightly, is filled with large birds. God is represented in the sky in Hebrew characters shining through the clouds in the center above the apple tree. The page is headed, "The creation of the world." Human history is foretold in this image.

Iopassus offered to tell Argall "the manner of their beginning," which the English judged "a pretty fabulous tale indeed." Iopassus said they had five gods, and the most important sometimes showed himself as a "mightie great Hare." The other four were the four winds; Iopassus made a diagram of the world with his hands to indicate their locations. The hare pondered what kind of creatures should populate this world, and so he created men and women but kept them temporarily in a great bag in order to protect them from some cannibal spirits, like great giants, who wanted to eat them. These bad spirits came to the Great Hare's home in the land where the sun rises, but he drove them away.

Argall told Henry to ask Iopassus what substance the people and other creatures were made of, but Henry refused because he thought interrupting the chief in the middle of his account would irritate Iopassus. Clearly Henry put his feelings ahead of Captain Argall's. Iopassus went on with his account in his own way. "That godlike hare" made the water and the land, stocked the water with fish, and put a great deer on the land. The other four gods became jealous and came from the four corners of the earth. They killed the deer "with hunting poles" and feasted on it, after which they returned to their corners. The Great Hare recovered the deer's skin and removed all the hairs, spreading the hairs over the earth "with many powerful words and charms whereby every hair

THE FIRST BOOKE OF MOSES,
CALLED *GENESIS.

* *This word signifieth the beginning and generation of the creatures.*

THE ARGVMENT.

MOses in effect declareth three things, which are in this booke chiefly to bee considered : First, that the world and all things therein were created by God, and that man being placed in this great tabernacle of the world to behold Gods wonderfull works, and to praise his name for the infinite graces, wherewith he had indued him, fell willingly from God through disobedience : who yet for his owne mercies sake restored him to life, and confirmed him in the same by his promise of Christ to come, by whom he should ouercome Satan, death, & hel. Secondly, that the wicked vnmindfull of Gods most excellent benefits, remained still in their wickednes, & so falling most horribly from sinne to sinne, prouoked God (who by his preachers called them continually to repentance) at length to destroy the whole world, Thirdly he assureth vs by the examples of Abraham, Izhak, Iaakob, and the rest of the Patriarkes, that his mercies neuer faile them, whom he chuseth to be his Church, and to professe his Name in earth, but in all their afflictions and persecutions he euer assisteth them, sindeth comfort and deliuereth them. And because the beginning increase, preseruation, and successe thereof might be only attributed to God, Moses sheweth by the examples of Kain, Ishmael, Esau and others, which were noble in mans iudgement, that this Church dependeth not on the estimation and nobility of the world : and also by the fewnesse of them which haue at all times worshipped him purely according to his word, that it standeth not in the multitude, but in the poore and despised, in the small flocke and little number, that man in his wisedome might be confounded, and the Name of God euermore praysed.

CHAP. I.

1 *God created the heauen and the earth,* 3 *The light and the darkenesse,* 8 *The firmament.* 9 *He separateth the water from the earth.* 16 *He createth the sunne, the moon, & the stars.* 21 *He createth the fish, birds, beasts.* 26 *He createth man, and giueth him rule ouer all creatures,* 29 *and prouideth nowriture for man and beast.*

Psal.33.6. & 136 5. ecclu.18.1 act.14.15. & 17.24. ‖Or, waste ‡Ebr. face of the deepe. ‡Ebr. face of the waters. Heb.11.3. ‡Ebr. be- tween the light and betweene the darknesse. ‖The first day. and it was so.

1 IN the beginning * God created the heauen and the earth.

2 And the earth was ‖without forme, and void, & darknesse was vpon the ‖ deepe, and the Spirit of God moo- ued vpon the † waters.

3 Then God sayd, * Let there be light : and there was light.

4 And God saw the light that it was good, and God separated † the light from the darkenesse.

5 Aad God called the light, Day: and the darknesse, hee called Night. ‖ So the euening and the morning were the first day.

6 ¶ Againe God sayd, * Let there be a ‖ firmament in the middes of the waters : and let it sepa- rate the waters from the waters.

7 Then God made the firmament, and separa- ted the waters which were vnder the firmament, from the waters which were ✲ aboue the firmament: and it was so.

† *Ebr. so was the euening, so was the morning. Psal.33.6. and 136. g.ier.10.12. and 51.15. ‖Or,spreading ouer, & arte.Psal 148 4.*

8 And God called the firmament, Heauen. ‖ So the euening and the morning were the second day.

9 ¶ God said againe, * Let the waters vnder the heauen be gathered into one place, and let the dry land appeare: and it was so.

10 And God called the drie land, Earth: and he called the gathering together of the waters, Seas : and God saw that it was good.

11 Then God said, Let ye earth bud forth the bud of the hearbe that seedeth seede, which beareth fruite according to his kind, which hath his seed in it selfe vpon the earth. & it was so.

12 And the earth brought forth the bud of the herbe, that seedeth seed according to his kinde, al- so the tree that beareth fruite, which hath seede in it selfe according to his kinde : and God saw that it was good.

13 ‖ So the euening and the morning were the third day.

14 ¶ And God said, * Let there be lights in the firmament of the heauen, to separate the day from the night, and let them be for signes, and for sea- sons, and for dayes, and yeeres.

15 And let them be for lights in ye firmament of the heauen to giue light vpon the earth. & it was so.

16 God then made two great lights : the grea- ter light to rule the day, and the lesse light to rule the night : he made also the starres.

17 And God set them in the firmament of the heauen, to shine vpon the earth.

‖ The se- cond day Psal.23.7. & 89.12. & 136.6.

Iob.38.4.

‖ The third day Psal.136.7. deut.4.19.

A 3   18 And

Engraving of Adam and Eve from *The Bible, That Is, the Holy Scriptures, Contained in the Old and New Testament* (London: Robert Barker, 1603). Courtesy of British Library Imaging Services.

became a deer." Then he opened the great bag and placed the people all over the earth, each country receiving one man and one woman: "and so the world took his first beginning of mankind."

Argall interrupted again, and this time Henry did ask his question: What happens to these people after death? Iopassus said they go up into a high tree, where they could see a "broad pathway" lined with "all manner of pleasant fruits, as Mulberries, Strawberries, Plums, etc." They follow the path to the rising sun, where the Great Hare lives. Once they are halfway there, they stop at a house where a goddess offers hospitality and always has all kinds of special delicacies for them to eat. "When they are well refreshed," they resume their journey to the sunrise, where they find their "forefathers living in great pleasure in a goodly field, where they do nothing but dance and sing, and feed on delicious fruits with that great Hare." They live there a long time, "until they be stark old men," when they die there and "come into the world again."

At the end of all this, Henry wrote, "Captain Argall gave the king some copper for me. . . . Thus was I set at liberty and brought into England." Argall obtained a great deal of corn as well in exchange for the copper. Argall sailed back to England in March 1611, and Henry accompanied him. After two years away, he once again experienced life in England.

KNOWLEDGE SOUGHT AND GAINED

L ONDON WAS FULL OF VIRGINIA NEWS when Henry Spelman arrived in July 1611. Shakespeare's *Tempest* was first performed that year. Henry and William Strachey, who returned to London in December of that year, understood it in a way few people in London could. They had been in the fleet that confronted the great hurricane of 1609, and Strachey sent home an account of the storm and its aftermath, "A True Reportory of the Wreck and Redemption of Sir Thomas Gates, Knight." The "Reportory," which arrived in London in September 1610, was not published until 1625; but Strachey and Shakespeare moved in the same literary circles, so Shakespeare had an opportunity to read the manuscript. *The Tempest* opened with a storm based on the "Reportory's" description.[1]

Shakespeare wrote *The Tempest* for the restored Blackfriars theater, where the King's Men, the company of which Shakespeare was part owner, performed. Both the theater and the lodgings were in a former monastery, which had been repurposed when England became Protestant; the complex included an alehouse and a music performance space. Before Strachey went to Virginia, he had been an investor in a company called the Children of the Queen's Revels, which occupied Blackfriars Theatre before the King's Men took over. Strachey attested that, as a shareholder, he had been at the theater "once, twice, and thrice in a week." Now back in London, he was living in "lodgings in the black Friars," the same complex where *The Tempest* was performed. The theater and its associated buildings were a magnet for writers; Ben Jonson also lived in the Blackfriars.[2]

The Globe, where Shakespeare's previous plays were staged, was open to the sky, but Blackfriars was an indoor space lit by candles in chandeliers. The storm with its loud noise and swirling action made effective use of the small enclosed space, and it must have been terrifying to the audience.[3]

The ship caught in the terrible storm carried the "usurping" Duke of Milan, who tricked his older brother, Prospero, out of his rightful office and sent him into exile on the island where the play takes place. Prospero, the true duke, was a powerful magician, and he took his revenge by directing his servant, Ariel, an "airy spirit," to create the storm that forced the ship onto his island.[4]

Strachey wrote about St. Elmo's Fire, the electrical effect that creates the illusion of flames playing around the mast in storms, and Shakespeare translated that into Ariel's magic. When Ariel reported back, he told Prospero how he burned in many places, "on the top-mast, the yards, and bowsprit, would I flame distinctly." It was so terrifying that one character jumped into the sea, exclaiming, "Hell is empty, and all the devils are here!"

When leaders among the passengers tried to come up on deck during the tempest, Shakespeare had the crew ordering them back down into the hold because they were in the way. In the brave new world of Atlantic enterprises, expertise trumped social class. Even for the high-ranking gentlemen, there was no escape from the hold, with its stench and the swirling water.

The Tempest presented many themes that stirred Henry's emotions. Like William Strachey, he had lived through the storm that opened the play, with its danger and uncertain outcome, and had seen the electrical effects playing around the mast, and he knew how terrifying it was. He could also understand the situation of Prospero's daughter, Miranda, torn from her family and normal social context and taken to live in a lonely place where her manipulative father pitted his magic against the powers of the land and its inhabitants. Miranda, who would have been played by a boy, was starting the transition from childhood to maturity and a degree of independence in this play. Henry, now sixteen, could hope for a similar transition for himself.

Another character with whom Henry must have felt some sympathy is Caliban, described in the list of characters as "a savage and deformed native of the island, Prospero's slave." Caliban insisted that the island belonged to him and that the "tyrant" Prospero had taken it from him. He said that at first Prospero had treated him well, almost as a member of his family, but then had turned against him. As Caliban put it, Prospero had taught him language, but Caliban's only benefit was that "I know how to curse."

Caliban also said that he would not build any more dams for catching fish, which shows how closely writers such as Shakespeare were following the news from America. In the earlier Roanoke colony, the Roanokes had built fish dams for the colonists, but then, as frictions grew, they threatened to tear them down. The colony's governor admitted that, had this happened, his men would not have been able to rebuild them because they just did not know how. Henry, because of his stay with Powhatan and Iopassus, knew the skill involved in creating those weirs.[5]

Playing on this same idea of English dependence, Caliban offered to show Stephano and Trinculo, survivors of the shipwreck engineered by Prospero, where the best springs were and to supply them with food and firewood. He was willing to serve Stephano and Trinculo as a way of getting away from Prospero's control. Henry would have found all these themes of friendship turned to anger, and dependence leading to conflict, familiar. Caliban's saying that Prospero had once treated him as a family member and then rejected him matched Henry's experience with Powhatan.

Caliban's statement that "the isle is full of noises" also awakened memories such as the voice that came out of the fire in the Huskenaw and the "howling and hubbub" made by the hidden men who suddenly attacked the Englishmen trading for corn. George Sandys, brother of Virginia Company head, Sir Edwin Sandys, later wrote of the loud noise made by the frogs all through the night in Virginia. The English called them "Powhatan's hounds" because of their "continual yelping."[6]

In the play, Stephano and Trinculo hatch a scheme to make their fortune by exhibiting Caliban at home. In England, as Trinculo says, although "they will not give a doit to relieve a lame beggar, they will lay out ten to see a dead Indian." A doit was a copper coin of very small value. Shakespeare knew that Londoners had flocked to see Namontack when he was in England, and his presence made news.

While Henry was in London, exotic Powhatans were even incorporated into royal pageantry. The lavish procession for the wedding of Princess Elizabeth in 1612 included one chariot carrying "the choice musicians of this kingdom in robes like to the Virginian Priests with sundry devices, all pleasant and significant."[7]

Everyone wanted to know about Virginia, and Henry Spelman was a key actor in the search for knowledge and understanding. His uncle, the historian Sir Henry Spelman, moved to London in 1612. Now that Henry was also in London and able to share his firsthand knowledge of both the Powhatans and the Patawomecks, Sir Henry got him to write it all down. As Henry put it, "To give some satisfaction to my friends and contentment unto others, which wish well to this voyage, and are desirous to hear the fashions of that country, I have set down as well as I can, what I observed in the time I was among them."[8]

Henry broke up his account into the kinds of categories scholars such as Sir Henry saw as important. The first was religion, what Henry called their service to their gods. He wrote that the priests could actually cause their gods to appear among them, and they had images of their deities that they kept in sacred houses. He distinguished between the Powhatans and the Patawomecks in his descriptions of their religious practices. He wrote that "the great Powhatan he has an Image called Cakeres," which was in the temple at Orapax. When the English leaders gave Powhatan gifts, they were placed in that same temple as offerings to the gods. The Patawomecks, Henry wrote, "have an other god whom they call Quioquascacke and unto their Images they offer Beads and Copper if at any time they want Rain or have too much."[9]

Marriage was one topic that scholars wanted to know about, because families are the bedrock of society. Henry wrote that the "custom of the country is to have many wives and to buy them, so that he which have most copper and Beads may have most wives." A man who wanted a woman for his wife would first "make love to her," by which Henry meant he wooed her to win her favor. The man then approached her father, or other male relatives if her father was dead, and agreed on a price for her. The idea of a bride price would not have sounded particularly strange to Henry's readers because dowries were usual in Europe. The difference in Virginia was that it was the groom who paid. When the agreement was made, the bride's family brought her to her new husband. In the marriage ceremony, the bride and groom joined hands, and the groom's best man broke a long string of beads over their hands and then gave it to the bride's father. "And so with much mirth and feasting they go together." When a child was born, the father assembled family and neighbors and announced the name he had chosen, and then the rest of the day was spent in feasting and dancing. Marriages with the "King of the country" cemented alliances or relationships with client tribes. In Europe, royal marriages firmed up links between ruling families in other countries and secured successions, and Henry told his readers that the same strategies held in Virginia. When the chief decided to marry, he sent his leading men out to bring him "the fairest and comeliest maids out of which the King takes his choice." Once one of his wives had a child with him, the Powhatan "puts her from him," but he made sure she had "sufficient Copper and beads to maintain her and the child while it is young." Once the child was old enough to leave the mother, she or he would go to live with the Powhatan, and the mother was now free to remarry.[10]

Henry also wrote extensively on sickness and death. He described a curing ritual he saw a priest perform over a very sick person. The priest set a bowl of water and a rattle on the ground, and then he scooped up water into his mouth and sprayed it over his own chest and arms. After this purification, he took the rattle in one hand and beat his breast with the other, making a "great noise." Then the priest rose, first one leg and then the other, "as loath to wake the sick body." He shook his rattle over the sick person's body and stroked the "grieved parts" with his hand. Finally, he sprinkled water over the person, "mumbling certain words," and then departed. If the patient had been injured or wounded, the priest cut open the wound with a flint knife to make it bleed, and then he sucked out the blood. After the wound was clean, the priest applied "a certain root beaten to powder" on it.[11]

The English, like the Powhatans and Patawomecks, believed in a wide variety of unseen forces at work in the world and thought that some people had special abilities to contact and control these forces. Alexander Whitaker wrote that the Powhatans had "great witches among them," recalling familiar English themes.[12] On both sides of the Atlantic, every village had a local healer—often called a "wise woman" or "cunning man" in England—who treated people with herbs but also used special words, prayers, charms, and incantations, and in England as in Virginia, priests often also acted as healers.

Clients went to cunning folk for aid: to be healed or for help in finding a lost article. The problem was that supernatural powers to do good could also be used for harm, and respect for shamans and witches always involved a degree of fear. Colonists' respect for Native shamans' powers were reflected in their burial of a small bottle filled with sharp stones under one of Jamestown's entrances; witch bottles were supposed to protect people from evil powers. Sometimes witches were prosecuted in England, but usually this happened only after a very long period during which people suspected the witch of using her or his powers to hurt people. Mostly people went to them because they could and did help those in need, and these powerful actors lived out their lives in peace.[13]

Magical healing extended to the top of English society. Henry described the priest stroking the sick body in order to heal. In England, the monarch, as God's representative on earth, cured people by touching them. English kings and queens cured people with scrofula, which in-

He Priefts of the aforefaid Towne of Secota are well ftricken in yeers, and as yt fee-meth of more experience then the comon forte. They weare their heare cutt like a crefte, on the topps of thier heades as other doe, but the reft are cutt fhorte, fauinge thofe which growe aboue their foreheads in manner of a perriwigge. They alfo ha-ue fomwhat hanginge in their ears. They weare a fhorte clocke made of fine hares skinnes quilted with the hayre outwarde. The reft of thier bodie is naked. They are notable enchaunters, and for their pleafure they frequent the riuers, to kill with their bowes, and catche wilde ducks, fwannes, and other fowles.

Priest. Engraving by the workshop of Theodor de Bry from a painting by John White. Courtesy of the John Carter Brown Library at Brown University.

The Coniuerer. XI.

Hey haue comonlye coniurers or iuglers which vſe ſtrange geſtures, and often cō-
trarie to nature in their enchantments: For they be verye familiar with deuils, of
whome they enquier what their enemys doe, or other ſuche thinges. They ſhaue
all their heads ſauinge their creſte which they weare as other doe, and faſten a ſmall
black birde aboue one of their ears as a badge of their office. They weare nothinge
but a skinne which hangeth downe from their gyrdle, and couereth their priuityes. They weare a
bagg by their ſide as is expreſſed in the figure. The Inhabitants giue great credit vnto their ſpeeche, which oftentymes they finde
to bce true.

B 3

Conjuror. Engraving by the workshop of Theodor de Bry from a painting by John
White. Courtesy of the John Carter Brown Library at Brown University.

volved swelling of the lymph glands in the neck. It was probably caused by tuberculosis, but people of the time called it the King's Evil. At certain times, people with scrofula would line up, and King James would touch each of them as they paraded by. Each person was given a special gold coin to keep for protection. This royal magic was powerful enough to cross the ocean and be valued by the Powhatans. Archaeologists have discovered the burial of a very young child at Werowocomoco with lavish grave goods including two king's touch coins.[14]

Henry wrote that if the priest's cure was unsuccessful and the ailing person died, the relatives built a scaffold about three or four feet off the ground on which the corpse was laid, wrapped in mats. All the people gathered and the bereaved relatives, who were singing and weeping, threw beads to the poorer people, who scrambled for the beads, sometimes even breaking arms and legs, "being pressed by the company." When the ceremony was concluded, all went to the bereaved relatives' home for a feast, after which they sang and danced joyfully all day with "as much mirth as before sorrow." Their joy sped the departed along the path, lined by luscious fruit trees, toward the place where the sun rises and the Great Hare lives, where they would live new lives of plenty and pleasure in company with all those who had gone before them. Ultimately, those who mourned knew, the dead would return back into the human world after living full lives in the other world in the endless cycle of death and rebirth. When the body had decomposed and only bones were left, they were taken down, wrapped in a new mat, and hung in a special building. Once the building decayed and fell, the bones were buried in it. Henry wrote that the deceased's goods were divided among his wives and children. The "wife he likes best" got the house for her lifetime, and then it went to the most loved child.[15]

Moving on to government and justice, Henry excused his own ignorance. First, his youth and "understanding" made him less able to understand these issues. Also, he had not actually sought much information about how the Powhatans and Patawomecks were governed because he started out with the assumption "that Infidels were lawless," that they did not have laws and government like "civil" people. But then, during his time living with the Patawomecks, he saw five people executed for crimes. Four were involved in the killing of a child: the mother, two others "that did the fact with her," and one further person who helped to cover it up. Henry said the fourth man had been bribed "to hold his peace." The fifth person executed had robbed "a traveler of copper and beads." Henry wrote that theft of a neighbor's corn or copper "is death," as also was having sexual relations with another man's wife "if he be taken in the manner." He then went on to describe the executions he had witnessed. The condemned person was brought to the front of the chief's residence bound hand and foot. One of the principal men then "with a shell cut off their long lock, which they wear on the left side of their head." The lock of hair was hung "on a bow before the Kings house." Meanwhile, a great fire had been set. Murderers were beaten with sticks until their bones were broken, and they were then thrown alive into the fire. Thieves were beaten until they were dead before their bodies were put in the flames.[16]

Henry presented this description in a matter-of-fact way. Although it may sound sensational and vicious to us, English people were accustomed to brutal punishments. Religious dissidents had been burned at the stake in the sixteenth century, and traitors were hanged, drawn, and quartered. "Hanging" meant being pulled up on a scaffold by a rope around their necks, after which they were cut down alive and had their chests and stomachs cut open so that their innards could be removed, or drawn, and burned in front of them. Finally, the traitors' bodies were cut into four pieces, which is what was meant by "quartered." These punishments drew huge crowds, and the authorities thought of the experience as educational, which it probably was. Spectators understood the "awful" majesty of the law, which meant at the time that they were filled with awe at the power and justice of the state.

Such punishments were not just something in England's past. The Guy Fawkes conspirators, who were convicted of planning to blow up the Parliament when King James was present, were sentenced to hanging, drawing, and quartering in January 1606, the same year the first ships departed for Virginia. It was also widely known that Guy Fawkes himself had been extensively tortured before his trial. So Henry's descriptions of the punishments he had witnessed did not create an impression of savagery but rather confirmed the Natives' concern for maintenance of the social order and therefore of their civility.

Henry's description of Patawomeck warfare centered on weapons and tactics. He said their weapons were bows and arrows and a tool resembling a hammer. Warriors carried shields made of tree bark on their left shoulders "to cover that side as they stand forth to shoot." He wrote that they lacked discipline in their fighting, which was never out in the open. They preferred to fight among high reeds or trees and hid behind trees as they prepared their arrows. Henry described a battle he had witnessed between the Patawomecks and some Massawomecks. The Powhatans and the Patawomecks were both Algonquian speakers, but the Massawomecks, who were from the northwest, possibly as far as the Appalachians, spoke a language belonging to the Iroquoian group. Henry said the Massawomecks arrived in canoes, "which is a kind of Boat they have made in the form of an Hog's trough but somewhat more hollowed in." The two sides planted themselves some distance from each other and, crouching down, "softly steal" toward the enemy. If an enemy was so badly wounded that he could not run away, "they make haste to him to knock him on the head." The warriors who killed the most were considered "the chiefest men among them." Actually, not many people were killed, according to Henry, and once the Massawomecks had shot all their arrows, they "were glad to retire," especially as they had no food. The discipline of European warfare involved massed troops advancing to the sound of trumpets and drums to maintain order. Henry particularly noted that the Patawomecks did not have either instrument but that each side had "a kind of Howling or Hubbub so differing in sound one from the other" that they could easily distinguish friends from enemies. Colonists in Virginia had already experienced such sounds coming out of the woods and knew they indicated an impending attack.[17]

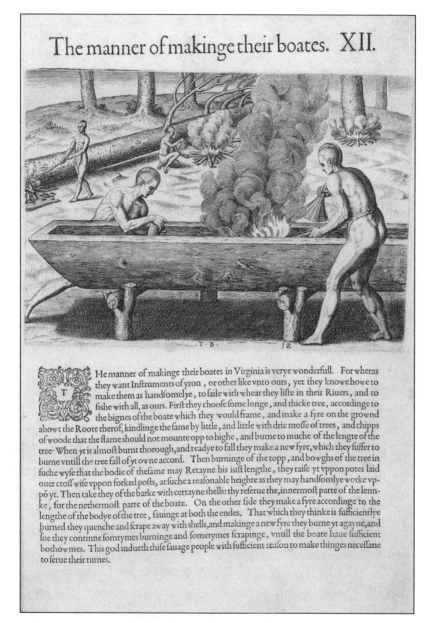

The manner of makinge their boates. XII.

He manner of makinge their boates in Virginia is verye wonderfull. For wheras they want Inftruments of yron, or other like vnto ours, yet they knowe howe to make them as handfomelye, to faile with whear they lifte in their Riuers, and to fishe with all, as ours. Firft they choofe fome longe, and thicke tree, accordinge to the bignes of the boate which they would frame, and make a fyre on the grownd abowt the Roote therof, kindlinge the fame by little, and little with drie moffe of trees, and chipps of woode that the flame should not mounte opp to highe, and burne to muche of the lengte of the tree· When yt is almoft burnt thorough, and readye to fall they make a new fyre, which they fuffer to burne vntill the tree fall of yt owne accord. Then burninge of the topp, and bowghs of the tree in fuche wyfe that the bodie of thefame may Retayne his iuft lengthe, they raife yt vppon potes laid ouer crofl wife vppon forked pofts, at fuche a reafonable heighte as rhey may handfomlye worke vppó yt. Then take they of the barke with certayne shells: thy referue the, innermoft parte of the lennke, for the nethermoft parte of the boate. On the other fide they make a fyre accordinge to the lengthe of the bodye of the tree, fauinge at both the endes. That which they thinke is fufficientlye burned they quenche and fcrape away with shells, and makinge a new fyre they burne yt agayne, and foe they continne fomtymes burninge and fometymes fcrapinge, vntill the boate haue fufficient bothowmes. This god indueth thife fauage people with fufficient reafon to make thinges neceffarie to ferue their turnes.

Making a dugout canoe. Engraving by the workshop of Theodor de Bry from a painting by John White. Courtesy of the John Carter Brown Library at Brown University.

Henry's final topic was his favorite: pastimes. He said that Native sports were like those in England. When the Natives came together for large feasts or other celebrations, they performed a dance like "our darbysher Hornpipe. A man first and then a woman, and so through them all, hanging all in a round, there is one which stand in the midst with a pipe and a rattle with which when he begins to make a noise all the rest Gigetts about wringing their necks and stamping on the ground." The man with the pipe and rattle resembled the taborer with his flute and drum who had so misled the Kecoughtans when Governor Gates attacked them and helps us understand their tragic misreading of English intentions.

Henry wrote that the Chesapeake Algonquians had a game like soccer, which was played by women and young boys, with goals like those in England. The big difference, according to Henry, was that "they never fight nor pull one another down." The men's sport involved dropping "a little ball" and kicking it with the top of the foot, "and he that can strike the ball furthest wins that they play for."[18] This was the end of Henry's account. He offered no general conclusion about Powhatans and Patawomecks and their ways. Perhaps he meant to return to the project at some later time.

As soon as William Strachey arrived in London at the end of 1611, he applied to the Stationers' Company for permission to publish the legal system established in Virginia, *The Lawes Divine, Morall and Martiall*, and it was published early in 1612. He then turned his attention to his more important work, completing the manuscript of his *Historie of Travell into Virginia Britania*, with its vivid descriptions of the colony and Powhatan life, and he enlisted Henry's help. Quoting Henry, he wrote a long passage about Captain Argall finding him living with Iopassus and the Christmas Eve exchange in which Henry described the creation of the world in the Bible and Iopassus told his own people's beliefs about the creation of humans and what happens to them after death. Strachey wrote that Henry had "despaired of ever seeing his native Country, his fathers house, (for he was descended of a gentle family)

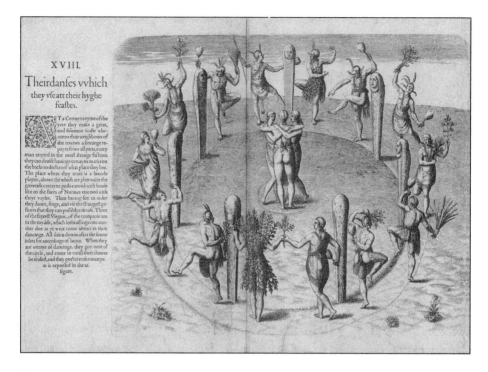

Religious ceremony. Engraving by the workshop of Theodor de Bry from a painting by John White. Courtesy of the John Carter Brown Library at Brown University.

or Christians any more." Samuel Purchas printed the part about the afterlife in his *Purchas His Pilgrimage* two years later.[19]

Several manuscripts of the *Historie of Travell* survive, and some include a very long list of Powhatan words and their English equivalents. Its length and specificity mean that Strachey must have had help from others with more extensive experience. Because we know Strachey interviewed Henry, it seems very likely that he drew on Henry's deep knowledge of both the Powhatan and the Patawomeck languages, so Henry's knowledge is represented here as well as in his own memoir.

Another source for this language project was Thomas Harriot. Early in the manuscript, Strachey singled out Harriot as "that true Lover of virtue, and great learned professor of all arts and knowledge," who was in the "first Colony," Roanoke, "spake the Indian language, searched the Country and made many proofs of the richness of the soil." By 1612, Harriot was a major scientist with a wide network of correspondents all over Europe. The American language that Harriot knew was coastal Carolina Algonquian, part of the same language family as those spoken in the Chesapeake, so Strachey, who praised him so highly, surely sought his help. The vocabulary, as Strachey wrote, would be an important source for future venturers to America, and that was a goal that Harriot cared about deeply. Harriot had actually invented a method to record languages phonetically to make communication possible around the world. He called it "An universall Alphabet containing six & thirty letters, whereby may be expressed the lively image of mans voice in what language soever; first devised upon occasion to seek for fit letters to express the Virginian speech. 1585."[20]

People in England were very eager to know more, and one subject of overriding interest was the American environment. Scholars all over Europe wanted to know about the American landscape and its plants and animals and to understand how they differed from familiar ones at home. The Virginia Company hoped colonists would find plants that might be useful and bring in some income, so they sent experts to look for them. Two apothecaries, Thomas Feld and John Harford, traveled in the same ship with Thomas Savage, and their job was to look for new kinds of medicines.

Medical care of the time was based on the theory that the human body contained four humors—blood, phlegm, black bile, and yellow bile—that mirrored the four basic elements in nature: air, fire, earth, and water. If your humors were well balanced, you had good health. If they became corrupted or off-balance, sickness ensued. So your doctor would try to extract the foul humors by bleeding or making you vomit. One disease that often prevailed in Jamestown was what they called the "bloody flux," terrible persistent diarrhea. Plants that could produce vomiting or that could stop the flux were potentially very valuable.

Dr. Lawrence Bohun (also written Boone) came in 1610, and he conducted many experiments using American plants and minerals. William Strachey mentioned "Saxafras, Galbanum, Mechoacon otherwise called Rubarbum Alba," and said Dr. Bohun had used them for "purging phlegm and superfluous matter" from colonists with "cold and moist bodies." Bohun also discovered a white clay that was useful against "pestilent and Malignant Fevers." Strachey also mentioned wax myrtle and sweet woodruff, plants with good medicinal properties. Wax myrtle, a southeastern America native, is also called the southern bayberry. Dr. Bohun experimented with the berries, which are "of so great force against inveterate disenterical fluxes," and, as Strachey said, gave them to "many of our men laboring with such diseases." The governor and council wrote home to the Virginia Company praising Bohun for his work in caring for colonists "struck with strange fluxes and agues." The good doctor was very versatile; he also made wine of the grapes produced by the "goodly vines" growing over every bush and tree, and Strachey affirmed that the wine was "full as good as your French-British wine." On his own, Strachey also reported other medicines, mostly from observation of Powhatan practices. He wrote that the "sharp and penetrable" juice of prickly pears was "powerful against the stone" (stones in the kidney or bladder). Powhatans used crushed wighsacan root to cure small wounds and bruises, and the root of another plant, pocoones, for joint pain and swellings; pocoones was considered "very precious." Strachey also mentioned "Pellitory of Spain and other simples" (medicinal herbs) and said "our apothecaries" had found them to be good medicine.[21]

John Tradescant, the king's gardener, collected plants from all over the world. He was a Virginia Company investor, and he also invested twenty-five pounds in a plan of Captain Argall's to send servants to Virginia. He and Capt. John Smith were friends, and Smith left a legacy of books to him in his will. Tradescant's son, also named John, went to Virginia three times, and he was said to have brought back more than two hundred previously unknown plants, including the "soon-fading Spiderwort of Virginia," now known as tradescantia.[22]

Engraving of tradescantia. From the collection of the author.

Exotic animals also found their way into reports. Among American animals, the most strange and interesting was the opossum, which is the American marsupial. Babies are born very small and then live in a pouch on the mother's abdomen until they are ready to enter the world. Some English thought they actually went back into the womb at will. Samuel Purchas, who gathered and published accounts of journeys to foreign lands and what the travelers found in these lands, presented a bizarre description of the opossum: "They have a monstrous deformed beast whose fore part resembleth a Fox, the hinder part an Ape, excepting the feet which are like a mans; beneath her belly she hath a receptacle like a purse wherein she bestows her young until they can shift for themselves."[23]

The Reverend Alexander Whitaker, who came on the same ship as Robert Poole, sent a report from Virginia in which he said there were two "most strange" animals, but his eyewitness description was more realistic than Purchas's. "One of them is the female Possum, which will let forth her young out of her belly, and take them up into her belly again at her pleasure without hurt to herself." Since everyone knew travelers made up bizarre stories, he insisted that his report was not a lying "Traveler's tale," and he testified, "my eyes have been witness unto it." Colonists sent several opossums and their babies to England, so some readers could see what Whitaker had seen with their own eyes. Whitaker also talked about the flying squirrel, another "strange conditioned creature . . . , which through the help of certain broad flaps of skin growing on each side of her forelegs, will glide from tree to tree 20 or 30 paces at one flight and more, if she have the benefit of a small breath of wind."[24]

European scholars wanted to know about the American environment and its products, but they were even more interested in learning about the people and their lives. They believed they could understand how human culture developed from its earliest beginnings by looking at societies they deemed primitive. Many thought the Americans were the descendants of the Ten Lost Tribes of Israel who were dispersed in ancient times, so studying them might reveal God's plan for the world. William Strachey wrote that Powhatan women withdrew from society "in the time of their natural sickness." Separation of menstruating women was important because it seemed to replicate a Jewish practice and therefore strengthened the argument that the Americans descended from the Ten Lost Tribes. Samuel Purchas considered Strachey's point important enough to include it in the second edition of his *Pilgrimage*.[25]

Alexander Whitaker was deeply interested in the spiritual elements of Chesapeake Algonquian life. He was a recent graduate of Cambridge University, where his father had been Regius Professor of Divinity, so he knew a great deal about scholarly conceptions of the supernatural. He endorsed the idea that the Natives were "sons of Adam . . . in whom there be remaining many footsteps of Gods image."[26]

Whitaker sent a letter about the episode in which the soldiers thought they had been bewitched and other strange happenings to the Reverend William Crashaw, a highly respected religious scholar in England. These events were potentially so meaningful that he needed a top scholar to help interpret them. In addition to the enchantment of the soldiers, Whitaker described "another accident" that happened to some soldiers moving up the Nansemond River. Suddenly they saw men on the riverbank doing a crazy dance like "our Morris dancers."[27] The men were led by a priest who "tossed smoke and flame out of a thing like a censer," a metal incense burner used by priests in England. Machumps, one of Powhatan's men who had been in England and now lived in the fort, told the soldiers that, because of this ceremony, it would soon rain hard. The dance did produce "thunder and Lightning and much rain within five miles," but there was not enough rain where the English were to make their "powder dank."[28]

This episode was important because the Powhatans knew that the matchlock muskets that the colonists carried required a "match," a smoldering piece of rope that soldiers used to ignite the powder in the pan and fire the musket ball. If rain extinguished the match or made their powder wet, the muskets were completely useless, and the soldiers were extremely vulnerable. Moving to bows and arrows required skills that most English did not possess, so the Natives' ability to make it rain through their supernatural powers meant the English soldiers were potentially in big trouble.[29]

Whitaker went on to mention other "such Casualties," such as when Powhatan captives in the fort, tightly bound and continuously watched, suddenly escaped. He introduced these events by saying that he would not insult Crashaw by writing about mundane things such as "what corn we have set, what boats we have built, etc." But he thought these apparently inexplicable things were worthy of Crashaw's consideration, and he wanted the doctor's learned opinion of them. Whitaker's judgment was that Chesapeake Algonquian priests were "very familiar with the Devil." Europeans believed that the Christian God was the only true God. Therefore, any other worship must involve the Devil. Readers back in Europe knew that God, for his own reasons, had not allowed people in the Americas to have access to knowledge of Christianity until now, so their worship of false gods was not their choice. As Whitaker wrote, "Oh remember (I beseech you) what was the state of England before the Gospel was preached in our Country."[30] John Rolfe echoed the same theme, emphasizing that "they bear the image of our heavenly Creator, & we and they come from the same mold." Like Whitaker, he wrote, "what were we before the Gospel of Christ shined amongst us?" In fact, teaching the Americans about Christianity and saving their souls was one of the main justifications for colonization.[31]

Whitaker argued God had sustained Jamestown through all its difficulties because he wanted the English to bring Christianity to the Americans. "I think the Lord hath spared this people and enriched the bowels of the Country with the riches and beauty of Nature that we wanting them might in the search of them communicate the most excellent merchandize and treasure of the Gospel with them." He begged Crashaw and his friends to send any young ministers looking for a good position, saying that the country was in great need of learned and zealous preachers and stipulating that young men would do best. And any ministers who did not like the restrictions that the Church of England placed on them would be happy to find that they could conduct worship as they pleased in Virginia.[32]

The Virginia Company, like English scholars, also wanted knowledge, but their quest was more practical. Investors pressed the colony's leaders to find out more about the land beyond the falls of the James and especially about valuable resources there. English boats, unlike the Powhatans' canoes, were too heavy and clumsy to be carried by land around the falls, so that was as far as they could hope to go at this point. But if they could plant a settlement below the falls now, then once they had become strong enough there, they could figure out a way to get beyond them.

Getting around the falls was so important because leaders in Virginia and in London continued to believe that they could find some network of rivers that would allow them to travel to the Pacific Ocean and the rich trade there. This was a hope that no amount of experience could kill, and it persisted until the transcontinental voyage of Lewis and Clark two centuries later. Although seventeenth-century Europeans could calculate latitude with pretty good accuracy, they were not yet able to estimate longitude at sea. Sailors, including Sir Francis Drake, had traveled down the east coast and rounded the tip of South America to sail up the west coast, but no one had any idea how far west they had gone. Wishful thinking led them to believe that North America was actually quite narrow, so getting across to the Pacific would be really easy.

Jamestown's leaders also wanted to follow up on rumors of rich mines in the interior. If they had been willing to listen to Thomas and Henry, they would have known that such mines were unlikely. The Powhatans had copper, which they gained in trade with people in the interior, but they did not actually know of any mines. But no one was looking for bad news. The Spaniards had found gold and silver, so why shouldn't they?

The most important fact for Jamestown's leaders was that the colony still had not made any money, and it was actually a drain on the Virginia Company's resources. How long would investors in London continue to pour money into a losing proposition? Creating an outpost to the west, in their minds, offered the best possibility for good gain with the least effort.

In pursuit of that goal, acting governor Sir Thomas Dale renewed plans to build a settlement at the falls of the James near modern Richmond in late summer of 1611, despite the frightening experience of the soldiers who believed they had been bewitched there. After four years of experience, Powhatan did not want the English penetrating so deep into his territory. Moreover, an outpost there would put the English close to the Powhatans' greatest enemies: the Siouan-speaking Monacans, who lived just beyond the falls. The Powhatans and the Monacans maintained a fragile peace, and Powhatan did not want the English messing that up.

Despite Powhatan's opposition, plans for a new settlement near the falls of the James did go ahead, and the town of Henrico was built. It was named for Prince Henry, the heir to the English throne, a young man who represented hope for a better future for many people in England, and Alexander Whitaker became the minister there.

As the colonists stepped up their efforts to find a valuable commodity or the passage to the Pacific, Spanish officials became concerned about what this would mean for their own settlements in Florida and in Mexico, especially its northern reaches. The Spanish ambassador in London, Pedro de Zúñiga, started snooping around for information from the time Jamestown was in the planning stage. Zúñiga sent a series of letters to the Spanish king Philip III in September and October 1607 about his efforts to put King James off from colonizing in Virginia. The Spanish king thanked him and told Zúñiga to "continue to keep an eye on it." Then, in June 1608, Zúñiga managed to procure and forward a letter that an English colonist, Francis Perkins, had sent to his supporters in England. He included another letter of his own to Philip III saying that the colony had no source of income, so their only goal was "to fortify themselves and carry on piracy from there."[33] Spain's wealth came from its American colonies, so a permanent English settlement that could serve as a base for future attacks on those colonies was deeply worrying. Zúñiga already had sources of information in government circles in London. What the Spanish really needed was someone inside Jamestown who would keep them informed, and while Henry was in London, they actually managed to plant a spy in Jamestown.

The Spanish were following up on the 1610 testimony of Francis Magnel, the Irish sailor who had been in Jamestown during its first eight months until the ships returned to England.[34] But Pedro de Zúñiga had already begun setting up a plan in 1609. He wrote the Spanish king that Thomas Arundell, Baron Arundell of Wardour, a Roman Catholic, was soon to undertake a fake voyage of discovery on which he would pick up a renegade Englishman on the Canaries or in Puerto Rico and then present him in Virginia as "a man who has fled from Spain." That man could then inform Philip III about the colony and its weaknesses. Zúñiga urged haste, as the colony was receiving many newcomers and needed to be removed soon. A few months later, he wrote, "Baron Arundell can be regarded with some suspicion because he has given such despicable satisfaction, but in this regard I think that he indicates a desire for them to order those people to leave there because they did not trust this business to him because he is a Catholic." Apparently nothing came of this plan at the time, but it was revived in early 1611, only to be discarded again because the English decoy was not then available.[35]

A new plan soon followed. In June 1611, a Spanish ship whose crew said they were searching for a lost vessel entered the mouth of the James River. Three men from the Spanish ship went on shore, including an aristocrat, Don Diego de Molina. In return, an English navigator named John Clark went aboard the Spanish ship. The whole thing was a ruse to plant Don Diego inside the fort, and as the conversation on land turned hostile, he and the other two men were seized. In response, the Spanish ship sailed away with John Clark. Don Diego stayed in Jamestown for five years, and John Clarke was a prisoner in Spain all that time.[36]

In November that year, Philip III wrote to Don Alonso de Velasco, who had replaced Zúñiga as ambassador, expressing his outrage that passengers on a peaceful Spanish ship had been seized and demanding their release. The same letter carried a secret passage written in cypher that revealed the letter's true intent: the king instructed Velasco to employ all "your skill and dexterity to prevent that king from finding out the purpose for which those three men went there."[37]

One of the Spaniards, Antonio Pereos, died fairly soon. Don Diego flourished and was allowed to send several unsealed letters home to Spain. Because they were not sealed, Virginia Company officials could read them before forwarding them to the Spanish ambassador Velasco. But Don Diego also managed to sneak out letters that gave a very different picture from his official ones. Although Jamestown's leaders thought of him as a prisoner, he functioned as a Spanish spy in the midst of the colony for five years.

The third man captured from the Spanish ship, Francisco Lembri or Francis Limbreck, posed a special problem. The English believed that he was an Englishman who had decided to serve the Spanish enemy, and Philip III identified him as an Englishman in his November 1611 letter to Velasco. George Percy called him "our hispanyolated Englishman Limbreck," and Don Diego wrote that the colonial authorities treated him extremely well, hoping "to make him confess that he is an Englishman." On the other hand, Don Diego believed Lembri's assertion that he was a native of Aragon in Spain, saying, "in truth no one would take him for a foreigner."[38] Like Thomas and Henry, he was a man with fluid identities, and no one, maybe not Francis/Francisco himself, could tell which was the "real" one. No one knew the truth: the English thought of him as a traitor; but some Spanish authorities thought that he might have been an English plant sent to spy on them. He replaced the unnamed renegade whom Ambassador Zúñiga had suggested recruiting.

Spanish authorities were extremely concerned about Jamestown evolving out of its disarray and finally becoming established. The issue for them was when to strike. In 1612, Sir John Digby, England's ambassador in Madrid, wrote to William Trumbull, the English representative in Brussels, that the Spanish king was displeased with "our plantation in Virginia," and if the English did not shut it down, he "will be forced to assay the removal of it." The letter also reported Spanish aggravation over the news that English mariners operating in the north had definitely discovered the Northwest Passage to the Pacific, which was not true.[39]

In 1613, Diego de Molina smuggled out a letter that was reportedly sewn into the sole of a Venetian gentleman's shoe. The English sources never mentioned a gentleman from Venice, so we have no idea who this man was. Don Diego wrote that the Venetian had fallen into "great and serious errors," meaning he had become a Protestant, but had now returned to the true religion and wanted to come to Spain to do penance. In this letter, Don Diego argued that he could be more truthful than in the ones he had to allow Virginia Company officials to see and strongly urged a Spanish attack on Jamestown. Like the English, the Spanish believed North America was not very broad, and Don Diego argued that once the English colonists got beyond the mountains, it would be simple for them to go over and attack New Spain, as well as attack Spanish shipping in the Caribbean. He warned authorities back in Spain that if they did nothing, the colony would eventually grow and become, as he put it, a "nest of pirates" that would prey on the Spanish colonies. The corsairs of North Africa had built a huge commerce by raiding ships in the Mediterranean and capturing Europeans for ransom, and Don Diego said the English were creating a "new Algiers in America."[40]

Don Diego wrote that it would be an easy matter to take over the fort. He said that the colonists were so miserable that many ran away to live with the Natives in preference to starving in the fort. Don Diego also said that ordinary colonists would actually join the Spanish if they came and offered an alternative to the present tyrannical rule. Moreover, it would be easy to take over the colony; the fortifications were so weak and poorly made that they could just be kicked down.

On the other hand, he advised the Spanish not to believe everything they heard from Virginia Company members, because they were deliberately undervaluing the region's potential. The English knew that there were good sources of gold and silver up the rivers, but they had not yet been able to find and exploit these sources. The colonists could also grow enough food if they were not so lazy and unskillful.

Clearly, as a man who had endured many years' captivity in Virginia, Don Diego de Molina wanted to capitalize on his insider knowledge and lead whatever expedition the Spanish authorities might put together. It was not unusual for someone in his position to exaggerate the benefits of such a venture and to minimize the risks.

Don Diego reiterated his claims the following year, in 1614, saying that the colonists felt like prisoners as much as he did. He immodestly compared himself to Moses, who had been sent to Virginia to help lead these people out to a better life. They all wondered, according to him, "What is the King of Spain doing?" Don Diego's argument, unfortunately for him, cut two ways. If Jamestown was doing as badly as Don Diego said, then why offend the king of England and waste resources taking it over? Spanish authorities chose to ignore his advice, and he and Francis Limbreck lived in captivity for a further two years.[41] Over that time, they witnessed momentous changes in English Virginia.

4

POCAHONTAS BECOMES REBECCA ROLFE

HENRY SPELMAN sailed back to Virginia with Samuel Argall in July 1612. This was a famous voyage, because their ship, Sir Robert Rich's *Treasurer*, made the crossing in record time, just fifty-seven days, so they landed in September. Henry had been reluctant to return to his role as the colony's servant; but Sir Henry arranged for him to have a salary when he returned to Virginia, so he would no longer be simply a servant at the beck and call of the colony's leaders. And Captain Argall promised him a return journey when Sir Thomas Gates went back to England.[1]

Pocahontas returned to Jamestown the next year, in 1613, several years after she had quit visiting the fort, but now the circumstances were very different. Capt. Samuel Argall discovered her whereabouts on one of his many voyages in search of food, and given that English demands and violence had alienated the people on the James and York Rivers, he targeted the people farther north on Chesapeake Bay.

At the end of 1612, Argall entered the Potomac River and encountered "the king of Pasptanzie a-hunting." Iopassus, who had adopted Henry into his family, again welcomed Captain Argall and told him the Patawomecks were his friends and that they had saved up corn for him. Actually the friendship was not quite so secure and happy. Argall casually mentioned that sealing the bargain and concluding peace "with divers other Indian lords" required the giving and taking of "hostages." And Argall left important people behind on the Potomac. In the margin of his report, he wrote these names: "Capt. Webb, Ensign Swift, Rob. Sparkes, and two boys." Capt. George Webb had been in Virginia since

1610, and at the time Argall handed him over as a hostage, he was the sergeant-major of James Fort. James Swift also arrived in 1610, and his rank of ensign made him an officer. Robert Sparkes's position is unknown, and the two boys were so insignificant in Argall's scheme of things that he did not even bother to name them. The take was eleven hundred bushels of corn, and Argall's party was at Pasptanzie for an extended period while Argall's crew built a "stout shallop" to carry the corn home.[2]

In March 1613, Captain Argall was back in the Potomac, and he learned "that the Great Powhatan's daughter Pocahontas was with the Great King Patawomeck." Pocahontas was there because she had accompanied a trading embassy to the Patawomecks. Colony secretary Ralph Hamor said she wanted to see her Patawomeck friends, and she stayed with them three months. So it was her bad luck to be there when Argall visited.[3]

Iopassus was soon to learn what a firm friendship with the English actually meant, and the account of what happened next makes painful reading even after four hundred years. Argall resolved "to possess myself of her by any stratagem that I could use." His justification was that she could be traded for various Englishmen held by Powhatan and some weapons and tools the Powhatans had gotten from Jamestown and also "some quantity of corn for the colony's relief."

Argall anchored his ship by Pasptanzie and sent for Ensign Swift and Iopassus, and when they came to his ship, Argall told Iopassus, "if he did not betray Pocahontas into my hands, we would be no longer brothers nor friends." Iopassus objected that if he helped the English capture Pocahontas, Powhatan would make war on him and his people, and Argall promised to join in his defense if that happened. Iopassus then said that he must consult with his brother, "the great King of Patawomeck."

The Patawomeck system was the same as the Powhatans': only the paramount chief could make such major diplomatic decisions. And even the paramount chief did not act without consulting his principal advisers, which is what the Patawomeck king did. After several hours of consultation, the Patawomecks decided to do as the English asked. Even though Iopassus had been forced into doing something he desperately wanted to avoid, colonial leaders' accounts turned the blame on him and portrayed him as eager to betray Pocahontas because of the loot he would get from the English.

Pocahontas was initially delighted to hear that some of the English people she knew were there on the Potomac. In setting up the plot, Iopassus "made his wife an instrument," which made sense to the English because that "sex have ever been most powerful in beguiling enticements." The plan called for Iopassus and his wife to accompany Argall and Pocahontas to the ship's mooring, where Iopassus's wife would insist that she really wanted to go on the ship to see it. Iopassus would pretend to be angry with his wife. She would then begin to weep, "as who knows not that women can command tears," and finally Iopassus would relent and agree to let her go on the ship if Pocahontas would accompany her. They played out this script, and finally, after "earnest persuasions," Pocahontas agreed; and "so forthwith aboard they went."

The party had supper on board the ship, and the English did their best to put on a good feast. Iopassus and his wife were particularly merry, and they repeatedly kicked Argall's shins to remind him that they had sealed the deal—they had delivered Pocahontas as promised. They all went to sleep. But Pocahontas was first up next morning, and she was very apprehensive about what was going on and asked to go back on shore. When Pocahontas realized that she was not going to be allowed to return to land, she "began to be exceeding pensive, and discontented." Capt. John Smith wrote that Iopassus and his wife kept up the show: "the old Jew and his wife began to howl and cry as fast as Pocahontas," but as soon as they had their stuff, they "went merrily on shore." Their loot for betraying Pocahontas was a small copper kettle and "some other less valuable toys so highly by him esteemed, that doubtless he would have betrayed his own father for them." Meanwhile, the English tried to sooth Pocahontas's feelings, and although it was very hard to convince

Pocahuntas Virginiæ Regis filia expatiatum profecta, astu
intercipitur, cap. 1. 2. 3.

Pocahuntas regis Powhatani filia, patri apprimè dilecta, ad quendam ex amicis Potaomeckam usque expatiata fuerat. Eodem venit Anglus quidam Capitaneus, Argoldictus. Quem cùm sub ignoto habitu virgo invisere cuperet, is re cum amico suo Japazeo communicata, illam astu in navem suam pellexit. Quamprimum navem conscenderat splendido convivio excepta, letis confabulationibus exhilaratur, posteáque in cubiculum somnum ibidem captura deducitur. Mane Pocahuntas in navi manere jussa, verborum blanditiis placatur; Japazeus verò donis ornatus cum uxore dimittitur. Postea, cùm Powhatani nuncius de captivitate filiæ allatus esset, ipse verò responsum ultra tempus distulisset, Angli unà cum Regis filia armata manu fluvium ascendentes in Regis ditionem progressi sunt, ut captivos suos vel permutatione facta, vel viatique armis in libertatem assererent: Toto hoc itinere sæpius à Barbaris petiti variisq; injuriis affecti sunt Angli, præsertim cùm angustias fluminis cujusdam ingressi essent, densum telorum imbrem in illos evomuerunt. Cum igitur unus ex Anglis in anteriore capitis parte leviliter esset sauciatus, reliqui, exscensione in terram facta, quadraginta exustis domibus, obvia quæque miserè deprædati sunt, sex insuper Indianis graviter vulneratis aut trucidatis.

Dum

The "inveigling" of Pocahontas to go on board the English ship. Courtesy of the John Carter Brown Library at Brown University.

her to bear her fate with patience, little by little she became resigned; "and so to Jamestown she was brought." Pocahontas would never see her husband, Kocoum, again.

Captain Argall immediately sent "an Indian" to inform Powhatan that his daughter was a prisoner in Jamestown and to deliver a list of the items he would have to supply in order to ransom her. The main things demanded in the ransom note were the Englishmen "whom he detained in slavery," the English weapons and tools that Powhatan had procured, and of course, more corn. Powhatan was naturally "much grieved" by this news; Ralph Hamor said this was partly because his daughter was being held but also because of "the love he bore to our men his prisoners." Argall wrote of Powhatan's reply, "he desired me to use his Daughter well, and bring my ship into his River, and there he would give me my demands." Once the exchange had taken place, he said, "we should be friends."[4]

Three months later, Powhatan sent seven Englishmen, each carrying a broken musket. They brought the message that when Pocahontas was safely back with him, he would return the remaining guns, five hundred bushels of corn, and "be forever friends with us." The English back at the fort said, in effect, "No guns, no Pocahontas." They heard nothing more from Powhatan for a year, and Pocahontas lived in Jamestown.[5]

Henry and Thomas were there with Pocahontas, and archaeological evidence suggests that other Powhatans may have been living in the fort as well. So she was not completely isolated from her own people.[6] Pocahontas was thus able to speak her own language with Henry and Thomas and with her compatriots in the fort. And perhaps they could resume their friendship even though their situations were now so different.

English Virginia was becoming an oddly cosmopolitan place when Pocahontas arrived, partly because people from all over Europe lived in the colony, including Don Diego de Molina and Francis Limbreck (Francisco Lembri). And soon a French Jesuit, Father Pierre Biard, joined them.

A separate Virginia Company had founded Sagadahoc in Maine at the same time as Jamestown, but it was abandoned after a few months. Despite that failure, English leaders did not want to give up the nation's claim to rights there. Early in 1611, a French ship intending to settle a colony, including Father Biard, was blown off course and landed on the Isle of Wight in the English Channel, so English authorities knew of French plans to settle North America's northern coast. The French went on to create the settlement of Acadia in modern Nova Scotia. So, in July of the next year, the Virginia Company commissioned Samuel Argall Admiral of Virginia, with orders to remove the French.[7]

Captain Argall sailed north in July 1613 to eliminate the French there, first attacking the newly founded mission of Saint-Sauveur at modern Castine on the coast of Maine. Half of the twenty French were allowed to return home, but Argall took the others, including Father Biard, back to Jamestown. Pierre Biard was a highly educated man, who had taught theology and philosophy in France, but he had little time to learn about Virginia.

In October that same year, Argall took Biard and some of his countrymen and returned to the site of Saint-Sauveur to cut down the Jesuits' cross, which he replaced with his English cross, proclaiming King James the true owner. He burned the buildings there and at another site, St. Croix, and then went on to the larger settlement of Port Royal in Nova Scotia. Port Royal's residents were away hunting, so, after taking all their farm animals, Argall and his men also burned it to the ground.[8] French people were settled at Quebec, and their traders were taking a major role in the northern fur trade; but the English wanted them to stay away from the southern part of the region. Argall's ship encountered a storm in its voyage back to Virginia and was forced eastward, first landing on the Azores and then Wales. Ultimately Father Biard was allowed to return to France.

Father Biard was in Virginia for only a few months, but the Spanish captives/spies were there for years. And Virginia also contained artisans from across the Atlantic. The German carpenters had been there a long time. Now Frenchmen skilled in silk production were imported because colony backers had high hopes that they could produce silk, which would be a huge source of income to help the colony pay for itself. Several colonists reported that they had seen mulberry trees growing in some places. They made a trial with some silkworms imported from Europe, and the worms seemed to do well but were eventually eaten by rats. No one mentioned that the rats were also imports: they had sneaked off the English ships and multiplied. Later efforts to produce silk also foundered. Virginia had red mulberry trees, and silkworms fed on white mulberries; so the whole scheme was another example of bad information and wishful thinking.[9]

French vignerons, winemaking experts, also lived in Virginia, because promoters hoped, following the lead of Dr. Bohun, that the native grapevines could be used to produce drinkable wine. England was spending a fortune buying wine from Portugal, so English-made wine would be a huge benefit.[10] Pocahontas came to live in a small international community, partly because the English had to import so many skilled artisans to make up for their own lack of knowledge.

Over the next months, Pocahontas apparently became accustomed to being among the Europeans, and Alexander Whitaker began to explain the basic beliefs of Christianity to her. Whitaker was a puritan, and puritanism differed from traditional versions of Christianity in rejecting their elaborate ceremonies and hierarchy and stressing personal acceptance of Christ's message. Through prayer, puritans were able to establish a close relationship with God, and this may have been especially appealing to Pocahontas. Whitaker wrote of the "great fear and attention" Natives showed in "their service of their God," and he offered her the chance of a similarly close relationship through prayer. Some puritan congregations allowed active participation of women in worship, which also made conversion more attractive to her. Whitaker began to win Pocahontas over to the idea of being baptized and becoming a Christian.[11]

John Rolfe, also a puritan, played a crucial role in this process. He and his first wife were among those who had been shipwrecked on Bermuda in 1609. Shortly after their arrival in Virginia, Rolfe's wife died; their infant daughter, named Bermuda in honor of her birthplace, had died in the island where she had been born. John fell deeply in love with Pocahontas and wanted to marry her, but he was concerned about what this marriage would mean for him as a Christian.

The Virginia Company had given the great Virginia fleet of 1609 a big ceremonial send-off, including a sermon by a very prominent preacher, William Symonds. As John Rolfe sat and listened to Symonds, the sermon made a huge and lasting impression on him. Symonds, citing passage after passage from the Bible, preached that God had sent Abraham to populate the world and bring God's message. Just as bees leave the overfull hive to go out and form new colonies, so God intended his people to do the same. But God also warned Abraham, Symonds preached, against intermarrying with heathens: "Abraham's posterity [must] keep to themselves."[12]

Rolfe described his feelings and intentions in a letter to Governor Dale, which he asked Ralph Hamor to deliver; Hamor and Rolfe had been together on Bermuda after the 1609 shipwreck. Rolfe wrote that his love for Pocahontas meant that "my hearty and best thoughts are and have been a long time so entangled and enthralled in so intricate a Labyrinth, that I was even awearied to unwind my self thereout." Remembering that dramatic sermon, he was concerned about "the heavy displeasure which Almighty God conceived against the Sons of Levi and Israel for marrying of strange wives," and he even worried that his love for Pocahontas might have been some strange temptation posed by the Devil. But as a result of his constant prayers for guidance, God had "opened the Gate and led me by the hand, that I might plainly see and discern the safest paths wherein to tread." God offered "an other but more gracious temptation," waking Rolfe from sleep with the question, "why dost thou not endeavor to make her a Christian?" Such a resolution was especially important given "her great appearance of love to me, her desire to be taught and instructed in the knowledge of God," and her capability of understanding what she was taught. Rolfe realized that the "vulgar sort" might think that his interest in her was purely physical, but he knew that it stemmed from much deeper, and more important, urges.[13] We do not know how he felt about her previous marriage to Kocoum; perhaps he thought it was not a true marriage.

Henry's account of marriage customs among high-ranking Natives along the Chesapeake gives us a way to understand Pocahontas's willingness to marry John Rolfe after her marriage to Kocoum. According to the customs of her own people, Pocahontas may have expected all along that she would not remain with Kocoum.[14]

During the spring of 1614, while John Rolfe was courting Pocahontas and Alexander Whitaker was instructing her in the tenets of Christianity, the acting governor at Jamestown, Sir Thomas Dale, decided to make another attempt to pry loose the weapons, tools, and runaways that stayed with Powhatan. He brought Pocahontas, "who had been long prisoner with us," in a large expedition up the Pamunkey River to Matchut, the even more remote place to which Powhatan had moved his capital from Orapax.[15]

Dale apparently had no idea that John Rolfe was courting Pocahontas and that she returned his affection, so his plan was to exchange her for what Powhatan had seized. As the governor put it, he was going to tell Powhatan to "render all the arms, tools, swords, and men that had run away, and give me a ship full of corn," and he would return Pocahontas to her father. If Powhatan did this, Dale said, "we would be friends, if not burn all."

As the English went on shore, fighting broke out, and they burned and pillaged a town; but they still claimed that their purposes were peaceful. The English learned that Powhatan was much farther inland but that his brother Opechancanough was nearby and would talk with them.

John Rolfe and Robert Sparkes, who had earlier been left on the Potomac by Samuel Argall, were then dispatched to confer with Opechancanough, and Thomas acted as interpreter. While Sparkes and Rolfe were talking with Opechancanough, Hamor gave Governor Dale Rolfe's letter expressing his desire to see Pocahontas converted and to

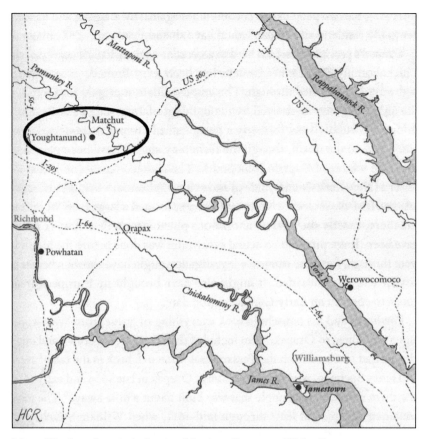

Map of Powhatan's capitals showing Matchut. Courtesy of Helen Rountree.

marry her. That letter changed everything; Dale and Hamor now piv-oted 180 degrees. Rather than use Pocahontas for the relatively trivial aim of forcing Powhatan to disgorge everything that had leaked out of Jamestown, they now had a much greater and far more important goal in sight: convert Pocahontas to Christianity and, through her, begin to fulfill the greatest aspiration for which the colony had been founded: the conversion of all her people. Her conversion as the "first fruits of Virginia" would really make skeptics in England take notice and support the colony.

Two of Pocahontas's brothers came on board the English ship to see their sister and find out how she was. They were satisfied that she had been well treated and assured Dale that Powhatan would make the exchange. But Dale had now discarded that option and wanted to make it seem that Pocahontas herself had rejected repatriation. Pocahontas went ashore, but according to the English accounts, she refused to talk to most people she met, saying that if her father truly loved her, he would not value a few weapons and tools more than he did his daughter and that she would stay with the English, "who loved her."

Powhatan then sent word that he would return the Englishmen who were still with him and send corn when the harvest was in. After five years of fighting, he needed to protect his people, so he wanted peace. According to Dale, he affirmed that "his daughter should be my child, and ever dwell with me."

Sometime in the spring of 1614, Pocahontas "renounced publicly her country Idolatry, openly confessed her Christian faith, [and] was, as she desired, baptized." The name she was given at her baptism, Rebecca, demonstrated the truly great hopes the English invested in this conversion. The name evoked the beginnings of the people of Israel in the book of Genesis and recalled the issues surrounding intermarriage that had so concerned John Rolfe.

God had called Abraham to move to Canaan, but when it came time for his son Isaac to marry, Abraham had a dilemma, because marrying a Canaanite woman was forbidden. He sent his servant back to his home country to find a wife for Isaac, and the servant devised a plan by which to identify the best prospect. He brought ten camels with him and stopped at a well where women came out of the town to draw water. Soon Rebecca came out with her jug on her shoulder, and Abraham's emissary, seeing how beautiful she was, asked her for a drink of water. She immediately said, "Drink, sir," and handed him her jug. Then she said she would draw water for his camels until they had drunk their fill.

Rolfe, who knew the Geneva translation of the Bible well, would have recalled the note printed in the margin by this passage: "Here is declared that God ever heareth the prayers of his, and granteth their requests." As the story went on, Rebecca not only gave Abraham's servant

Dum Indiani ab Anglis inducias impetrant, duo Regis
Powhatanis filii sororem suam invisunt. cap.3.

Osteaquam Angli ad præcipuam Regis Powhatanis sedem, vicum quendam Matzkot dictum pervenissent; qua-
dringenti barbari probè armati aditu illos vultu verbisque minacibus prohibere sategerunt: Nihilominus Angli,
licet iniquiore essent loco, in terram enituntur. Barbari rerum suarum securi ne latum quidem unguem ipsis cedunt,
sed sursum deorsum, hac illácque inter Anglos obambulantes, præcipuos ex illis de Anglorum rege, quò animo in
istas regiones devenissent, num ferro decernendum putarent, percontabantur, interim inducias exposcentes donec ad regem
res deferretur. Quæ quidem certis conditionibus ipsis concessa sunt. Siquidem enim minus ex ipsorum voto Rex responsurus
esset, tubâ classicum datum iri, ut signis collatis hostiliter inter se congrederentur. Interea Pokahuntas in terram delata, à duo-
bus fratribus invisebatur, qui optimè illam inter Anglos habri conspicati, omnem operam apud patrem se daturos
polliciti sunt, ut demum certa firmáque pax utrinque sanciretur. Atque ita Angli ab
armis discesserunt.

Cichoho-

The captive Pocahontas meeting her brothers, with Thomas Savage interpreting.
Courtesy of the John Carter Brown Library at Brown University.

water but also invited him to stay in her father's house. When the man explained his mission to Rebecca's family, they agreed that she should accompany him and marry Isaac; Rebecca also consented. Her family prophesied that her progeny would grow into "thousand thousands." The descendants of Isaac and Rebecca's son Jacob, later named Israel, would become the twelve tribes of Israel.[16]

In naming Pocahontas Rebecca, Alexander Whitaker expressed his hope that the children produced through her union with John Rolfe, whom Whitaker described as "an honest and discreet English Gentleman," might be the beginning of a new people combining English and American roots. Powhatan sent word accepting the marriage of his daughter to John Rolfe. Despite many invitations, he never went to Jamestown; as Henry said, "he goes not out of his own country." Powhatan sent Pocahontas's uncle to represent him at the marriage ceremony. Even the grizzled old soldier Thomas Dale wrote, "were it but the gaining of this one soul, I will think my time, toil, and present stay well spent."[17]

In the period of good feelings that followed the wedding, a new English embassy visited Powhatan. It was led by Ralph Hamor, soon to return to England, who wanted to visit Powhatan so he could describe him from personal experience when he was back home. He was accompanied by Thomas, who "speaks the language naturally, one whom Powhatan much affecteth," and two Native guides. When the two men came face to face, Powhatan at first ignored Hamor and turned to Thomas, saying, "My child you are welcome, you have been a stranger to me these four years." Just as he had agreed that Pocahontas could be considered Governor Dale's child, he affirmed, "you are my child by the donative of Captain Newport."[18]

Powhatan also complained that Namontack, the young man given in exchange for Thomas, had not returned to him after Namontack's second voyage to England: "though many ships have arrived here from thence, since that time, how you have dealt with him I know not?" The sources are spotty on Namontack's fate. The few mentions we have seem to indicate that he had been accompanied by Machumps, another Powhatan man, on his second transatlantic trip and that they were returning on the ship that was wrecked on Bermuda in the great hurricane of 1609. Capt. John Smith, drawing on eyewitness reports, wrote, many years later, that Machumps killed Namontack in Bermuda and buried him secretly, and Samuel Purchas also mentioned the murder in a marginal note. Machumps continued to function as a go-between for Powhatan, and Alexander Whitaker quoted him on the rainmaking ceremony they both witnessed in 1611. Clearly, whatever happened to Namontack, the English did not tell Powhatan.[19]

After Powhatan had complained about his loss of both boys, Thomas and Namontack, he then turned to Hamor, feeling around his neck for the "chain of pearl" that he had sent to Governor Dale. The pearl chain was supposed to be worn by any official ambassador, so Powhatan could be sure of the visitor's status; and he said Dale had agreed that any ambassador who did not have it should be tied up and sent back to Jamestown. Clearly Powhatan was fed up with people roaming the countryside, coming to his capital, and claiming that they spoke for the colonial government. He insisted that the English must get a grip and control ambassadorial status. Captain John Smith had previously mentioned pearl chains given by Powhatan, but the English thought they were just gifts meant to impress.[20]

Hamor covered up by saying that the governor's "page" had forgotten to give the official chain to him. Presumably the negligent page was another unnamed boy working as a servant in Jamestown. Hamor argued that, because he was accompanied by one of Powhatan's own councilors, the chain was unnecessary as proof of his official status, and Powhatan decided to accept Hamor as ambassador. As they entered Powhatan's residence, the paramount chief offered "a pipe of tobacco." Smoking was becoming popular in England, and people called it "drinking smoke." So Hamor described how Powhatan "first drank, and then gave it me, and when I had drank what I pleased, I returned his pipe, which with his own hands he vouchsafed to take from me."

Dn. Thomas Dalenus per fecretarium Raphe Hamor adhuc
aliam Powhatanis ambit filiam. c. 14. 15. 16.

T Powhatan eò magis ad pacem fanctè colendam obligaretur, Dn. Thomas Dalenus Secretarium Raphe Hamor, unà cum puero interprete, duobúsque Indis conductoribus, ad regem amandavit qui minimam natu filiam in uxorem sibi exposceret. Ubi ad regem ventum, is statim manum jugulo legati admovens, ac si fauces ipsi interclusurus esset, quàm arctiffimè collum ejus apprehendit; siquidem is ex pacto catenulam ex margaritis contextam geftare debuerat. Cum verò abundè sese regi purgasset Legatus, rex eum in ædes suas ad lapidis jactum à flumine diffitas deduxit. Hic vilibus storeis insidens Rex, uxorum agmine utrinque claudebatur, quarum unam, & quidem natu minimam reliqua reginam suam salutabant. Præ foribus centum sagittarii excubabant. Postquam igitur Legatus dona, duas nimirum cupri laminas, quinque coralliorum series, quinque ligneos pectines, decem piscatorios hamos, ac cultrorum par unum obtulisset; ac capita legationis suæ proposuisset, repulsam tulit, quod filiam istam jam pridem alii ex primoribus suis nupsisse prætenderet. Tandem legatum aliquoties convivis exceptum, ac cervinis quibusdam pellibus affabrè elaboratis donatum ad suos bona cum gratia dimisit.

c 3   Equeftris

Powhatan searching Ralph Hamor's neck for the ambassadorial chain, with Thomas Savage interpreting. Courtesy of the John Carter Brown Library at Brown University

In this comfortable atmosphere, Powhatan inquired about "his daughter's welfare, his unknown son, and how they liked, lived, and loved together." Hamor said that she was so happy that she never wanted to leave the English and return to her own people, at which Powhatan "laughed heartily, and said he was very glad of it." He then asked the purpose of Hamor's visit. Hamor replied that it was private, so Powhatan ordered everyone to leave except for his two wives, who were always with him.

Then Hamor gave a great deal of presents and promises of more to come and, through Thomas, revealed the purpose of his embassy. He said that Governor Dale wanted another of Powhatan's daughters to be his "nearest companion, wife, and bedfellow" (he did not mention that Dale already had a wife in England). Powhatan thanked Hamor courteously but absolutely refused. The daughter whom Dale wanted was already promised to another, and Powhatan firmly said that it was enough for the English to have one daughter of his. He said it was not a "brotherly" act "to desire to bereave me of two of my children at once."

They all ended the day with a meal, for which Powhatan brought out a "great glass of sack [wine] some three quarts or better, which Captain Newport had given him six or seven years since, carefully preserved by him, not much above a pint in all this time spent, and gave each of us in a great oyster shell some three spoonfuls." Powhatan had welcomed his guests with a traditional pipe of tobacco, and now he was enacting his version of an English ritual. The next morning, they had a huge feast at breakfast.

While Hamor was with Powhatan, "by great chance" he saw another person caught between cultures. He was an Englishman named William Parker, who had been captured three years before. Now, Parker had "grown so like both in complexion and habit to the Indians" that Hamor recognized him only because he spoke English. The Powhatans had previously said that Parker had died, and the prisoner now begged Hamor to do anything he could to bring about his release. Powhatan was angry about it, saying, "You have one of my daughters with you, and

I am therewith well content, but you can no sooner see or know of any English man's being with me, but you must have him away, or else break peace and friendship."

Powhatan agreed to allow Parker to return to the English but said that he would not give them any guides. If they got lost or ran into danger, that would be their problem. He left them alone, but once his anger subsided, Powhatan reconsidered. That night, he sent a man to say that the English party could have guides as they went home. When they met again with Powhatan, he presented a list of items he wanted from the English, including copper pieces, a grindstone (he specified the exact size he wanted), a large axe to split wood, a hundred fish hooks or, if the English "could spare it, a fishing seine." He also asked for more personal items: a shaving knife, two bone combs, and a cat and dog. Powhatan was concerned that Hamor could not remember the whole list and had him repeat it. Still unsatisfied, he brought out a notebook that someone had given him and told Hamor to write everything down. Hamor was impressed by the notebook and asked Powhatan for it, "it being of no use to him." But it actually was useful: Powhatan "told me, it did him much good to show it to strangers which came unto him."

Powhatan told Hamor that if the English "offer me injury my country is large enough, I will remove my self farther from you." He had already made two moves that made his capital increasingly inaccessible, so the English knew this was no idle threat. As they were parting, Powhatan gave the party several gifts including dressed deerskins for them and for Pocahontas and "his son" Governor Dale and demanded that Hamor again repeat the list of the items he wanted. Then he reiterated what he would do if Dale was not satisfied with this exchange of gifts and promises of peace: "I will go three days journey farther from him, and never see English man more."

In their conversations, Powhatan told Hamor, "I am now old and would gladly end my days in peace." In fact, he turned over the paramount chiefship to Opechancanough a few years later. While Pocahontas was becoming further entangled with the English, Robert

Poole was sent to live with Opechancanough. He had arrived with his father and brother in 1611, so he had already been in America for three years. As a member of Opechancanough's court, Robert was in on the ground floor with the new leadership when the change came.

The partnership of Pocahontas and John Rolfe made a huge impact on the Virginia colony in many ways. By 1614, the devastating drought had lifted, and experimenting with crops became more feasible. Jimsonweed, with its hallucinogenic effects, never caught on, but another mind-altering drug, tobacco, was already becoming popular in Europe. Rolfe is credited with growing the first marketable tobacco in an English colony, but the real credit should go to Pocahontas. Women were the agriculturalists in Chesapeake Algonquian society, so she was the one who understood the environment, and she was the experienced planter. The colonists thought the native tobacco was too harsh for European consumers, but Rolfe had brought tobacco seed from his forced sojourn in Bermuda. Experiments with growing tobacco before Pocahontas arrived in the colony had all failed, but by 1614, Pocahontas and Rolfe produced a crop that Europeans would actually buy.

Pocahontas's expertise was crucial because tobacco cultivation was very different from English farming, and it involved painstaking work. Rather than planting in the spring, they sowed the seeds in late winter in specially prepared seedbeds, which they covered with brush to protect them. During the next months and following native practice, servants created mounds or hills across the fields, twenty-five hundred per acre, into which the seedlings would be planted.

In May, the sprouts were transplanted to the hills. This was both an arduous and an exacting job. The little plants, which could be transplanted only on rainy days, would die if not watched and cared for constantly. The Algonquians planted corn around the tobacco, and once the corn was high enough, the leaves would shade the growing tobacco and discourage weeds. Daily tilling got rid of weeds and, if the workers were careful and lucky, the worms and bugs that could attack the plants. Once the plants took hold and began to grow, the workers cut off the tops so they would not flower and carefully removed some leaves so that the remaining ones would grow as big as possible.

Harvest time also required a lot of knowledge that was not easily acquired. Planters had to know just when the crop was completely ripe, and this judgment had to be made plant by plant. An experienced cultivator would look at and feel the leaves and decide when they were ready. The cut leaves were laid on the ground where they had grown and covered with dried grass or other plants; later servants attached the leaves to poles. Finally, the leaves went into tobacco houses, where they hung from rails to finish curing. If not fully dried, leaves could become moldy, and all that year's effort would be wasted.[21]

Under the tutelage of Pocahontas, John Rolfe produced sweet-scented tobacco, and this became the gold that colonists had sought from the beginning. Tobacco made Virginia sustainable as an enterprise. Now the colony had money for supplies and new colonists, and newcomers could be put to productive work.

As hope for the future blossomed with this new crop, Henry was uncomfortable and could not foresee a good prospect for himself in Virginia. The old rivalry with Thomas had not gone away, and Thomas was in a much stronger position than he was. While Henry had been with the Patawomecks and then in England, Thomas had become established as *the* interpreter in Jamestown. Not only was he in solidly with the colony's leaders, but he, and later Robert, was always going to accompany any embassy to the Powhatans. Pocahontas was a married woman, and she and Henry could not hang out together as pals. Henry was now twenty and ready for an adult role. He needed a future.

In 1615, Henry wrote an anguished letter to his influential and rich uncle in London, begging for help in getting back to England. Thanking Sir Henry for his recent letter and "those things which you were pleased to send me," he wrote, "Sir all my hopes for returning into my home country do now consist in your worthy self for now I rest altogether void of any means which may anyway afford me any future benefit" in Virginia. Henry was quick to add that, despite his own situation, Virginia was a "good and fruitful country." If two or three thousand dedicated workers were sent over, the land would flourish. In fact, "in short time England would more stand in need of us (and our commodities) than we should want them." He was glad to report that God favored the enterprise, and everything now prospered.[22]

But Henry felt he had been left out of this prosperity as he transitioned from boy to man. Even worse, he had been cheated of the income and position he had been promised when he was back in England in 1612. He "humbly" asked his uncle to "talk with Captain Argall, concerning my wages which I should have for the time which I am out of England." Argall, as he sailed eastward again, had promised Henry that he could return with Sir Thomas Dale, but that did not happen; Sir Thomas stayed on in Jamestown. Now Henry believed that his uncle's aid was his only hope for the future. Otherwise, he felt "utterly lost." He had heard that, far from helping him return, Sir Henry was making sure that he was kept in America. Unfortunately for us, someone tore off the side of the letter at this point, so his specific accusations were destroyed.

Though the paper was torn and some of Henry's writing is lost, he appears to have argued that if he could be back in England, he could bring honor to himself and his family. At the top of the next page, he asked to be remembered to his mother and grandmother and all his kindred and friends. He signed himself, "your obedient nephew till death." Sir Henry's reply, if any, does not survive. The letter may have been saved among his papers because someone apparently used a piece of it for a shopping list that began, "gold leather for shoes," and went on to list the silk and linen necessary for a set of fine clothes to the amount of ten pounds. Ten pounds is reckoned to be the minimum amount necessary to keep one person fed, housed, and clothed for one year, so this was a pretty expensive suit of clothes.

Sir Henry Spelman apparently did not intervene on behalf of his nephew, but Henry did return to England in a spectacular way as part of the escort for the Lady Rebecca Rolfe. In 1615, Pocahontas gave birth to

Thomas Rolfe, and the Virginia Company decided to bring the Rolfes to London to show off the colony's success.

Pocahontas was royalty, the daughter of the Powhatan. She was also the first, and celebrated, Christian convert in Virginia. The Virginia Company printed Ralph Hamor's account of her conversion and the events that led up to it with Sir Thomas Dale's, Alexander Whitaker's, and John Rolfe's letters to announce their success in 1615. As presented by the Virginia Company, Whitaker and Dale used identical language in saying that Pocahontas had "renounced publicly her country idolatry." Now as the wife of an English gentleman and mother of a Christian child, she was living proof of what had been accomplished, and the company wanted everyone to see it.

The *Treasurer*, bound for England, carried an array of people. Pocahontas was surrounded by an entourage of her own people. She had several women to attend her, including her sister Mattachanna and Mattachanna's husband, Uttamattomakin, the chief priest among the Powhatans. Henry Spelman went as interpreter. Diego de Molina, the Spanish aristocrat who had been captive in Jamestown, was on board, headed for repatriation to Spain. Once the ship arrived in England, Don Diego was exchanged for the English pilot John Clark, who had been a captive in Spain all the time Don Diego had been in Virginia. Francis Limbreck was not so lucky. This "English . . . Judas" was hanged from the ship's yardarm as they came in sight of English land.[23]

ENGLISH EXPERIENCES

SIR JOHN CHAMBERLAIN was an independently wealthy gentleman who spent his time writing the news to correspondents all over
Europe, and he reported the *Treasurer*'s arrival in June 1616: "Sir Thomas
Dale is arrived from Virginia and brought with him some ten or twelve
old and young of that country, among whom the most remarkable person is Poca-huntas (daughter of Powhatan a king or cacique of that
countrie) married to one Rolfe an English man." Chamberlain high-
lighted the exotic nature of the visitors by using the term "cacique,"
meaning ruler, which appeared in reports from the Spanish colonies.[1]

The Virginia Company's strategy was working. Pocahontas and her
company were already attracting favorable attention. No one mentioned
what she and her party thought of London and its crowds.[2]

The Virginia Company was determined to present Pocahontas properly. Native men who were brought to London were displayed wearing their traditional garb, because they were seen as exotic specimens.
Pocahontas was now the Lady Rebecca Rolfe, and her clothing needed
to show her status as a Christian gentlewoman. Her huge challenge was
getting used to the clothes she had to wear.

For a woman used to the relative freedom of her own native clothing,
putting on her new English lady clothes was a horrible shock. Ladies
had an experienced maid to do all the lacing, tying, and hooking involved in these complicated clothes. First you put on a smock, a long
shirt-like garment made of linen. Over that, your maid tied on a pair
of bodies, what we would call a bodice or corset, that the maid laced
together down your front or back. Bodies had channels sewn into them

that were filled with whalebone or bundles of reeds, called bents, in the channels that ran up and down. After it was all laced together, a piece of horn or wood, called a busk, was pushed down the front to stiffen it.

Then a petticoat was tied to the bodice, and over that, the maid placed a roll of cloth, called a bumroll, that went around your waist so your skirt would stick out all around you. Pocahontas wore a "high-bodied" gown that had buttons at the top and a skirt, which is what the English called the tabs that hung from the waist. The wings that extended out from the shoulders covered the line where the sleeves joined the gown. At the top, your maid tied on a large starched collar that was supported by a network of wires. So your clothes poked and scratched you throughout the day, not to mention how heavy it all was. No woman could afford to slouch ever. Add to that the discomfort of wearing hard-soled shoes, maybe even with small high heels.[3]

One advantage of all this elaborate clothing was that it covered up Pocahontas's tattoos. George Percy wrote that women in Virginia "pounce and race their bodies, legs, thighs, arms and faces with a sharp Iron, which makes a stamp in curious knots, and draws the proportion of Fowls, Fish, or Beasts, then with paintings of sundry lively colors, they rub it into the stamp which will never be taken away, because it is dried into the flesh." Only tattoos on her face would have been visible to curious Londoners, and no one mentioned seeing them.[4]

Pocahontas also had to get used to wearing her hair up. Married English women wore their hair pinned into coils on their heads. They covered it with a linen cap, referred to as a coif, and then a hat with a tall crown and brim over the cap.

English food was also very strange. Having beer or wine with every meal was disorienting to people used to fresh water, and they began the day with an unaccustomed wooziness. The variety of foods was much more limited than the Virginians were used to, and their preparation was definitely unappetizing.

In the absence of refrigeration, there were only three ways to preserve food: drying in salt, boiling in vinegar, or making a jam with sugar. Salt and vinegar were used to preserve meat and fish. So except in the summer months, Pocahontas's party ate a lot of salted or pickled food, but they would have had roast beef and roasted or boiled chicken as well as salt cod and beef. Their vegetables in winter were mainly roots: carrots, parsnips, and turnips.[5]

Apples and pears could be kept in cool cellars, and plums could be dried into prunes; but other fruits were only available preserved in copious amounts of sugar. England did not yet have its own sources of sugar from Caribbean plantations, and imported sugar was very expensive; so most people had little fruit in the winter. Some medical experts claimed that fruits were dangerous to eat anyway, so lack of them in the winter was no problem.

As you progressed down the income and status scale, bread became a larger and larger part of your diet. Everyone ate bread and butter for breakfast, and the richer you were, the whiter the bread. In England as in Virginia, these years saw many poor harvests and consequent food shortages. There was a harvest failure once every seven years, according to one source. In the worst times, the poor ate bread made of acorns rather than wheat, oats, or rye. Acorn bread, if the visiting Powhatans saw it, would have been familiar to them because they ate it at home. A character in Shakespeare's *Julius Caesar* refers to the "stinking breath" of the common people, which was a result of their poor diet. Low consumption of fruits and vegetables also contributed to chronic low-level scurvy, caused by vitamin C deficiency.[6]

London was a rapidly growing city: from fifty thousand inhabitants in 1500, its population had increased to two hundred thousand by 1600.[7] When Pocahontas and her entourage were in London, they stayed at the Belle Sauvage Inn on Ludgate Hill, near St. Paul's Cathedral. It was originally called the Bell Inn, and an early owner, named Savage, added his own name. So it is pure coincidence that the inn name seems to echo the way Londoners saw Pocahontas. The inn's courtyard was a playhouse, and the Belle Sauvage was a place of constant traffic of Londoners going in and out.[8] The government made persistent efforts to stop performances of plays in inns, but it is unclear how effective the ban actually was.

In Ben Jonson's play *The Staple of News*, a character says, "I have known a Princess, and a great one, come forth from a tavern." When challenged, the character retorts, "the blessed Pocahontas (as the Historian calls her and great Kings Daughter of *Virginia*) hath been in womb of a tavern." The historian referred to here was Capt. John Smith.[9]

The Virginians were thrust into a bustling part of London. The cathedral bell would have kept them in time with the passing hours, and they would have seen London's busy and varied population. The courtyard of St. Paul's Cathedral was not the quiet place of contemplation we might associate with a churchyard. Rather, it was the center of the English publishing industry. Printers and more than two hundred booksellers crowded the area, and their patrons created a constant flow of people. That is where you went to hear the news and all the latest gossip.[10]

St. Paul's was in the western-most part of the old City of London, enclosed in the wall originally built by the Romans. Ludgate was one of seven gates in the wall, and because it was adjacent to the cathedral, it had a singularly important role. To the west was Westminster, then a separate city and the seat of government, so "Ludgate was the threshold between St. Paul's and Westminster, between spiritual and earthly power." Coronation processions passed through Ludgate on their way to Westminster, and the gate was closed on the death of Queen Elizabeth. And Ludgate also served as a debtors' prison to separate debtors from common criminals. Ludgate Hill became Fleet Street as it moved down the hill, and Fleet Street eventually turned into the Strand.[11]

Just outside the gates of St. Paul's was a huge market where farmers brought vegetables for sale. In addition to locally grown produce, London also imported onions, carrots, and cabbages from the Netherlands. This market grew so big that it was moved to Covent Garden, newly rebuilt by Inigo Jones, a few years later.[12]

The Blackfriars Theatre was just a few blocks away. Shakespeare had been a member of the King's Men, the company that played there, but

Nineteenth-century engraving of the Belle Sauvage Inn from Henry C. Shelley, *Inns and Taverns of Old London* (Boston: L. C. Page, 1909).

he died in April 1616, just two months before Pocahontas's arrival. His *Tempest*, with its echoes of American experiences, was performed at the Blackfriars. The nearby Mermaid Tavern saw regular gatherings of poets and playwrights, including Ben Jonson, John Donne, and Inigo Jones. Cheapside, center of London's commerce and home of its wealthiest goldsmiths, runs along the northeast side of St. Paul's. This is another misleading name; rather than being a place for the thrifty shopper, its name comes from an old English word, *ceap*, that meant bargaining or a place where bargaining took place.[13]

Prisons were also near neighbors. The Fleet, where political prisoners were housed, and the large Newgate Prison were both close by. Bridewell, where the poor were kept out of the way, was also right there. Poor children from Bridewell were later sent to Virginia as servants. On the other side of St. Paul's was Bethlehem Hospital for the insane, whose name was compressed into "Bedlam."

The Fleet River, for which the prison was named, ran nearby, and the Virginians were not far from the Thames, with its constant traffic of boats and ferries. London had no sanitation system, so all the by-products of industry and the waste of daily life ultimately ended up in the rivers. As they compared the crowded, noisy, and dirty city to their own Werowocomoco, the Virginians had a lot to think about.[14]

Prince Henry, the golden youth for whom the Henrico settlement in Virginia was named, had died in 1612, not long after his namesake town was settled. Henry was very athletic, and rumor had it that he had in-

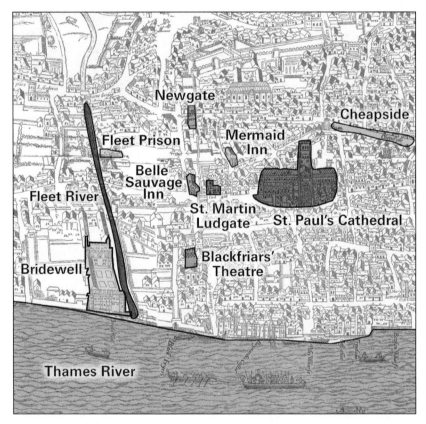

Pocahontas's London. Designed by Scott Walker from *The Map of Early Modern London*, edited by Janelle Jenstad. Map derived from the Agas Map, produced in ca. 1633, depicting the City of London in the 1560s.

Pocahontas engraving, by Simon van der Passe, 1616, National Portrait Gallery (Accession Number: NPG.77.43).

sisted on swimming in the foul Thames, where he caught his fatal illness. Queen Anne, in her extreme distress, had sent to Sir Walter Ralegh to make a "cordial" of the medicines he had brought from Guiana in the 1590s. Ralegh sent his balsam of Guiana, and Henry briefly seemed better.[15] He was eighteen years old when he died, and his younger brother, Charles. now became the heir apparent.

The Virginia Company, insisting that it was bringing new royalty to England, rushed an engraved portrait of Pocahontas into print. Rather than having her portrait painted, something that would have been seen by a very few, the company chose to have a large number of engravings created for wide distribution. Inexpensive engravings were the social media of the day, and her image was seen by people of all classes.

Other Natives from North America had been in England, and people had flocked to see their strange dress and manners. As Shakespeare's *Tempest* testified, people wanted to experience the exotic.[16] Pocahontas, on the other hand, was presented as the ultimate English lady. What mattered was that she was the daughter of an emperor and a Christian gentlewoman married to an English man. Her portrait showed her in the most expensive and elaborate dress. Her hat was of felt made from beaver fur that had been bleached white, an expensive process that only the wealthiest could afford. She wore an elaborate brocade gown with a wide starched lace collar, drop pearl earrings, and a fan of three feathers. No one could doubt that she was an important personage, someone to be looked up to and admired.

Immediately beneath Pocahontas's figure in the engraving, it says that she is in her twenty-first year, 1616. Around her image is a ribbon of text that says in Latin, "Matoaka als Rebecca Filia Potentiss: Prince: Powhatani Imp: Virginia." Below the portrait is the translation, "Matoaka als Rebecka daughter to the Mighty Prince Powhatan Emperour of Attanoughkomouck als Virginia, converted and baptized in the Christian faith, and wife to the worthy Mr. John Rolfe." "Als" here means something like "aka" or "alias." Attanoughkomouck was one of the names for Powhatan's territory that the English had learned. The more commonly used one was Tsenacommaca.

One of the most remarkable things about the portrait is that the name Pocahontas does not appear anywhere on it. This shows how closely the printer was watching the emerging story. Samuel Purchas, the man who made a profession of collecting and publishing travelers' accounts, wrote that the leading intellectuals in London seized the chance to learn more about Virginia Algonquian religion. Sir Theodore Goulston, an important London physician and scholar and Virginia Company member, held salons several evenings at his home, where Uttamattomakin, the Powhatans' chief priest and Pocahontas's brother-in-law, talked with these learned men about his people's religious beliefs and practices. Henry Spelman, identified by Purchas as "Sir Thos. Dale's man," acted as interpreter for these meetings. Uttamattomakin revealed that Pocahontas's real name had been concealed from the English because of fears they could harm her if they knew her name. Pocahontas was a nickname they had been told to use to protect her. Now that she was baptized with the name Rebecca, her real name, Matoaka, could be known. Alexander Whitaker had written in his letter of 1614, published in Ralph Hamor's *True Discourse* in 1615, that after her baptism, he knew that her name was Matoa.[17]

Over the evenings of meetings, Uttamattomakin, according to Purchas, sang and danced "his diabolical measures," and he was very happy to answer questions and to describe his people's beliefs fully. The one thing he warned his hosts against was trying to convert him. Purchas wrote that he was "very zealous in his superstition, and will hear no persuasions to the truth." Uttamattomakin described how priests were able to make the deity Okeus appear among them when they gathered in a secret place and performed the rituals. He actually said the secret words that would cause Okeus to appear, but Henry was unable to translate them. Uttamattomakin said that Okeus was a "personable Virginian" in his appearance and had a long lock of hair on the left side reaching down almost to his foot. Uttamattomakin maintained that it was in imitation of their God that Virginia Algonquian men wore their hair this way. Purchas was scandalized that the lovelock now so fashionable among London dandies was actually an imitation of a deity that he considered to be the Devil.[18]

Many of the scholars and intellectuals gathered at Goulston's salon had been associated with the famous English mathematician and scientist John Dee. Dee died in 1609, so he was not present; but he certainly came to mind as they watched Uttamattomakin's rituals. Dee was known all over Europe for his learning, and Queen Elizabeth consulted him many times. Elizabeth summoned Dee when a very bright comet appeared in the night sky in 1577, and they spent three whole days discussing its significance. Some people, who were suspicious of his activities, called him the "Queen's Conjuror."

Dr. Dee was like Uttamattomakin in that he "conversed" with angels in person, including the archangels Gabriel and Michael, and received instructions from them. Just as Uttamattomakin used special words to call Okeus, Dee summoned the angels using special prayers. He used three crystal stones to concentrate the rays of light in which the angels appeared, and one of the crystals had been left for him by the angels outside his study window. He set up his crystals and their table according to the instructions the angels gave him. He believed that the angels were bringing him knowledge direct from God and that, using that knowledge, he and other scientists could begin to restore the earth to the way it was at the first creation. Queen Elizabeth actually came to his house to see the crystals for herself, and some said that Dee was the model for the magician Prospero in Shakespeare's *Tempest*.

The revelation of the American continents, previously unknown to Europeans, was one indication that God was encouraging the creation of new knowledge. Studying the newly revealed people, plants, and animals was already contributing to greater understanding, and Dee, who was the first to use the term "British Empire," was deeply interested in America. He wrote a book, now lost, on ways to convert American Natives, and he was an adviser to several voyages to the far north searching for the Northwest Passage that would allow ships to cross through to the Pacific Ocean.

As a reward for all Dee's efforts, Queen Elizabeth issued a patent that gave him, on paper, ownership of most of Canada. One of his last acts was to write a report on the blazing star, Halley's comet, seen by the first supply fleet carrying Thomas Savage, and he sent the report to Thomas Harriot. Both men were deeply involved in the study of optics or light, partly because light, in which the angels appeared to Dee, was God's first creation.[19]

As scholars sought understanding of this previously unknown culture and its deepest meanings, English elites honored Pocahontas as visiting royalty, and John Rolfe faded to the background. Samuel Purchas described how she was honored: "I was present when my Honorable and Reverend Patron, Lord Bishop of London, Dr. King entertained her with festival state and pomp beyond what I have seen in his hospitality to other ladies."[20]

Pocahontas and Uttamattomakin were "graciously" received at court, where they were in the audience for *The Vision of Delight*, a masque written by Ben Jonson, staged by Inigo Jones, and performed on Twelfth Night (January 6, 1617). It was part of the court's Christmas celebrations, and the two Virginians were "well placed" among the spectators; "well placed" meant near the royal family.[21] Being near the king meant that Pocahontas and Uttamattomakin had the ideal view of the scene. People seated on the sides had to crane their necks to see.

Masques presented allegorical characters that represented good and bad forces. *The Vision of Delight*, which was set at night and in midwinter, opened on a life-size streetscape, with a "fair building." Delight entered first, followed by Grace, Love, Harmony, Revel, Sport, Laughter, and Wonder, and they sang of the pleasures of spring. Then suddenly some antimasquers entered. These were the bad elements. A she-monster gave birth on stage to six "burratines," grotesque characters from Italian comedy. In addition, there were six outlandish older men, called pantaloons, who danced with the burratines.[22]

The speeches were shot through with double meanings and sly hints of lechery and gluttony. Pocahontas and Uttamattomakin may not have caught the allusions from English popular culture, but they certainly took in the strange and wonderful events unfolding before them. Night rose in a "chariot bespangled with stars" and trailing a train of flames. The moon also hovered over the scene. Soon clouds covered the skyscape, and Fantasy broke forth with a long speech about all the kinds of dreams he could provide. The wild antimasquers broke onto the stage again.

Then suddenly, with a burst of loud music, the scene changed to a spring setting. Green countryside replaced the London street, and lambs and flowers dotted the landscape of green plants and flowing rivers. The masquers danced, and they and the audience experienced a waking dream of the spring to come. The character Wonder asked how this transformation could have come about. The air was suddenly mild, fields had their "coats," and winter was banished underground. Wonder posed the question, "Whose power is this? What God?" Then Fantasy stepped forward and gestured toward King James, saying, "Behold a King, Whose presence maketh this perpetual Spring."

Masques presented order and disorder as opposing forces vying for control. At the conclusion, the king always restored proper order. In this particular masque, the dancers were presented as figures in dreams, and the audience was invited to see themselves as dreamers also. The first lines of the masque were sung, so Pocahontas and Uttamattomakin could see real connections with worship in their own community, which was conducted in song. Did Pocahontas think back to the dance performance with which she and her friends had welcomed Capt. John Smith? Smith called it a "Virginia Masque," and it shared many elements with this English one.

Uttamattomakin and Pocahontas would have understood and responded to the dreaming dancers. Dancing could produce a dream state, and, in their worship, dancing allowed them to connect with the world of spirits. Dreams were powerful for them, and Uttamattomakin, as a priest, was the carrier and interpreter of dreams because he was able to move between the human and spirit worlds. English people could also experience dreams as important links to the supernatural. John Rolfe had written in his letter explaining why he wanted to marry Pocahontas that God came to him in his sleep urging him to spend all his effort to make her a Christian. The visitors from Virginia found powerful and familiar themes in *The Vision of Delight*.

Masques were extreme costly and lavish productions, and they often had only one performance. Sets were large and intricate, and the masquers wore costumes in the most expensive fabrics. They were accompanied by large numbers of professional musicians. *The Vision of Delight* required ten French musicians. Because masques were meant to show off the importance of the king and his courtiers, the expense was part of the show. *The Vision of Delight* did have a second performance later in the month. But two performances were little enough for the £1,500 or so (over £100,000 in modern currency) that it was said to have cost. The caustic letter writer John Chamberlain wrote, "I have heard no great speech nor commendation on the masque neither before nor since."[23]

Uttamattomakin was not impressed either. When he met with Capt. John Smith toward the end of his stay in England, Smith reported that Uttamattamokin said Powhatan "did bid him to find me out, to show him our God, the King, Queen, and Prince, I so much had told them of." Smith did his best to describe the Christian God, and he told Uttamattomakin that he had seen the king for himself. Uttamattomakin refused to believe that the unimpressive man he had met was actually the powerful monarch of whom he had heard such reports.[24]

English observers always described Powhatan as a man of immense dignity, and as Henry said, he did not dress differently from other men because he was set apart by the great honor his people showed him. English royalty gained respect in the opposite way, through lavish display. King James's coronation robe cost £2,172, and that for his queen, Anne, was £1,996, the equivalent of hundreds of thousands of pounds today.[25]

James I was awkward, not dignified, in his self-presentation. Sir John Oglander, a staunch supporter of the monarchy, began his "Note on King James" with the statement, "King James the First of England was the most cowardly man that ever I knew." Oglander did praise his learning and wisdom and his concern for his people's welfare. Oglander also recorded that James loved men more than women, "loving them beyond the love of men to women," and singled out the royal favorite, the Duke of Buckingham. James hated the fact that ordinary people thought they had a right to see their king. When the public pressed around him, his courtiers told him they "came out of love to see him," and his reply was, "God's wounds! I will pull down my breeches and they shall also see my arse!"[26]

Capt. John Smith described the very formal way that Powhatan washed and dried his hands before and after eating, but James I was said to have hands as soft as silk because he never washed them. The Duke of Buckingham once closed a letter to the king saying, "And so I kiss your dirty hands."[27]

When Smith finally convinced Uttamattomakin "by circumstances" that the man he had met really was the king, Uttamattomakin remarked on James's stinginess, a serious defect in a man who wanted to be thought great. Powhatan earned the respect of his subjects partly because he distributed everything he had to his people, but as the fabulously expensive masque showed, James I accumulated wealth for himself and his favorites. Uttamattomakin reminded Smith that he had given Powhatan a white dog, which Powhatan kept with him always, "but your King gave me nothing, and I am better than your white Dog." His report when he returned to Virginia must have been really interesting.[28]

Other Virginians were in London then. Squanto, the man who later became famous as the Pilgrims' adviser and interpreter in New England, was in London at the same time as Pocahontas. The English applied the name "Virginia" to the entire east coast of North America, so Squanto, a Patuxet from New England, was also a Virginian in English eyes. Several different people wrote his story, and each telling was slightly different; so our understanding of what had happened to him is a bit murky. Patuxet was on the Massachusetts coast near where Cape Cod begins, and many ships ranged those waters. The northern New England and Newfoundland coasts attracted huge transatlantic attention because the rich fishing grounds provided badly needed protein for Europe's burgeoning population. The French explorer Samuel de Champlain had traveled around Massachusetts Bay early in the seventeenth century, and his map showed the site of Squanto's village.

Capt. John Smith, after his departure from Jamestown, felt that his contributions had been undervalued, so he turned his attention to New England, which he argued was a better place for English people to prosper. He actually invented the name "New England" as a promotional tool. He wanted his readers to see that the more northern sections of North America's east coast were better suited to English bodies than hot Virginia was, and he published his first book promoting the region in 1616, when the Virginia Company was working hard to garner support for its colony.[29]

Smith had gotten backing for two ships to scope out possibilities in 1614. They planned to hunt for whales and to look for mines with valuable ore. If neither worked out, they would try to get fish and furs. They did manage to get some fish, and Smith's ship returned to England to sell some of their take.

The other ship, captained by Thomas Hunt, stayed behind, supposedly to salt and dry the rest of their fish for sale in Spain. But Hunt actually had a very different plan. This "worthless fellow" lured twenty-four young Native men onto his ship and then took "these poor innocent creatures" prisoner. Squanto was one of the twenty-four. Hunt was "more savagelike than they," and his scheme was to sell his captives into slavery in Málaga in Spain. But Hunt's plan was thwarted when Spanish authorities intervened, and his captives were turned over to Roman Catholic priests to be instructed in the Christian religion.[30]

Málaga is on Spain's Mediterranean coast, so it is surprising to learn that there was a small community of English merchants there. The merchants' ships brought fish from Newfoundland, which was especially important to Spain's Roman Catholic population for their fish days. In return, the ships carried wine and raisins back to England. This was a mutually beneficial connection, and the authorities did not want rogue traders like Hunt messing it up. The presence of the English merchants in Málaga solves another mystery about Squanto's life: how he got to England. He traveled on one of the merchants' ships with the all-important wine shipment.

One thing about Squanto's life that we do know for sure is that he was living in England in 1616 and 1617 when Pocahontas and Henry Spelman were there. He stayed with John Slany, treasurer of the Newfoundland Company, at his house on Cornhill, a short distance from Ludgate, where Pocahontas and her train were lodged.[31] At that time, plans to colonize in Newfoundland were not going well, largely because the fishermen went there in the spring and returned in the fall and did not need an expensive permanent residence. And after Sagadahoc in Maine had been abandoned, there were no English colonies in New England. So the Newfoundland Company had no incentive to trumpet Squanto's presence with the kind of publicity and show that advertised Pocahontas and her entourage.[32]

But given the few short blocks that separated their living quarters, it is tempting to imagine that Pocahontas or Uttamattomakin met Squanto.[33] The Powhatans and the Patuxets spoke languages of the Algonquian language family, so they might have been able to communicate on some level, just as Spanish and Italian speakers can. Squanto's experience recalled Paquiquineo, the Paspahegh man tutored in Christianity by priests in Spain before his return to the Chesapeake, and Uttamattomakin would have valued better understanding of those experiences.

The Newfoundland Company may not have been interested in fundraising in 1616, but two huge campaigns competed for the public interest that year, one by the Virginia Company and the other for a Guiana venture by Sir Walter Ralegh.

The Virginia Company tweaked a project it had had in the works since 1612, a lottery scheme to bring in revenue. The company's 1612 charter had authorized a lottery; it was held in London, and the company tried to create a stir around it. The Virginia Company set up its lottery house at the west end of St. Paul's churchyard to catch all those who were looking for the latest news. Agents created a broadside advertising the 1612 lottery, and the new Spanish ambassador, Diego Sarmiento de Acuña, Count of Gondomar, was interested enough to secure one and send it to Spain. It is now in the archives in Simanca as the sole surviving copy. But this lottery and the ones that followed were disappointing. There was a large time gap between a person's buying a ticket and the announcement of the prizewinners, sometimes many months or even years, and there had also been charges of corruption among the managers.[34]

In 1615, the company decided to hold another "Great Standing Lottery," with high ticket prices and lavish prizes promised. For this lottery, the company commissioned a ballad, "London's Lotterie," to the tune of "Lusty Gallant."[35] And in February 1616, just a few months before Pocahontas's arrival, the Virginia Company published a prospectus for its new and improved lottery that carried pictures of two men: Eiakintomino and Matahan. Eiakintomino was displayed in St. James's Park, and a Dutch visitor did a watercolor painting of him that was used in this prospectus.[36] Both men are holding bows, and each has a turtle by his feet. The poster, which also carried an image of King James I and the Virginia Company seal, advertised the lottery and the cash prizes it offered, illustrated by bags of money. It showed a man sitting between two huge bins, from which the winning tickets would be drawn. Patriotism had not worked as well as the Virginia Company hoped in attracting money, so it thought appealing to people's greed and love of gambling would be better. It all sounded perfect, but this one still failed to sell enough tickets.

Lottery poster, Society of Antiquaries, London.

So, in 1616, the Virginia Company again revamped its plan. The previous lotteries had been in London and were called "standing lotteries," but now company officials created what they called a "running lottery." Company agents went to cities and towns all over England and proposed holding a lottery in them. The town would benefit, and part of the proceeds would go to charity. Delays in announcing winners had discouraged prospective ticket holders, but the running lotteries offered instant results and real rewards. The running lotteries created a festive atmosphere, and they brought Virginia to popular attention all over the country. They also brought in money.[37]

Meanwhile, Sir Walter Ralegh was soliciting funding for a venture to Guiana on the Caribbean coast of South America. He had been freed from a very long imprisonment in the Tower of London in March of that year in order to carry out his plan. Ralegh had been the backer (and owner) of the ill-fated Roanoke colonies in the mid-1580s. Although he never went to Roanoke, he did lead an expedition to Guiana in 1595, and he returned convinced that the fabled golden city of El Dorado was there, as he argued in *The Discovery of the Large, Rich, and Beautiful Empire of Guiana, with a Relation of the Great and Golden City of Manoa (Which the Spaniards Call El Dorado)* (1596).

When James I came to the throne after Queen Elizabeth's death in 1603, he believed that Ralegh had conspired to block him from becoming king, and he committed Sir Walter to prison on a suspended sentence of death. From 1603 on, Ralegh campaigned to be allowed to return to Guiana in search of the wealth he was certain was there, and his appeal was finally effective in 1616. His permit stipulated that there would be no violent clashes with the Spanish. King James was not going to rekindle the war with Spain from Queen Elizabeth's time through some hotheaded actions over there.

During 1616 and the first part of 1617, Guiana and Virginia dueled for a place in the public imagination. Ralegh gathered £30,000, a sum close to what the Virginia Company had raised over the previous decade, and his expedition set sail in June 1617. His ship was aptly named *Destiny*.[38]

Ralegh had left two English boys in Guiana in 1595, but neither was present in 1617. Ralegh had promised to return in 1596, but as often happened with this kind of plan, events in England prevented it. Francis Sparrey had been captured by the Spanish and taken into prison in Madrid, where he became Francisco Espari. Hugh Goodwin had been killed by tigers, according to Spanish reports.[39] Thomas Savage and Henry Spelman would have been abandoned in the same way if Lord de la Warr had not arrived in the nick of time when the Jamestown colonists gave up and headed for home in 1610.

Ralegh's new expedition did not find the hoped-for gold, and some of the men attacked a Spanish fort while they were in Guiana, violating the king's instructions. Ralegh's 1603 death sentence was carried out after his return in 1618, and his execution made many people unhappy. Chamberlain wrote three weeks later, "We are so full still of Sir Walter Ralegh, that almost every day brings forth . . . ballads" and other "stuff."[40]

The search for American gold had once again ended in tragedy with Ralegh's execution, but the Virginia Company also faced negative publicity. The Virginia Company was certain that tobacco was going to be the gold to finance its colony, but tobacco still seemed to be a problematic product. Ideally, the colony would have produced something essential to life, such as the medicines that the apothecaries looked for, and enhanced England's economy that way. Tobacco was clearly not essential, and many people thought it was corrupting.

Pocahontas's people used tobacco for ceremonial purposes and to sustain themselves when on long journeys, but in Europe, tobacco was swiftly becoming a big exotic fad. Tobacco had been coming into England from the Spanish colonies for decades, but it was expensive and only for the ultra rich. Soon, with tobacco cultivation spreading over the land in the Chesapeake, it was a product almost everyone could buy. Drinking tobacco smoke, as they put it, was Europe's first huge consumer craze.

Some people argued that tobacco was actually beneficial to health, as the exhalation of hot and dry smoke would help eliminate excessive cold and moist humors from the body. Thomas Harriot, in his book on the people and land of the Carolina coast, had praised tobacco, saying, "it purgeth superfluous phlegm and other gross humors, openeth all the pores and passages of the body, . . . whereby their bodies are notably preserved in health." He also testified, "we ourselves during the time we were there used to suck it after their manner, as also since our return, & have found many rare and wonderful experiments of the virtues thereof." To detail all tobacco's healthful qualities, he wrote, would require a whole book in itself.[41]

Others, including King James, considered smoking both filthy and dangerous.[42] In 1604, long before there was an established tobacco industry in English-claimed territory, James had written *A Counterblast to Tobacco.* In 1607, as Jamestown was first planted, Cambridge University authorities forbade students "taking tobacco," which they associated with excessive drinking.[43]

When Pocahontas and her party were actually in London, Thomas Deacon published, with the king's official stamp of approval, *Tobacco Tortured; or, The Filthy Fume of Tobacco Refined: Shewing All Sorts of Subjects, That the Inward Taking Tobacco Fumes, Is Very Pernicious unto*

Their Bodies; Too Too Profluvious for Many of Their Purses; and Most Pestiferous to the Public State. Deacon linked the derangement caused by tobacco smoking to all kinds of public disorder, up to and including the "Gunpowder Treason" of 1605. Another author claimed that the imprisoned Gunpowder Plot traitors "took tobacco out of measure" and were so drugged that they seemed to have no fear or feelings as they faced their terrible executions.[44] Capt. John Underhill in New England later reportedly said that he had actually had a religious experience uniting him with God while "taking a pipe of Tobacco."[45] With its consciousness-altering properties, tobacco continued to be problematic, especially as it was considered an American, and therefore alien, substance.

Everyone was soon able to buy tobacco because, as the Virginia crop grew, the price continued to drop, making it available to the masses. In 1592, the Earl of Northumberland, George Percy's older brother, paid four pounds for a pound of tobacco, and John Aubrey, writing later in the seventeenth century, remembered his grandfather saying that a pound of tobacco had cost a pound of silver. In his grandfather's day, the gentry had pipes made of silver; "the ordinary sort made use of a walnutshell and a straw." By 1618, a pound of tobacco cost two or three shillings (there were twenty shillings in a pound). And a decade later, the price had dropped to a few pennies (there were twelve pence in each shilling). A satirical book called *The Honesty of Our Age* claimed that a survey found seven thousand stores and taverns selling tobacco in London and its suburbs at the time Pocahontas was there. And the Virginia colony benefited immensely from it. John Pory wrote in 1619, "All our riches for the present do consist in Tobacco."[46]

Meanwhile, the Virginia Company was making plans to move Pocahontas and her party out of London. They may have made one short trip to Norfolk, to John Rolfe's home in the village of Heacham; local tradition there maintains that he brought Pocahontas and their son to visit his family. Pocahontas would have welcomed the chance to see some of the landscape away from the dirt and noise of London, especially after seeing the countryside portrayed in *The Vision of Delight*.

Image of tobacco shop window, 1617. Richard Braithwaite, *The Smoaking Age.*
Courtesy of the British Library Imaging Services.

Henry Spelman's home was also in Norfolk, and he presumably met with some of his family during his time in England and persuaded his fifteen-year-old brother, Thomas, to go to Virginia. Thomas, who was identified in the records as a gentleman, paid his own way in 1616 and therefore was eligible for a land grant. Maybe the three pounds he had received in the will of his great-uncle Francis Saunders early in 1614 had helped pay the cost of an ocean crossing. In 1625, the court records show that he left a boy with a planter named Luke Eaden in exchange for a barrel of corn; he intended to redeem the boy when he was able to repay the debt.[47]

Pocahontas and her party did move away from London to Brentford, a suburb to the west of the city next to where the royal botanical gardens at Kew would be founded in the next century. The Virginia Company decided that a healthier and cheaper environment would be better for the visitors, and George Percy helped arrange the move. Brentford was the site of Syon House, the London home of the Percy family. George's older brother Henry, the present Earl of Northumberland, was confined in the Tower of London on suspicion of involvement in the Gunpowder Plot, but George was living in Brentford.

Although the sources do not mention their meeting, another man with American experience was also present. Thomas Harriot had his own cottage at Syon House, where he carried on his scientific work.[48] The Earl of Northumberland's interest in science had earned him the nickname of the Wizard Earl, and Harriot, who had become one of the leading practitioners of the new science of the day, worked with him, bringing him materials and expertise for his experiments in the Tower.[49]

Harriot and the Virginia visitors probably met many times while they were all in Brentford. Harriot himself had learned coastal Carolina Algonquian from Manteo, the Carolina Native who stayed with the Roanoke colonists. Because Harriot could speak and understand the language, he wrote that he had had "special familiarity with some of their priests." The chance to talk with Uttamattomakin and further his own understanding of the Algonquians' religion and beliefs about creation and the afterlife was a wonderful opportunity for Harriot.[50]

Capt. John Smith also seized the opportunity to visit Pocahontas in Brentford. While she was in London, the Virginia Company had kept close tabs on her and decided who could visit her, but Smith had access to her in the country. Now that she had become a celebrity, he played up his earlier association with her. He wrote a letter to Queen Anne, James I's wife, about Pocahontas and about the help she had given to the Jamestown colony in its most difficult time. In writing about Pocahontas, he was also highlighting his own role in the colony's early years, and his account was filled with personal tags to elicit an emotional response. For an ordinary Englishman to write to the queen of England was a bold move, and he took the further liberty, several years later, of publishing the letter.[51]

Smith also published an account of his meeting with Pocahontas in Brentford. At first, it was disappointing, because when Pocahontas saw Smith, she "turned about, obscured her face, as not seeming well contented." She was angry at him for staying away while she was in London. Rolfe suggested that they leave her alone, which they did for several hours, during which time Smith was "repenting myself for having writ that she could speak English." When they rejoined her, Pocahontas began to talk, and she chided Smith, reminding him of all she had done for the colonists, and said, "You did promise Powhatan what was yours should be his, and he the like to you."[52]

Pocahontas remembered that Smith had referred to Powhatan as "father, being in his land a stranger," and she said that now that the situation was reversed, she would call Smith father. He said that he did not dare to allow that in England because she was a king's daughter, at which Pocahontas exploded. He had acted without fear in Virginia, and yet in his own country, he was afraid of a word! She insisted that she would call him "father" and he would call her "child and so I will be for ever and ever your Countryman." She wanted to restore the close friendship they had had in America.

Then Pocahontas went on to set the record straight. The colonists had told the Powhatans that Smith was dead, but Powhatan had directed Uttamattomakin to seek him out and learn the truth: "because your Countrymen will lie much." Smith was clearly proud of his relationship with Pocahontas and her people. Smith wrote that he visited her several times with various friends and courtiers, and he reported that all those sophisticated men told him that she exceeded many English ladies in both her appearance and her behavior.

As spring approached in 1617, the Rolfes made preparations to return to America. The Virginia Company had invested heavily in making the visit a success in order to attract the favorable attention that its project needed. Chamberlain, ever scornful, spoke for at least some of the investors when he sent Pocahontas's picture to his correspondent in the Netherlands: "Here is a fine picture of no fair Lady and yet with her tricking up and high style and titles you might think her and her worshipfull husband to be sombody, if you do not know that the poor company of Virginia out of their poverty are fain to allow her four pound[s] a week for her maintenance."[53] Four pounds was a lot of money. Still, it was a bit much to think that Pocahontas and her entourage, torn from their own country, should be self-supporting. And the four pounds presumably was to keep her entire household in London.

As the time for the party's return to Virginia neared, the Virginia Company revealed the great scheme that was behind Pocahontas's lavish treatment and the important people she had met. In February 1616, even before the Rolfes had arrived, King James had ordered the two archbishops, of Canterbury and York, to direct every parish in the country to take up a collection for money to set up schools and churches among the Powhatans in Virginia, "for the education of the children of those barbarians." Uttamattomakin had told Samuel Purchas that he was too old to be converted and said that the English should start with the children; his thinking matched what English leaders had already decided. The royal command said that the collection was to occur every six months for two years, four collections in all. Some bishops suggested to the parish officers that the collection should be done house to house to make sure that everyone contributed. Just as the Rolfes were awaiting a favorable wind, the Virginia Company did something remarkable. On March 2, the company received £300 that had been raised in the parishes all over England. A week later, it appropriated a third of that sum to the Rolfes to be used in educating Powhatan children and in converting the Powhatans to Christianity. The actual grant said that it was £100 "for the Lady Rebecca . . . for sacred use in Virginia." The company recorded that John Rolfe promised "in behalf of him self and the said Lady, his wife," to use all "good means of persuasions and inducements" to win the Virginians to the "embracing of true religion."[54]

These plans came to nothing. Pocahontas died as the ship that would have carried her home sailed down the Thames, and she was buried in the chancel of St. George's Church at Gravesend on March 21, 1617. Burial in the chancel was reserved for people of high rank, so her status was reaffirmed in this final English scene. As with the inn the party lived in, the Belle Sauvage, the name "Gravesend" seems to have a special affinity with Pocahontas's story, but just as the inn name derived from previous owners, the name "Gravesend" originally referred to the medieval office of landgrave, or count, and the edge of his jurisdiction.[55]

The sources are frustratingly skimpy on how or why Pocahontas died just as she was entering her twenties. Her lungs had been troubling her, and pneumonia or even tuberculosis may have been the cause. But there are also reports of her profound unhappiness with the prospect of returning to Virginia. Chamberlain, reporting the gossip, wrote that the Rolfes were waiting for a good wind to take them back across the Atlantic but that it was "sore against her will."[56] It seems highly possible that she was suffering great inner conflict because of that Virginia Company grant and the promise that she would devote herself to converting her people to Christianity. As long as she was in England, or even in the English colony, she could occupy the role of the celebrated first convert. But to go among her own people and try to subvert the very basis of their culture and traditions must have seemed impossible to her.

Pocahontas remembered Paquiquineo's story of having been trained by Spanish priests and returned to Virginia to convert his people. Paquiquineo solved his problem by destroying the mission that brought him back in the 1570s, but Pocahontas, as the mother of young Thomas, was tied to the English in ways that were quite different. Her inner turmoil over what would happen once they were back in Virginia must have been intolerable. What we call stress-related illness seventeenth-century people called a broken heart, and some said Pocahontas died of a broken heart. Whatever physical illness she had was made far worse by the stress she felt.

Henry Spelman had seen death before. His father died when he was eight, and early death was common in the England of his time. He had been so good with Iopassus's young child, and we can imagine him coming forward to comfort Thomas Rolfe and soothe his crying as the baby longed for his mother. Thomas was apparently inconsolable, and even Henry's efforts were not enough.

As soon as Pocahontas was buried, the ship carrying Henry, John Rolfe, and baby Thomas traveled on, with Samuel Argall once again in command, but they stopped at Plymouth on England's west coast. Thomas was not doing well, and Rolfe and Argall feared he would not survive the rigors of the ocean passage. He was sent to live with his uncle Henry Rolfe, so the boy grew up in John Rolfe's home in Heacham. He never saw his father again.

Uttamattomakin and Mattachanna also sailed with the company, although some of their people stayed behind. One man lived with George Thorpe, who later went to Virginia with big plans for mass conversion. The Virginian was baptized with his protector's name two weeks before he died, and the records of St. Martin's in the Fields noted the burial of "Georgius Thorp, *Homo Virginiae*," on September 27, 1619.[57]

Two of the women who attended Pocahontas remained in London. Both were Christians, and they had taken the names Mary and Elizabeth. Mary, who had worked as a servant for a while, became "very weak of a consumption," which was how the English described tuberculosis. The Virginia Company allocated twenty shillings a week for her medicine to Rev. William Gough, who "hath great care and taketh great pains to comfort her both in soul and body." Reverend Gough was pastor of St. Anne's in the Blackfriars and cousin to Rev. Alexander Whitaker. He was the cousin to whom Whitaker had written in 1614 about Pocahontas's conversion and marriage.[58]

By 1621, the company was chafing at the cost involved in keeping the two women. It decided to send them to Bermuda, which belonged to a spin-off from the Virginia Company, and the company sent them off in state. Each woman was provided with two servants, which would make her more attractive to a potential marriage partner, and clothes and bedding, soap and starch, food, a Bible, and a psalter. The total cost was over seventy pounds. The company instructed Nathaniel Butler, the Bermuda governor, to be especially careful in "bestowing of them," as they were daughters of viceroys in Virginia.[59]

Mary died on the ocean voyage, but Elizabeth was married in the Bermuda governor's front room to "as agreeable and fit husband as the place would afford"; the ceremony, witnessed by over a hundred guests, was followed by a lavish feast of "all the dainties" that could be provided. The governor described the bride as the sister of Opechancanough and a princess in her own right. Officials hoped that she and her husband might eventually go to Virginia and take on the conversion job they had planned for Pocahontas and John Rolfe.[60]

Henry Spelman now returned to Virginia with the rank of captain, so he had achieved the recognition of his adult status that he had craved. As he moved out of nonage, he hoped for a new, more independent life in Virginia and one in which his special skills would be recognized and valued.

6

VIRGINIA'S TRANSFORMATION

JOHN ROLFE AND HENRY SPELMAN arrived back in Jamestown in mid-May 1617, an even faster crossing than Henry's earlier one. Even though they had been gone just over a year, they found things quite different in Virginia. The most important change was the departure of Powhatan, who had relinquished his power and moved away from the capital. Opechancanough took control of the Powhatans and directed their policies for almost three decades.

Rolfe wrote to the Virginia Company official Sir Edwin Sandys about the sea voyage and saying, "My wife's death is much lamented, my child much desired when it is of better strength to endure so hard a passage." He explained his decision to leave his son behind and asked Sandys to continue to pay the stipend that the company had allocated Pocahontas and "some estate of land" for Thomas's future, "being the living ashes of his deceased mother."[1]

Capt. Samuel Argall was installed as acting governor in Jamestown, a post he held until April 1619. Argall turned out to be a poor governor, but Opechancanough, with Robert Poole as interpreter, was very effective as leader of all the Powhatans.

Meanwhile, the Virginia Company back in London was making major changes over the next couple of years as it planned for Virginia's future. Now that it had an assured source of income with tobacco, the company wanted to put the colony on a much more secure foundation. It transformed the government and encouraged the colonists to work hard by giving them a real stake in the future. One major step was to give each colonist land of his own; those who had come as servants up to this time would have land once their servitude was finished. Henry Spelman and Samuel Collier both received grants of land under this new system.

The company appointed George Yeardley as governor early in 1619. He had been in and out of the colony since 1610 and had been acting governor in the past. Now, he received a knighthood from King James, who signaled his approval of the company's new scheme. Yeardley was to preside over a very changed system, because the revised plan called for a general assembly to make laws for the colony. For the first time, backers in England were committed to trying to build a true English society in Virginia in place of the military establishment that had worked so poorly. The entire plan came to be known as the Great Charter, a name echoing England's own foundational Magna Carta.[2]

The plan solved one persistent problem: how to get a lot more colonists in Virginia. People who invested in the colony, whether they stayed in England or came to America, were allowed to join together to form companies of their own to create large plantations. These companies received land for the money they put in and fifty acres for every servant they brought over. With these incentives in place, and with a crop they could sell, investors brought over hundreds of servants to work on their land. Passage for one servant cost five pounds, and servants served seven years. If they survived, servants were a very good investment.

The company decided that owning land would not mean much unless colonists had families to work with them and children to inherit their stake, so it also made arrangements to import virtuous women to be wives for the colonists.[3]

The Virginia Company encouraged the City of London to send a hundred children "of twelve years and upward" annually to help populate the colony. These children were to be assembled out of the "multitudes that swarm" in the streets of London. When the company learned that some of the proposed deportees were "ill-disposed" and reluctant to go, it asked for authority to force them onto the ships, and the king's Privy Council was happy to grant the company the right to ship them off against their will. They were bound to servitude when they arrived;

the boys would be servants until they reached the age of twenty-one and the girls until they married or turned twenty-one.[4]

The poet John Donne, who was the dean of St. Paul's, preached a sermon before the Virginia Company praising the policy of forcing poor children to go to America. He compared Virginia to Bridewell, the prison and hospital where the indigent and disorderly were placed, and said the project "shall sweep your streets and wash your doors, of idle persons, and the children of idle persons, and employ them." Drawing on the medical lore of the day, he pictured Virginia as a spleen to drain England's foul humors and a liver to breed good blood. Sending children from the streets and minor lawbreakers would rid England of a burden, and Virginia would offer those unfortunates the chance of a new productive life. John Chamberlain, writing the news to Sir Dudley Carleton, declared that sending starving children to Virginia was "one of the best deeds that could be done with so little charge."[5]

Longtime colonists were not so happy with the changed situation and the new market for servants. John Rolfe wrote of the many complaints against the colony's leaders "for buying and selling men and boys" and changing the agreements that had been made with tenants, concluding that these kinds of practices were "in England a thing most intolerable."[6]

Two versions of Rolfe's letter survive. In one version, Rolfe wrote that a Dutch ship had come into the James River toward the end of August in 1619 and had sold "20. and odd Negroes" to the governor in exchange for food for the ship's crew. These Africans, probably newly arrived from Africa and captured in the Caribbean from the ship that had brought them across the Atlantic, added another complement of young men and women to the colony's population. Slavery was not yet established as a labor system; so some of these Africans would eventually become free, and some became planters in their own right. But they served very long terms of servitude.[7]

So in this period of transition, the colony saw two sets of young and unwilling new arrivals, as well as all the young men and women who had signed themselves up as servants. Because the Virginia population was now so young, all the newcomers posed a management problem, and the solution was to get them onto plantations and working. Suddenly, the plantations spread all along the James River and some on the Eastern Shore. Native communities were pushed back away from the waterways that were Virginia's highways, and their lives were radically disrupted by the growing plantations. Neither the Powhatans nor the colonists had foreseen this dramatic development.

As the colony expanded in Virginia and tobacco became an ever-growing sensation in England, the situations of Thomas, Henry, and Robert were problematic. Governor Yeardley arrived with his wife, the former Temperance Flowerdieu, in April 1619, and as he began to put the Virginia Company's new plan into operation, a central issue was how to deal with the boy interpreters now that they were growing into men. Robert, who was barely noticed earlier, was now the key interpreter with Opechancanough. And his position was growing increasingly difficult as the plantations spread and relations worsened. Thomas Savage also continued as interpreter, but he was increasingly directing his attention to the Accomacs, who lived on Virginia's Eastern Shore on the other side of Chesapeake Bay. Colonial leaders said that he was the first to establish trading relationships there.[8] Henry did not know where he stood. He had been a central figure in the colony's relations with the Powhatans and Patawomecks, and he resumed his relations with the Patawomecks; but now he was marginalized. His position was quite unclear in the new regime.

Henry and Thomas argued that they were now adults and should be treated as such, especially as they had knowledge that made them essential to the colony's success. Colonial leaders recognized that their period of servitude was over but wanted to keep them in service to the colony. Their solution was giving the go-betweens military rank. Being officers did not necessarily mean that they were expected to perform military service, only that they were on call when their service was needed.

Henry had already been made a captain. Thomas was given the rank of ancient, or ensign, in 1618 and placed under the command of Capt.

John Martin, who became Master of the Ordnance, in charge of all the guns and military equipment, in 1619. Ensign was the lowest rank among officers, and in this case, it probably signaled Thomas's relatively lowly birth. Social status also explained why Henry, with his connections to the illustrious family of Sir Henry Spelman, was given the rank of captain.

Powerful men competed to control and direct the young men despite their new ranks. As Master of the Ordnance, Captain Martin asserted that Thomas, "my ancient," answered only to him. Martin was perpetually at odds with the authorities in Virginia, and he was furious when Governor Yeardley called for Thomas to do some interpreting for him. He actually sued Yeardley and included his request for Thomas's services in the list of complaints. Thomas was so important to Captain Martin because of his connections to the Accomacs on the Eastern Shore and the corn he was able to procure from them, and he wanted to establish that it was Thomas who had made these alliances "before Sir George Yeardley came in." The governor said in his reply to the court that he had not known that Thomas was Martin's servant and instead considered him a "public interpreter."[9] Thomas clearly was not in control of his own life.

The situations of Henry and Robert were also highly problematic. The high point of 1619 was the first meeting of the new assembly, for which each plantation elected a representative, on July 30. For the first several days, the assembled representatives debated and decided issues involving parceling out of obligations for the colony's roads and defenses. Then, in a stunning development, tensions between the boy interpreters who were growing into men exploded onto the public stage. On the assembly's final day, it transformed itself into a court for the purpose of hearing treason charges against Henry Spelman, based on information supplied by Robert Poole.

Robert's testimony about "what passed between Opechancanough and Captain Henry Spelman" demonstrated the deep rivalry between the two interpreters. Henry was the senior interpreter, but he had been away from the scene, first on the Potomac with the Patawomecks and then in England, for a long time. Robert had been with Opechancanough for many years and had good reason to believe that his relationship with the great chief was the crucial one.[10]

Robert testified that Henry had sent a Powhatan man to Opechancanough to ask Opechancanough to send a messenger asking Henry to come to see him, just to give Henry a plausible reason to go and visit the paramount chief. So Henry had created a pretext for going to Opechancanough, which was the kind of operation Powhatan had tried to avoid by giving the governor the chain of pearls to be worn by any truly official ambassador. Robert said that he encountered Henry at Opechancanough's court but that "Capt. Spelman would not speak to him nor so much as look upon him not being (as it should seem) well content to see him there." Opechancanough asked Henry why he would not speak to Robert, and "his answer was let him first speak to me."

Robert testified that Henry and Opechancanough spent the next day in private conference. A Powhatan man was placed at the door as sentinel, and no one, not even Robert, was allowed to enter. When their conference was over, Opechancanough called for Robert and asked him "what great king was shortly to come from England." Robert said that he did not know and referred him to Henry, who said it was "my Lord Rich, who meant to plant at Kiskiack and Captain Spelman to join with him."

It was true that Sir Robert Rich was planning to come to direct the entire Virginia enterprise. Now that it was on a solid footing and with large numbers of colonists going over, he wanted to make it into the place he thought it could be. Rich played a large role in England's expansion into the Atlantic. He had his own fleet, and he was a very big investor in the Virginia Company. As a leading puritan, he wanted to see England take its place as an Atlantic power alongside Spain and to make England the true leader of the Protestant nations, as Spain was of the Roman Catholics. He also hoped to engage in privateering, seizing Spanish ships carrying the riches the English believed they had stolen from the Native people. King James had forbidden any attacks on Spain or its people, but leaders such as Rich hoped this policy would end soon.

Rich was patron to a number of people involved in Atlantic ventures, including Samuel Argall and Henry Spelman, and his ship, *Treasurer*, made many crossings on behalf of the company. Presumably it was through Argall that Henry learned of Rich's decision to take up the governorship of Virginia. Rich knew that the present governor, Sir George Yeardley, intended to investigate Argall's actions as governor, so he had sent a ship to carry Argall home before that could happen.

So Henry was left in Virginia with the knowledge that Sir Robert Rich would soon be there and that he would play a role in the new administration, and he talked about it to Opechancanough with Robert listening. Then Henry said to Robert in English that he "would give £40 my lord were come for then he would trample upon all his enemies." The assembly that heard this testimony included many people whom Henry considered his enemies, and they did not like the prospect of being trampled by him.

According to Robert's testimony, Opechancanough intervened and asked whether this new governor would be greater than Sir George Yeardley. Henry answered that he was far greater than Yeardley and that once Sir Robert was present, Sir George would be "but a Tanx Werowance, that is a petty governor not of power to do anything." Henry may have felt he was doing the best he could for Opechancanough, so the chief would not overcommit to a regime that was soon to end. He warned Opechancanough that Rich could abrogate at will any treaties or alliances that Yeardley might make. Robert told Henry that "he had done very ill to speak such words and that Sir George would not take it well at his hands." Henry defiantly suggested that Robert tell Yeardley what he had said, "if he thought it good so to do."

Opechancanough was disturbed by the tension between the two interpreters and also by what Henry had told him. He wondered why "so many Governors were sent, one upon the neck of another out of England, which made the Indians uncertain what to trust unto," because each new governor overturned what his predecessor had set in place.

As Henry was departing, he made a bizarre request: he demanded that Opechancanough give him the medal with the image of King James that Gov. Sir Thomas Dale had entrusted to Powhatan. Dale and Powhatan had exchanged tokens, the chain of pearls and the medal, as a way of fixing the problem of people falsely claiming that they had been sent by their own leaders and spoke with authority. Only a person carrying the official symbol would be accepted as an ambassador.

Now Henry demanded the medal for the very odd purpose of sending it to Capt. John Bargrave, "to invite him to an Indian dancing." Bargrave was a recently arrived planter, who quickly built a reputation as a troublesome man. The problem with Henry's request was that he wanted "to send it from him self a private person by a private Messenger to Captaine Bargrave a private gentleman only to invite him to an Indian Dancing." His request "violated the dignity and honor" of the royal image, which was supposed to be carried only between "the king and the governor as a sacred token of peace and Amity and that by the hand of some public and principal person." Opechancanough refused to hand it over, but Henry "would not cease importuning him till he had obtained it: Saying that this Governor would soon be out of place and that he needed not care for his displeasure."

Henry knew that asking for the medal for his private use was out of bounds, and no one said what or where the "Indian dancing" was to be. Clearly he was completely frustrated by Robert's preeminence with Opechancanough and by his own marginal status. His firm belief that he would soon be elevated with the coming of Sir Robert Rich and his frustration had made him reckless.

Once Henry had departed, Opechancanough invited Robert for a private talk. First, he said that he had promised Sir George Yeardley to send him some corn when Yeardley was last in Virginia and that he would send it before the "arrival of that great new governor." If Sir George would let him know when he was settled, he would send the corn so that it "might not be taken away by his successor." He also said that if Yeardley would come to visit him, he would "discover [reveal] some other conference that Spelman had had with him."

Clearly, Opechancanough was made uncomfortable by these exchanges and was uncertain about how to react. Whom should he trust? Both Opechancanough and Henry faced the great problem of the times: the need to trust in arrangements that were chancy at best. All overseas ventures were risky, and all arrangements could be overturned at a moment's notice by storms or political change or a hundred other causes. The ocean voyage that separated England and Virginia took many months, so the colonists were always behind the curve.

In this case, events in England had already destroyed Henry's hopes. Sir Robert Rich's father, the Earl of Warwick, died, and Sir Robert became the earl in March 1619. Now that he had ascended to very high rank, Rich had many more kinds of enterprises to oversee, and he shelved the plan to go to Virginia. All this had happened before the Opechancanough interview, but no one in Virginia knew about it. So Henry, who had been so incautious, was now left facing a treason charge instead of advancement under a new and powerful governor.

John Pory, another client of Rich, was secretary of the Virginia colony, and he kept the official record of the assembly proceedings. He recorded that Robert charged Henry with speaking "very unreverently and maliciously against this present Governor," not only ruining Yeardley's reputation but also bringing contempt on the whole colony and thereby inviting "mischiefs . . . from the Indians." According to Pory's account, Henry confessed to some of the charges, "but the most part he denied, except only one matter of importance, and that was that he had informed Opechancanough that within a year there would come a Governor greater than this that now is in place." The result was that "he hath alienated the mind of Opechancanough from this present Governor, and brought him in much disesteem." Now the whole colony was "in danger of their slippery designs."

The assembly then debated the punishment. It could have executed Henry as a traitor, and some assembly members called for very harsh penalties; but most wanted a more lenient sentence. Calling his behavior a misdemeanor, they took away his rank of captain and required him to serve the colony for seven years as interpreter to the governor. The Virginia Company back in London recorded that he had been "degraded" and made a servant. Pory's assembly notes had referred to Henry as a private person when he asked Opechancanough for the medal, which meant that they no longer considered him in service to the colony. As a result of his sentence, he was back to being a servant and a public person.

We know that Henry was already unhappy about his difficulties in making the status transition from boy to full adulthood in the colony. Now, when he had finally achieved the rank of captain, he was again pushed down. When the sentence was passed on him, Henry, "as one that had in him more of the Savage than of the Christian, muttered certain words to himself neither showing any remorse for his offenses, nor yet any thankfulness to the Assembly for their so favorable censure." Pory wrote that they could only hope that he might redeem himself, "God's grace not wholly abandoning him." Pory also wrote in a letter to the new Virginia Company head, Sir Edwin Sandys, that he wondered how Robert Rich, the new Earl of Warwick, would feel about Henry's "unadvised using of his lordship's name to Opechancanough."

Clearly Henry was not satisfied with his role in Virginia, and in Robert's testimony, he comes across as a self-important little prig. After all, he came to Virginia with a reputation as a troublemaker. But there may be other ways of looking at his behavior that make it more understandable. By 1619, he had been closely involved with Virginia's Native people for a decade. They had treated him as one of them, even as a son of the king. When Pory wrote that Spelman was more savage than Christian, he spoke to a fear common among colonial leaders. If someone, particularly someone very young, lived on intimate terms with the Natives and learned their language and culture, would that person remain wholly committed to an English viewpoint? Henry certainly had a keen understanding of how Opechancanough saw things, and he may have wanted to save him and his people from what Henry saw as a crucial mistake. His conversation with Opechancanough may have involved more than just bravado and rivalry with Robert. And it may have revealed an area of ambiguity that Jamestown's leaders did not want to think about. Delighted as they were by Pocahontas's conversion to Christianity and English culture and by the prospect of many future conversions, the idea that the process could work the other way was profoundly disturbing.

The one positive outcome for Henry was that, as John Rolfe reported, the governor quickly rescinded his sentence. He was soon up north with the Patawomecks, so he was back with people he knew well and where his skills were valued. But the remission of his sentence was a blow as well as a blessing; Governor Yeardley was now inclined, according to Rolfe, to see Henry's transgressions as stemming from "childish ignorance." Youth was characterized by impetuous behavior and acting out, and Jamestown's leaders were saying that Henry's behavior demonstrated that, even at the age of twenty-five, he had not yet transitioned into adulthood. He was back in his original status.[11]

The colony's leaders soon had further concern about those who were caught between cultures. In January 1620, both John Rolfe and John Pory wrote to Virginia Company leader, Sir Edwin Sandys, with disturbing news about Robert Poole. Robert seemed to be deliberately manipulating the colony's relationship with Opechancanough and had "even turned heathen" and was "proving very dishonest." They feared that he was playing both ends against the middle. For example, he told the governor that if he sent two men to Opechancanough, the Powhatan "king" would come to Jamestown for a visit. But when Yeardley sent the two emissaries, they were given "frivolous answers" and found that Opechancanough had said no such thing and had no intention of going to Jamestown.[12]

Governor Yeardley then sent Rolfe and another leading colonist, Captain William Powell, with a new message explaining that he had issued his invitation for Opechancanough to come to Jamestown because Robert had said that he had requested it. The emissaries anchored a few miles from Opechancanough's capital and entrusted Yeardley's message to Henry and a recently arrived boy named Thomas Hobson.

At first, Opechancanough was unwelcoming to Henry and his companion; Robert was already there. But after Henry delivered the governor's message, Opechancanough's attitude changed. Not only were the two emissaries sent away "lovingly," but Opechancanough now "accused and condemned" Robert and believed that he had "sought all the means he could to break our league." Rolfe remarked that the Powhatans "also seemed to be weary of him." The problem for the colonists was what to do about Robert. They did not dare simply to remove him from his roles for fear of the damage he might do. They were already convinced, according to Rolfe, that he was altering the messages he carried in order to manipulate the relationships. Pory reported that Governor Yeardley had decided to punish Robert but changed his mind when he came to Jamestown carrying the medal with the king's portrait that Henry had previously demanded. This meant that he was an official emissary from Opechancanough, and therefore Jamestown's leaders "counted him a public, and as it were a neutral person." They decided not to "call Poole to account" for fear of offending Opechancanough.[13]

Pory's choice of words was telling. Because Robert carried the medal at Opechancanough's direction, his role was "public," whereas Henry had sought to use the medal for a "private" mission. Public and private were the most important distinctions, as when Governor Yeardley explained his calling Thomas to do a mission for him after Thomas had been assigned to work for Captain Martin by saying that he thought Thomas was a public interpreter. Robert had to be treated with respect as an official emissary from Opechancanough. But the word "neutral" seemed to indicate that Robert stood in between the colonists and the Powhatans and that his allegiance was fluid.

Thomas, Henry, and Robert faced increasingly difficult situations as they tried to define their own roles. For one thing, they were no longer youths and wanted to be treated as adults. But even more importantly, the entire situation had changed dramatically. Now that the plantations were growing so rapidly and pushing Native communities out, relationships were fraught; and Henry and Robert were caught in between as tensions between Powhatans and colonists mounted. They could no longer just carry messages and stay on good terms with everyone. And often the messages they did carry were meant to manipulate the other side. The blame could easily be turned on them if messages were false.

Neither Opechancanough nor the leaders in Jamestown really trusted Thomas, Henry, and Robert anymore. Many would have agreed with Rev. Jonas Stockham when he wrote, "We have sent boys amongst them to learn their Language, but they return worse than they went."[14]

As colonists continued to arrive and farms spread over the land along the rivers, Opechancanough worked to broaden and consolidate his influence with Chesapeake Algonquians. The Patawomecks were one group that he tried very hard to make his firm allies, and the colonists were not sure how successful he had been in bringing them along. John Rolfe reported that Capt. Thomas Ward had sent a ship up to the Potomac in October 1619, possibly with Henry acting as interpreter, and Ward believed that Iopassus "had dealt falsely with them." Iopassus offered them little corn, so they took what they wanted "by force." Rolfe did say that they had peaceful relations with other tribes along the Potomac, and at their departure, they "also made a firm peace again with Iopassus."[15]

Thomas discovered how far Opechancanough's influence extended when he accompanied John Pory on two trips up to the northern reaches of Chesapeake Bay. Pory was an educated man and a dedicated traveler. A former member of Parliament, he had translated the work of the celebrated Moroccan scholar al-Hasan al-Wazzan, known to Europeans as Leo Africanus, from Italian into English, and he had taught Greek at Cambridge University. Unsurprisingly, he found life in Jamestown dull and, as he put it, uncouth. He even had to drink water in place of wine![16]

Travel was Pory's solution to boredom in America as it had been in Europe. He traveled south into the region described by Thomas Harriot of the Roanoke colony and north as far as the Patuxent River, with Thomas acting as interpreter.[17] Pory wrote that Governor Yeardley sent him northward to find a good place to make salt, with Thomas and "Estinien Moll a Frenchman." When they got to the northern part of

Chesapeake Bay, the Patuxents said they wanted to renew their friendship with Thomas. Thomas had made previous reconnaissance voyages up there as he was establishing relationships on the Eastern Shore. The Virginia Company in London noted one report from him saying that French traders were carrying on "a great trade in furs" in the northern parts of Chesapeake Bay.[18] Pory wrote that not long after his party's arrival, Namenacus, "the King of Patuxent, came to us to seek for Thomas Savage our Interpreter." Namenacus put on a show to impress Pory. When they were all sitting down, he did something bizarre: "he showed us his naked breast; asking if we saw any deformity upon it." When Pory told him that he saw no mark, Namenacus said that on the inside his breast was also "as sincere and pure." He invited Pory and Thomas to visit him in his country anytime; Pory was really impressed and promised that they would. This demonstration was supposed to convince the English that Namenacus wanted to be their firm friend, but events proved otherwise.[19]

On their second trip north a few weeks later, Pory and Thomas visited Namenacus and his brother Wamanoto. They exchanged many gifts, and then they went hunting with "the two kings." Pory was completely taken in and believed Namenacus's claim that he had given strict orders that "none should offend us." The two Englishmen visited Wamanoto's house and met his wife and children and saw his cornfields. After a hunting excursion, Namenacus took them back to his home and, Pory wrote, treated "me as kindly as he could, after their manner." The next day, Namenacus presented Pory with a canoe and twelve beaver pelts. Pory gave Namenacus gifts that pleased him so much that he said he would keep them always and that they would be buried with him when he died. As in the exchange between Argall and Iopassus on the Potomac, Namenacus wanted to know about the Christian Bible and especially the first chapter of Genesis and the story of Adam and Eve "and simple marriage." Thomas interpreted the biblical creation story for him; Namenacus said that he was "like Adam in one thing, for he never had but one wife at once," but he found the rest of the story hard to understand. Pory thought everything was going swimmingly, and then the next day, for reasons he did not understand, it all fell apart.[20]

The "two Kings with their people" came on the ship, but they were empty-handed. Thomas understood what was going on and took center stage now. "Ensign Savage challenged Namenacus the breach of three promises, viz. in not giving him a Boy, nor Corne, though they had plenty, nor Moutapass a fugitive, called Robert Marcum, that had lived 5 years amongst those northerly nations, which he cunningly answered by excuses." A sailor named Robert Markham had arrived in Virginia with the first settlers and participated in Capt. Christopher Newport's initial voyage up the James River in search of a passage through the continent.[21] This mention in 1607 is the only time Markham's name appeared in the records until Thomas confronted Namenacus. His commitment to life with the Patuxents made him lost to the English records.

Thomas understood Chesapeake Algonquian diplomacy very well, and he knew that the chiefs' former friendliness was a pretense hiding hostile intentions. Pory, however, continued to believe that his diplomatic skills would conquer all.

Wamanoto stayed on the ship after the others had left, and Pory decided he was not to blame for his brother's actions. Pory asked him "if he desired to be rich and great," to which Wamanoto replied that every man wanted these. Pory then said that he would achieve wealth and greatness if he would follow Pory's directions, and Wamanoto gave Pory "two tokens" to be carried by any messenger. That way he would know for sure that the messenger came from Pory. Wamanoto also restored some items that had been stolen from the English as a sign of his good faith. Pory thought that he had really impressed the chief.[22]

Wamanoto gave Thomas and Pory a man to guide them up the Patuxent River, but there they ran into difficulties and got a glimmer of what was in the works. Pory had been played by the two leaders, and his inexperience showed. Native people upriver had "an old quarrel with Ensign Savage," but Pory thought that had been patched up. Two chiefs guided them further upriver and urged them to go ashore. Pory and

Thomas did briefly go on land but then suspected "some treachery." They were right: "a multitude" of warriors came out of the woods shouting insults and threats.

Pory and Thomas rushed back downriver and across Chesapeake Bay to the Eastern Shore, where they learned the truth from Thomas's friend, the chief of the Accomacs. Chief Esmy Shichans, called the "Laughing King" by the English, had become the colonists' firm friend largely through Thomas's efforts. The Laughing King told them that the trip up the Patuxent River had been planned by Namenacus as a ploy to kill Thomas.

The Patuxents were seeking the protection of the Powhatans, so they were carrying out Opechancanough's orders in targeting Thomas. The Powhatans blamed Thomas for opening up the trade with the Eastern Shore and lessening their own control over the colonists. The shift in trade coincided with the great influx of new tobacco-planting colonists who displaced Native communities along the James and the other rivers and made their lives increasingly difficult, so they were doubly angry.

Opechancanough also blamed Thomas for a personal humiliation he had suffered earlier. Opechancanough had sent some of his men to the Eastern Shore to capture an Englishman named Thomas Graves. Thomas Savage, along with three other Englishmen, rescued Graves by challenging the thirteen Powhatans who were holding him, including Opechancanough's son, to a fight. More than a hundred of the Accomacs watched as Opechancanough's men refused the challenge. Because they "durst not" fight a much smaller number of Englishmen, the Accomacs just laughed at them, and "they came no more."

Pory acquired land on the Eastern Shore and set about placing tenants there. He concluded his account of this Eastern Shore visit by praising the Accomacs as far superior to the Powhatans and other tribes on the western side of Chesapeake Bay. He was particularly impressed with how the Laughing King had divided his authority with his brother Kiptokepe, who actually governed the people. These very "civil" people had much higher agricultural yields than those on the west, and they even had a kind of record-keeping using little sticks.

Thomas became firmly attached to the Eastern Shore. The Laughing King gave him a huge grant of land, including the site that is still called Savage Neck. So he became one of the largest landowners among the English, and he was the first English resident landowner on the Eastern Shore.[23]

Despite Thomas's removal across the bay, he kept sending information to the colonial authorities in Jamestown. But the closer Thomas was to the Accomacs, the more doubtful the authorities back in Jamestown were about trusting him. Just a couple of years after Henry's trial and with their doubts about Robert growing, official mistrust led the colonial government into making a disastrous mistake about Thomas. The Laughing King informed Thomas that Opechancanough had asked for a deadly poison that grew on the Eastern Shore. His plan was to invite the colony's leaders to a huge gathering for the "taking up of Powhatan's bones," where the English would be served poisoned food. Powhatan died in 1618, an event marked by three large comets, and now in 1621, there was to be a great ceremony bringing Natives from all over to honor his permanent interment.[24] The Laughing King also said that Opechancanough was planning a mass assault on the English plantations. The Accomac chief refused to make the poison available, and Jamestown's leaders decided that the whole thing had blown over.

In fact, as the governor and his council reported to London, Opechancanough continued to demonstrate good will. He welcomed the missionary-colonist George Thorpe into his domain and encouraged Thorpe to think that his people were ripe for conversion, saying that they knew God loved the English more than the Powhatans. The Powhatans made other moves to assuage colonists' fears, including sending "one Browne," who had been living with the Weraskoyacks "to learn the language," back to his master, Ralph Hamor, "in a friendly manner." Jamestown's leaders decided that they understood the situation better than Thomas and the Laughing King, so they dismissed their warning.[25]

Over the next months, Opechancanough continued to plan for a great strike against the colonists. George Thorpe happened to mention in his first report home that Opechancanough had changed his name to Mangopeesomon, and that should have set off alarm bells. In the Roanoke colony a few decades earlier, the colonists learned that the Roanoke leader Wingina had changed his name to Pemisapan just before a gathering of all the people to honor and rebury a dead leader. That name change had signaled a planned attack on the English. And the Laughing King had made clear that Opechancanough was focusing his plans on the occasion of Powhatan's reburial. Names were intensely meaningful for these people, as the English had learned when Pocahontas's true name was revealed after her baptism. But wishful thinking trumped all evidence to the contrary, and Jamestown's leaders ignored what the Laughing King and Thomas had to tell them.

Jamestown's leaders also dismissed concerns over the death of an extraordinary man called Nemattanew. He was a leading warrior and close to Opechancanough, but even more importantly, he was a charismatic religious leader. George Percy wrote that the colonists called him "Jack of the feathers, by reason that he used to come into the field all covered over with feathers and swan's wings fastened unto his shoulders, as though he meant to fly." Nemattanew convinced his followers that his spiritual powers made him invulnerable to English guns and that he had a special ointment that would render them impervious to bullets as well.[26]

As it turned out, Nemattanew was all too vulnerable. Colonists said that he had killed an Englishman named Morgan and that Morgan's servants, seeing him wearing the slain man's cap a few days later, killed him. Colonists reported that he begged the men to bury him secretly so his followers would not know he had been killed by a bullet. Opechancanough hid his distress over Nemattanew's death. He sent word to the governor that the death of "one man should be no occasion of a breach of the peace, and that the sky should sooner fall than the peace be broken on his part."[27]

Two weeks later, the colonists' false sense of security was shattered.[28] On the morning of Good Friday, March 22, 1622, the Powhatans carried out an ambitious plan to attack all the plantations at once and wipe the

English off the face of their land. English reports said that the colonists had welcomed Powhatans into their home that morning and shared their breakfast with them, and then suddenly the visitors had seized their hosts' own weapons and killed them.

Henry was up on the Potomac when it happened; he captained one ship, the *Elizabeth*, on this voyage, and longtime colonist Raleigh Crashaw captained the other. A Patawomeck came onto Henry's ship and, telling him about the attack, warned him to be wary. This unnamed man reported that Opechancanough had tried to enlist tribes along the Potomac in his plan. He said that the Patawomecks had refused but the Wiccomicomicos near the river's mouth had agreed. Henry and Crashaw went down the river to them and found them appearing friendly. They freighted Henry's ship with corn. So Henry returned to Jamestown, and Crashaw went back upriver to the Patawomecks, where he and his men constructed a small palisaded area to stay in.

Opechancanough sent a messenger to tell the Patawomeck chief about his successful attack; the messenger carried two baskets of beads and Opechancanough's request that Crashaw be killed. The Patawomecks should be assured that "before the end of two moons, there should not be an Englishman in all their Countries." After a long conversation with Crashaw, the chief refused and returned the beads to the messenger.[29]

Although hundreds of colonists were killed on that day, Jamestown and other plantations were spared because some Native boys had warned them. Like Henry, Robert, and Thomas, these boys were torn between loyalties. One, who worked for William Perry, was a Christian convert and lived with Richard Pace in his plantation called Paces Paines; he always appeared in the records simply as "Perry's Indian." The boy's brother came to him and told him that Opechancanough wanted him to kill Pace and that "by such an hour in the morning a number would come from divers places to finish their execution." The boy agonized for several hours and then told Pace about the plan; according to the accounts, Pace had treated him as his own son, and the boy regarded Pace as a father. Pace immediately rowed across the river to warn Jamestown, so the governor was able to close the fort and call out his men. Two years later, William Perry went to London bringing the boy, and the Virginia Company took up a collection to maintain him as a Christian and prepare him for "some good course to live by."[30]

Chauco, who "had lived much amongst the English," warned the men on a small English ship that was trading on the Pamunkey River, up near Opechancanough's capital, and they spread the word; so several more lives were saved in the upriver plantations. George Thorpe was also warned by a young Powhatan who lived with him, but he chose not to believe that the Powhatans he knew would do such a thing. Not only did he die in the attack, but his body was singled out for mutilation. His great plan to turn young Powhatan men into European-style Christians in the school he hoped to build died with him.[31]

The events of March 22, 1622, began ten years of war between the Powhatans and the colonists. Samuel Collier, Capt. John Smith's "page" who had left with the Weraskoyacks early in Jamestown's history, was killed by friendly fire. Smith wrote that he was killed by an English sentinel who accidentally fired his gun. Clearly the colonists were on edge and trigger-happy.[32]

The services of Thomas, Henry, and Robert became more essential than ever in the colonists' extreme need. Meetings of the governor and his council in 1623 record many times that Thomas procured corn from his contacts on the Eastern Shore for the colony, and the Patawomecks promised corn as soon as their harvest was in.

Despite Henry's strong ties in the region, or maybe because of them, he, like Samuel Collier, was a casualty of the early years of this war. It was very hard to distinguish friend from enemy among the people along the Potomac, and all loyalties were fluid. The choices people made often depended on what was happening at that exact moment. Robert and Henry were both thrust into circumstances in the north that neither they nor anybody else really understood, and they were doing their best to figure out whom to trust and how to act.

While Raleigh Crashaw was with the Patawomecks, Ralph Hamor came with two ships looking for corn. The Patawomeck king convinced Hamor and Crashaw to mount an attack on his own enemies, the Anacostians (also called Nacotchtanks), who he said had plenty of corn. The joint party of Patawomecks and English looted and destroyed the Anacostian town, and Hamor returned to Jamestown with the corn.

Capt. Isaac Madison soon took Crashaw's place with the Patawomecks, and Robert accompanied him. Madison did not continue Crashaw's policy of living comfortably with the Patawomecks and instead built his own separate place, "so that they were not so sociable as before, nor did they much like Poole the Interpreter." Madison sent Robert and three other men to seek two Englishmen who had absconded, and they encountered "a King beat out of his Country" by "the Necosts" (Anacostians). The "expulsed King" was angry because the Patawomeck chief would not aid him in his revenge, "but to our interpreter Poole he protested great love." The search party took "this Bandyto" back to the Potomac, and he then had "private conference" with Robert, making him "swear by his God" that he would not reveal what he was told. The king then described an elaborate Patawomeck scheme to kill all the Englishmen there.[33]

Robert broke his oath and told Captain Madison of the plot, and Madison immediately set in motion a plan to capture the Patawomeck chief and his leading men. He sent for the chief, who came "and brought him a dish of their daintiest fruit." Madison, after interrogating the Patawomeck leader, suddenly left his "strong house," locking the door, "leaving the King, his son, and four Savages, and five English men inside." He then led an attack on the town, killing thirty or forty men.

The king demanded to know why this had happened, and Robert "told him the treason" but also cried out "to intreat the Captain cease from such cruelty." The Patawomeck chief's answer was, "This is some plot of those that told it, only to kill me for being your friend." After the fact, the colonists were convinced that the chief had indeed been the victim of a plot hatched by the Anacostians and that he was completely innocent.

A few months later, and a year after the great 1622 attack, Henry led a trading party on the Potomac. According to a report forwarded by a colonist named Peter Arundel, the English wore armor, and a Native leader asked why they approached their friends that way. As colonist George Sandys wrote about this episode, Henry was "a man wary enough and acquainted with their treacheries." Henry told the leader that they had been warned to expect treachery and rashly pointed to the man who had warned them. The king's response was alarming. He immediately seized the man who had warned the English and had his head cut off and thrown into the fire. The next day, Henry's party came ashore again expecting to trade, but they were attacked and all the English were killed or taken prisoner. There were differing reports about the identity of the killers, but they may have been Anacostians.[34]

Peter Arundel wrote, "We ourselves have taught them how to be treacherous by our false dealings with the poor king of Patawomeck that had always been faithful to the English, whose people w[ere] killed, he and his son taken prisoner, brought to Jamestown, returned home again ransomed, as if [he] had been the greatest enemy they had. Spelman's death is a just revenge. . . . It is a great loss to us for that Captain was the best linguist of the Indian Tongue of this Country."[35] Henry Spelman's life had spanned twenty-eight years. Another Henry, a young, recently arrived colonist named Henry Fleet, was captured in this encounter, and he lived with the Anacostians for several years. After he was ransomed, he became a key interpreter and a very important colonist.[36]

The next month, April 1623, Chauco came to Jamestown with a message from "the great King" Opechancanough saying that "blood enough had already been shed on both sides" and that the Powhatans were in great need because so much of their food supplies had been destroyed. They asked for peace to settle down in their homes again and do their spring planting. The English remembered Chauco for his warning before the great attack and honored him. Their reply was that if Opechancanough would return the twenty women taken prisoner during the attack and would refrain from further fighting, both sides could plant in peace. Two weeks later, Chauco brought back one prisoner, Sara Boyce, and the Powhatans wanted the English to note that she was "apparelled like one of their Queens," a huge mark of respect. The others were not returned then because Robert, frustrated by all the tangled politics and fearful for the future, had, according to the council's letter to London, "given out threatening Speeches." That was the English leaders' excuse. The council sent another messenger to Opechancanough saying that the Powhatans could plant in peace; but it was all a lie, and Robert's threats had actually warned Opechancanough about what was coming. The council revealed its duplicitous strategy in its letter to the Virginia Company back home: once the Powhatans were resettled around their cornfields, it would be easier to attack and kill them.[37]

Of the remaining nineteen women captives, some were returned a few months later, after interested parties got together a collection of beads for their ransom, and a few others came back the next year; so seven had been repatriated. Anne Jackson was brought back years later, and she was put under lock and key until she could be sent to England, presumably because colonial leaders feared that she would return to her Native family if she could. The others were never heard of again.[38]

The Virginia Company itself was a casualty of the fallout after March 1622. As news of the disaster trickled into England, word spread quickly. John Chamberlain sent word to his correspondents, and, of course, he blamed the colonists for being so weak and stupid. A poem called *Mourning Virginia* was registered with the authorities, but no copies survive. Christopher Brooke, who was a Virginia Company investor, wrote *A Poem on the Late Massacre in Virginia*. And Edward Waterhouse, the company's secretary, compiled an account out of the various reports sent home, and he published it with the title *A Declaration of the State of the Colony and Affaires in Virginia*. All these publications blamed the victims. They portrayed the Natives as savages and the colonists as ineffectual in controlling them. The next year, a play was performed, *A Tragedy of the Plantation of Virginia*. In licensing it for performance, the Master of the Revels stipulated, "the profaneness to be left out, otherwise not tolerated." It was not published, so we have no text of it.[39]

In fact, the colonists were suffering, and life was very hard following the great assault. There was a "general sickness," which was said to have killed more people than the attack, and John Rolfe was one of those who died in the epidemic. As information began to trickle into London, people slowly began to understand that the problem lay not with the colonists so much as with the policies of the Virginia Company in London.

A twelve-year-old boy named Richard Frethorne, whose ship left England in 1622 before news of the calamity had arrived, wrote his "Loving and Kind Mother and Father" about his suffering. "This is to let you understand that I your Child am in a most heavy Case." He wrote that the land itself was making colonists sick with diseases such as scurvy and bloody diarrhea. And the colony had no food or medicine to help restore patients whose bodies were weakened by illness. Since he landed, he had eaten only peas "and loblollie (that is, water gruel)." John Jackson, a gunsmith in Jamestown whose sister Anne had been taken captive and would return years later, took pity on Frethorne and made him a small cabin to stay in and gave him some food. Richard wrote, "[Jackson] much marvelled that you would send me a servant to the Company; he saith I had been better knocked on the head." Richard begged his parents to pay off his servitude indenture and bring him home: "if you love me." Their response, or if they even got his letter, is unclear; it was certainly used as propaganda against the Virginia Company. Like most of his shipmates and many earlier arrivals, Richard Frethorne soon died.[40]

Others wrote more public reports of what was going on. Nathaniel Butler, the governor of Bermuda who presided over the marriage of Pocahontas's companion, spent the winter of 1622–23 in Virginia, and he wrote a scathing description of life there, "The Unmasked Face of Our Colony as It Was in the Winter of the Year 1622." His report, which was presented to the king's Privy Council, described people starving while the men in charge had plenty to eat. Butler said the fortifications were laughable. And further he wrote about the many deaths: people dying in the woods and under hedges, and their corpses left to rot. The company commissioned an answer written by people who had been there, but when they responded with arguments such as that the deaths were God's will and, besides, there were no hedges in Virginia, their response just added to the feeling in England that something needed to be done.[41]

The colonial government investigated how the Powhatans had obtained English weapons and knowledge of how to use them. In 1624, the General Court called Robert Poole to testify on this point. He said that when he first went to live with Opechancanough, the chief had shown him trees with bullet holes in them and said that Capt. John Smith had taught some of his men to shoot. Robert also mentioned other Natives who had been taught to shoot by servants living on the plantations and said that Sir Thomas Dale gave a gun to a man named Kissacomas and that he often sent Robert with powder and shot to replenish Kissacomas's supply. He said the Natives also acquired guns when they attacked English parties. Robert testified that he went to Pamunkey at the governor's request in 1618 to steal the firing mechanisms from the Powhatans' guns. When the guns were sent to Jamestown to be repaired, the authorities kept them.[42] So, from the beginning, the colonial leadership had contributed to the debacle.

Factions within the company in London were angry over the way shipments of food and new colonists had been handled, especially too little food and too many colonists, and condemned the company leadership. Some of these disgruntled investors appealed to the king to investigate what had gone wrong. Capt. John Martin, to whom Thomas Savage had been assigned, sent home a proposal, "How Virginia May Be Made a Royal Plantation," in December 1622. He recommended that every shire in England should send men to occupy the lands that Opechancanough controlled and outlined a new plan of government for these lands.[43]

The royal government was growing increasingly dissatisfied with news from Virginia and with the Virginia Company in London. Early in 1621, the crown revoked permission to operate the lottery, which had been the chief source of income to support the colony.[44] Not only had the colony been mismanaged and thousands of English people sacrificed, but those in power in England thought that having tobacco as the principal, almost the sole, commodity from Virginia was simply wrong. England expected colonies to produce real, solid commodities that would help build the English economy, not something that vanished in smoke as soon as it was purchased. Moreover, there were rumors of corruption and kickbacks that lined the pockets of company officials in London.

King James's Privy Council set up a royal commission to investigate in May 1623, and the commissioners interviewed people who had been in Virginia, including Capt. John Smith, who followed events there closely. He testified that too much money had been spent aggrandizing the government in Virginia, replacing experienced colonists with newcomers. He echoed Opechancanough's earlier complaint about inexperienced governors being sent one after another. And, Smith testified, company members had sent over too many raw colonists, badly provided for, as a way of making more money for themselves. He recommended ending the Virginia Company so that King James could take the colony into his care. Smith published his great history of all the colonies while the investigations were proceeding, and he included his testimony in it.[45]

While the commission studied, tensions ran high in the Virginia Company, including a thwarted duel between the Earl of Warwick and Lord William Cavendish. When the Privy Council received the commission's report, it decided that the Virginia Company should be reconstituted with a new charter and a more rational government both in London and in Virginia. It asked the company members to approve the plan, but those who attended the meeting utterly rejected it. So the royal government moved to revoke the company's charter altogether. Further investigation went forward, including a small commission that included John Pory; the commissioners went to Virginia to see conditions for themselves. All was still in process when King James died in March 1625, and in May his son Charles I declared Virginia a royal colony. The Virginia Company was finished.[46]

ATLANTIC IDENTITIES

I N VIRGINIA, THOMAS SAVAGE AND ROBERT POOLE lived on into
adulthood under the new administration. Thomas was safe on the
Eastern Shore, living on the acres that Esmy Shichans had given him.
By 1624, he had a wife, Hannah, and a son named John. Hannah had
come over in 1621, and because she had paid her own way, she received
fifty acres in her own name. By 1625, Thomas had two servants of his
own. He continued to act as interpreter for the authorities in Jamestown
and to help his Eastern Shore neighbors, as when he asked Accomacs to
help planters round up feral cattle.[1]

Despite all of Thomas's service and his status as an independent landowner, however, he was still vulnerable to the whims of those in authority, and his experiences show clearly the kinds of malfeasance being
investigated in London. A violent and unpredictable man, William
Eppes, was given command of the Eastern Shore, and Thomas ran afoul
of him. Eppes's high position is strange because he had previously killed
a man in a drunken rage. He had a fight in 1619 with Edward Stallings,
who had recently arrived, and hit Stallings so hard with his sword still
in its scabbard that he split the man's skull. He was tried before the
General Court and found guilty, as John Rolfe wrote, of "manslaugh-
ter by chance medley." "Medley" is an old-fashioned word for combat. Eppes was stripped of his offices, but he had powerful friends in
England and was soon restored to his offices with the rank of captain.
He took charge of Nicholas Grainger, a ten-year-old boy swept from
the London streets and sent to Virginia in 1619. Nicholas was listed as a
servant in Eppes's household in the Virginia Muster of 1625.[2]

Eppes was given military command of the Eastern Shore in 1623, and he soon picked a fight with Thomas Savage. In 1624, Charles Harmer testified before the Virginia General Court that he had accompanied Eppes when he went to Thomas's plantation. Eppes had heard that Thomas said he feared for his life with Eppes in command, and Eppes accused him of slander. He "laid the said Ensign Savage neck and heels," which meant that he tied Thomas in an unbearably excruciating position with his back bent backward for his interrogation. Harmer testified that he personally had never heard Thomas slander Eppes. Nonetheless, the General Court stupidly decreed that Thomas should have no contact with his Eastern Shore Native friends unless Eppes personally ordered it. If Thomas talked to the "Indians of those parts" without permission, he was to pay Eppes the enormous sum of £200. Once again, the authorities in Jamestown sacrificed all the intelligence they might get through Thomas's connections with the Accomacs for the illusion of control. And clearly Eppes, although he was known as "a mad ranting fellow," had very influential connections. After several more scandals, including evading his debts and drunken, adulterous sex with a woman named Alice Boyse, Eppes departed for the Caribbean, where he presumably expected to be more at home.[3]

Luckily, interventions in Eastern Shore affairs by the Jamestown authorities were few, and planters there were able to forge their own path. The Eastern Shore was not as good for tobacco growing as the land along the James was, so planters such as Thomas moved into the much more solid provisioning business. They grew cattle and pigs and corn, wheat, and other food crops for sale to colonies up and down the coast. This was a very smart move because it made maximum use of their acres and also freed them from the problems of the tobacco trade. Tobacco growers often felt frustrated because the price moved up and down wildly and also because they loaded their tobacco on the ships of transatlantic merchants who returned a year later and told them how much their tobacco had been worth. It is not surprising that they always believed they were being cheated.

Getting involved in the coastal provisions trade was far less frustrating and risky because food grown on the Eastern Shore was sold in New England, New Netherland, and other recently founded colonies, including the earliest Caribbean settlements. The planters knew the merchants whose ships carried their products, and they got quick returns from them. And people always needed food, so the market was steady and growing.[4]

Capt. John Smith published his grand history of all the colonies in 1624, and in it, he said that Thomas "with much honesty and good success hath served the public without any public recompence, yet had an arrow shot through his body in their service."[5] Thomas died sometime between 1632 and 1633, when Hannah appeared in the records as a widow. In 1635, the nine thousand acres given Thomas "by the King of the Eastern shore as by deed calling himself Esmy Shichans" was confirmed by legal patent. Hannah, who had patented her own fifty acres in 1627, married a planter named Daniel Cugley in 1638. Thomas and Hannah's son, John, was still alive to testify in a case in 1677.[6]

Robert stayed in Jamestown and experienced acute financial difficulties. Early in 1624, he presented a petition to the governor asking for compensation for his services the previous year and saying that he had many debts that he could not pay and that his creditors were threatening him with arrest. He said he was owed 563 pounds of tobacco and twelve barrels of corn. The court awarded him 500 pounds of tobacco so he could pay off his creditors.[7]

Soon Robert lifted himself out of poverty by getting involved in the trade up north in Chesapeake Bay. Late in 1624, Robert, now identified in the records as a gentleman, was called to testify before the Virginia General Court about a trading mission he had accompanied as an agent for t colony treasurer George Sandys, brother of the Virginia Company leader Sir Edwin Sandys. Robert was on the defensive and began his testimony by denying that he had kept for his own private use any of the beads that Sandys allotted him for trading. And he specified exactly what the expedition got in trade and exactly how many beads had been paid for each commodity. Robert said that everyone on the voyage traded for furs, but he was not sure where they came from. He person-ally acquired "7 great bear skins, 6 deer skins, 2 wildcat skins, 9 otter skins, 2 young bear skins, 8 or 9 muskrat skins, 1 lion skin," but no black fox skins. The lion skin was a gift from "the great man of Patuxent," il-lustrating that Robert had important connections in the region.[8]

The fur trade became, for a time, an important part of the Virginia economy. When Capt. William Claiborne set up a fur-trading enterprise on Kent Island in the northern Chesapeake in 1631, he initially employed Thomas as his interpreter.[9] Henry Fleet became involved in this lucra-tive and highly competitive trade after he returned from his life with the Anacostians, and his translation skills were very valuable. He boasted that he was "better proficient in the Indian language than mine own."[10]

Robert Poole made a trip back to England in 1625 before returning to settle down.[11] He continued to make regular appearances before the governor and general court to testify in cases where his special knowl-edge was important. Robert's father and brother were both dead by 1627, so he applied for and received a patent for the land they were owed as well as his own, three hundred acres in all, in Newport News.[12] In 1629, the Virginia Assembly identified him as Captain Poole and gave him a grant of £1,200 in compensation for a leg wound that "he received in the Country's service."[13]

As Thomas Rolfe, the son of Pocahontas and John Rolfe, grew up back in England, his thoughts turned to Virginia. His father had mar-ried Joan Peirce after his return to the colony, and now Joan's father, Thomas Rolfe's stepgrandfather, took an interest in the young man's welfare. Capt. William Peirce had been shipwrecked on Bermuda in 1609 along with John Rolfe and his first wife. Both men had become important figures in the colony, and they often worked together on colony business. Rolfe and Peirce had been sent to meet the ship that brought Africans to the colony in 1619, and one of those, a woman named Angelo, came to live in Peirce's household. In 1635, Peirce paid for Thomas Rolfe's passage back to Virginia. Thomas was about the same age his mother had been when she died. Once he was in Virginia, he married Jane Poythress and took up the substantial lands that his father had left him.

Thomas Rolfe settled in among the English, but he did make one effort that we know of to contact his mother's people. The court records say that in December 1641, he petitioned the governor for permission to go and see Opechancanough, "to whom he is allied and Cleopatra his mother's sister." As was so often the case, the records tell us nothing more, not even if the meeting took place or the identity of the woman whom the English called Cleopatra. If there was a meeting, no one saw fit to make a record of what happened or of what they said to each other.[14]

Relatively peaceful conditions prevailed when Thomas Rolfe arrived in Virginia. For ten years after the 1622 attack, the colonists had tried to make the Powhatans' way of life impossible by destroying their food crops. But both sides had had enough by 1632. The peace then allowed more and more English to come into the colony, and new plantations were being opened up every year, spreading over the land. By the time Thomas Rolfe came back home, the English outnumbered the Natives in the region.

If we could know what Opechancanough and Thomas Rolfe said to each other in 1641, we might understand the next series of events better. In 1644, Opechancanough, who was by now a very old man, led another concerted attack on all the colonists. This attack killed more of the English than the 1622 one had, but there were so many more colonists now that it had far less impact. The ensuing conflict ended two years later, with Opechancanough's capture by a force led by Gov. Sir William Berkeley.

Opechancanough was brought to Jamestown, and people came to gawk at him in his jail cell. According to Robert Beverley, who wrote a history of Virginia in the eighteenth century, Opechancanough "continued brave to the last Moment of his Life, and showed not the least Dejection at his Captivity." One day, when he heard the noise made by the crowds of people coming to look at him, he indignantly called for the governor. When the governor came, Opechancanough scornfully told him "that had it been his Fortune to take Sir William Berkeley Prisoner, he should not meanly have exposed him as a Show to the People." Beverley said that Berkeley had hoped to bring Opechancanough to England to show off his royal prisoner, but one of the guards "basely shot him through the back" and killed him.[15] In reality, it would have been difficult to present Opechancanough across the Atlantic because England was torn by civil war at the time.

As things now stood, Thomas Rolfe did not have the possibility of a life between English and Native society that Thomas Savage, Henry Spelman, and Robert Poole had had. Despite his descent from the Powhatan ruling family, he felt forced to make a firm commitment to life in English territory. He became a lieutenant in the militia, and in 1646, as his great-uncle was being brought a captive to Jamestown, he signed a contract to build and man a fort on the peninsula between the James and York Rivers north of Jamestown. It was a good site from which to monitor what the Powhatans were doing, and this commitment showed that Thomas Rolfe had made his choice.

৽

Thomas, Henry, and Robert spent their lives trapped between cultures. The more they knew, the less the powers that be trusted them. One piece of advice given to great lords in England was that they should not blindly trust people who served under them. The Earl of Northumberland, George Percy's brother, wrote in a book of advice for his son, "the oath of a mechanical man is not to be trusted." Mechanicals were laborers or artisans, like the "rude mechanicals" in Shakespeare's *Midsummer Night's Dream*. Capt. John Smith declared, "in the most trust was the greatest treason." A man foolish enough to trust his inferiors deserved what he got.[16] And elite men were advised not to employ servants who were knowledgeable because, if they knew too much, servants would not simply follow orders. After all, as everyone knew, knowledge is power.

The problem in Virginia was that those who were in charge of the colony knew a lot about European warfare but almost nothing about anything else. Thomas, Henry, and Robert came to know a great deal about the country they were all trying to live in and about the politics of that country. It was obvious that they would not just follow orders, particularly when the orders were stupid.

Not only did the three interpreters have to do what they considered best, which could mean disregarding or modifying orders, but they also sometimes unwittingly carried false messages on both sides. When the English attacked Powhatan towns or when leaders on either side sent deceitful vows of peace, they pulled the rug out from under the boys, who then carried the blame.

Manipulation and double dealing using young go-betweens happened everywhere in the Atlantic. Squanto suffered from the same kind of distrust after he finally returned to New England in 1619. He arrived to find his town of Patuxet deserted after a devastating epidemic that had swept through the region between 1616 and 1619. Like the other surviving Patuxets, Squanto went to live with the Wampanoags, a neighboring tribe.

The Pilgrims came in 1620 in the *Mayflower*, piloted by the same John Clarke who had spent so many years as a prisoner in Spain while Don Francisco de Molina was in Jamestown.[17] Because they arrived in late December, which was not a great time of year to begin a settlement, the Pilgrims decided to occupy the abandoned town of Patuxet. The newcomers, starting with just over a hundred people, lost half their population that first winter. They were in a desperate state by March 1621, when an English-speaking Native named Samoset walked into their town. Samoset had learned English from fishermen on the Maine coast, and his name was probably Somerset, given to him by the fishermen. A few days later, he brought Squanto back to his own town, now occupied by the Pilgrims, and Squanto stayed with the English and acted as their intermediary, interpreter, and source of knowledge about how to fish and farm in New England.

The Pilgrims' very survival depended on Squanto, and yet they came to mistrust him just as the English in Virginia had doubted Thomas,

Henry, and Robert. Because these young men with fluid identities controlled the relationship between the English colonists and their most powerful friends/enemies and because they understood the feelings and culture of both sides, they were always seen as potential betrayers. And Squanto had become a Roman Catholic convert in Spain, so these extreme puritans had another reason for mistrusting him.

The first incident occurred when Squanto conveyed a warning that Massasoit, the Wampanoag sachem, was planning to attack the fledgling colony. When the Pilgrims found out that the rumor was untrue, they were angry with Squanto. Then later they were told that Squanto had convinced the neighboring Algonquians that he was in charge of deciding when the English would attack them. The Pilgrims believed that he had falsely warned nearby towns of impending attacks and then told them that he had used his influence with the English to prevent those attacks. He also claimed, they were told, that he was in control of the Pilgrims' stockpile of the terrible diseases that had wreaked such havoc a few years earlier and that the germs would be let loose among the Natives if he gave the word.

Whether these reports about Squanto were true or came from other people trying to manipulate the relationships, the Pilgrims reported that both they and Massasoit had come to distrust him. And yet they had little alternative, because, as Edward Winslow wrote, Squanto was "so necessary and profitable an instrument, as at that time we could not miss him." Pilgrim leaders knew that "if he were dead, the English had lost their tongue." But Squanto did die after a year and a half with the Pilgrims. Plymouth governor William Bradford recorded that Squanto asked him "to pray for him that he might go to the Englishman's God in Heaven," and he bestowed several of his belongings on English friends "as remembrances of his love."[18]

Pocahontas's position had been equally ambiguous. The colonists thought that she had become an English gentlewoman. But when she renewed her acquaintance with Capt. John Smith in Brentford, she said, "*Your* countrymen will lie much." The English were not *her* countrymen.

The last straw for her was the Virginia Company's insistence that she go among her own people and subvert their culture by trying to convert them. But because of her death, her son grew up a thorough Englishman.

ᔥ

Early modern Europe and its Atlantic contained countless people who chose, or were forced into, a life that required a fluid identity. Europe was full of double agents who spied for their birth country but also, in order to get access to the information they needed, spied for the country or countries they were supposed to be spying on. If they were to function well, their identities had to be ambiguous. The English government knew that their spies were double agents, and the issue always was which sponsor was the agent actually deceiving and which was she or he really telling the truth. And was it the full truth? Often agents withheld some of the information they had garnered in order to preserve their position. They would then dole it out if they sensed they were in trouble.

These double agents, or intelligencers, as contemporaries would have called them, also competed for information and recognition, so they sometimes told their "handlers" about their rivals' bad actions, as Robert had informed on Henry. If spies were deemed to have sold out to the other side, or if their usefulness was compromised, they could expect the harshest treatment.

This world of spies illuminates the situation of Thomas, Henry, and Robert in Virginia because it was the context in which Jamestown's leaders evaluated what the boys had to tell them, and they were con-ditioned to expect treachery or at least partial revelation.[19] Powhatan understood the double game equally well. Adam and Francis, two of the Germans who had been sent to build a house for him, tried to return to Powhatan when Lord de la Warr arrived as governor in 1610. Powhatan refused to accept them, saying, "You that would have betrayed Captain Smith to me, will certainly betray me to this great Lord for your peace," so he had them executed.[20]

Jamestown's leaders constantly faced the problem of determining people's true allegiances, and they employed the categories they had learned at home. Huge numbers of people in Europe had undergone experiences or made choices that rendered their identities questionable. The English were fascinated and distressed by the thousands of their fellow countrymen who were captured by North Africans in the Mediterranean and in the Atlantic and even on the west coast of Britain, who then converted to Islam or, in the language of the day, "turned Turk."[21] Campaigns to raise money to ransom them kept the issue before the public eye, and their returns were marked by special sermons. Alexander Whitaker's cousin Rev. William Gough preached a sermon on the restoration of a renegade named Vincent Jukes, and it was published in 1639 as *A Recovery from Apostasy, Set Out in a Sermon Preached in Stepny Church Neere London at the Receiving of a Penitent Renegado.*

John Rawlins, whose ship was captured in the Mediterranean by Algerian pirates, described the cruel tactics they used to force Christians to convert, but he also said that some "for preferment or wealth very voluntarily renounced their faith and became Renegados." Moreover, many of the sailors and officers he met in Algiers were Christians who had converted to Islam. In fact, sometimes half the captains of the corsair ships were renegade Christians.[22] "Turning Turk" became a synonym for treachery, as when Hamlet worries about what will happen to him if "the rest of my fortunes turn Turk."[23]

"Turk" plays, centering on English captive-converts, were popular on the London stage in the first decades of the seventeenth century. Robert Daborne's *A Christian Turn'd Turke* (1612) centered on the story of two pirates, John Ward and the Flemish Simon Dansiker, who accepted Islam after being captured. They were in the public imagination at the time because of two pamphlets and three ballads about them, plus a royal proclamation against pirates that singled out Ward. One ballad, "The Seaman's Song of Captain Ward, the Famous Pirate of the World, and an Englishman Born" (to be sung to the tune of "The King's Going to Bulloigne"), contains this stanza:

At Tunis in Barbary
Now he buildeth stately
A gallant palace and a royal place,
Decked with delights most trim,
Fitter for a prince then him,
The which at last will prove to his disgrace.

In the play, Ward died miserably, lamenting his bad choice in abandoning his faith. But in reality, as in the ballad, he lived in great wealth in Tunis with the name Ioussef Reis (*Reis* means "captain"), as was attested by English travelers who met him. In Philip Massinger's *The Renegadoe* (1624), the central character realizes his folly and repents. Not only does he reject Islam for himself, but he also converts the woman he loves. The plays offered endings that suited their audience's tastes; but, like Ward, many converts lived on in their adopted countries as Muslims, and some held positions of authority.[24]

One counter story also captivated English readers: al-Hasan al-Wazzan was a diplomat from Fez in Morocco who was captured in the Mediterranean by Christian pirates in 1518 and taken to Rome. The pirate captain was Spanish, Don Pedro de Cabrera y Bobadilla, and his brother was the bishop of Salamanca. Once Bobadilla realized al-Wazzan's high status, he decided to present him as an offering to Pope Leo X, who was dedicated to defeating Islam and hoped to be able to contact ancient Christian communities within Africa, such as that said to have been established by the legendary Prester John.[25] At that moment, the papacy was facing even more threatening religious developments in the challenge being launched by Martin Luther in Germany, but the scale of that threat, which would rend Christianity asunder, was not yet clear. Two years later, al-Wazzan was baptized by the Pope, who gave him a version of his own name, Johannes Leo de Medici. After his baptism, al-Wazzan translated his new name into Arabic as Yuhanna al-Asad, Yuhanna the Lion.

Yuhanna al-Asad had traveled extensively throughout Africa in his ambassadorial role, and he was an avid reader; so he composed an

A
Chriſtian turn'd Turke:

OR,

The Tragicall Liues and Deaths of the two Famous Pyrates,

WARD and *DANSIKER.*

As it hath beene publickly Acted.

WRITTEN

By ROBERT DABORN, Gentleman.

Nemo ſapiens, Miſer eſt.

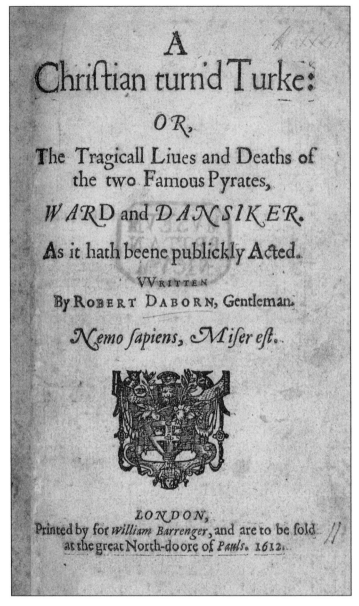

LONDON,
Printed by for *william Barrenger*, and are to be ſold
at the great North-doore of *Pauls.* 1612.

Title page of *A Christian Turn'd Turke*. Courtesy of British Library Imaging Services.

extensive history of Africa at the Pope's urging. He entered English consciousness when John Pory, later to be the secretary in Virginia, published his own translation of the book "written in Arabic and Italian by Iohn Leo a Moor, born in Granada, and brought up in Barbary" in 1600, as *A Geographical Historie of Africa*. Europeans of the time knew almost nothing about the interior of Africa, so the work was extremely valuable; and its author became known in England as Leo Africanus.[26]

Captivity drove many people to write. Miguel de Cervantes, the author of *Don Quixote*, had begun, like John Smith, as a soldier fighting against the Turks. As he was making his way back to Spain, he was captured by pirates in 1575 and lived in captivity in Algiers until 1580. After four unsuccessful escape attempts, he was ransomed, mainly through the efforts of his mother. Before he left Algiers, Cervantes wrote an account of his captivity and included testimony from twelve witnesses to certify that he had not apostatized and had remained loyal to Spain and his Christian faith. In this document, the *Información de Argel*, and in much of his writing, he referred repeatedly to the experience of captivity. His work was known in England, and the first part of *Don Quixote*, published in Spanish in 1605, was quickly translated and available in English by 1612.[27]

Capt. John Smith first told the story of his captivity in the Muslim Ottoman Empire in print in his autobiography, *The True Travels, Adventures, and Observations of Captaine John Smith* (1630). In it, he told of his brave and effective exploits on the side of the Hapsburgs against the Ottoman army, which resulted in his being given the rank of captain and a coat of arms on the field of battle; his arms included three Turks' heads commemorating his defeat of three Ottoman soldiers in single combat. Despite his skill and bravery, he was captured and taken into Turkey. Most of the Turk plays involved a beautiful young woman who allured the hero, and Smith fitted his story into the genre as he described being given to a highborn young woman in Istanbul whose name he rendered as Charatza Tragabigzanda (probably "girl from Trebizond"). He rebelled and escaped when her brother tried to force him into the harsh training regime for the Janissary corps. He made his way through Europe after his escape and arrived back in London just as the Virginia Company was planning its colony.[28]

Smith must have told his story to friends many times before he published it. In 1623, a play by Richard Gunnel called *The Hungarian Lion* was registered with the Stationers Company; it was to be performed by the Palsgraves Players at the new Fortune Theater. The text of the play is lost to us, but many references indicate that it was about Smith's eastern adventures. In the dedication to the *True Travels*, Smith explains why he decided to set the record straight: "they have acted my fatal Tragedies upon the stage and racked my Relations at their pleasure." A dedicatory verse in the same book by Richard James mentions audiences seeing Smith's "worth advanced" in Gunnel's Fortune.[29]

Smith claimed that he never capitulated or abandoned his Christianity. Captives who were redeemed and returned to England always claimed that they had not really converted and had only feigned allegiance to Islam. But male converts would have been circumcised, so they were forever marked by their experience. If Smith had been circumcised, the telltale evidence was destroyed when his powder bag exploded in his lap.

The term *renegade*, which originally applied specifically to Christians who turned to Islam, began to be used in Virginia to describe colonists who absconded to join the Powhatans. Edward Maria Wingfield, Jamestown's first governor, wrote that during that first year, the Paspahegh leader and other chiefs sent back "our men runnagates," including the "boy that was run from us." One of the "runnagates" may have been William White, the laborer with the first colonists who told his impressions of the Huskenaw. Later, Governor Dale wrote home complaining about Simons: "who had thrice played the runnagate, whose lies and villany much hindered our trade for corn." And when John Rolfe reported concerns about Robert Poole, he used the language of "turning Turk," saying that Robert had "even turned heathen."[30]

In Jamestown, leaders were constantly worried about the colonists' commitment to the project and feared betrayal by those who only feigned loyalty. Sometimes it was the leaders who were treacherous. Smith reported that Gov. Edward Maria Wingfield hatched a plot to escape for England in the colony's pinnace while the newly planted colonists waited for the first supply in misery. As that first horrible summer merged into autumn, George Kendall, a gentleman who had been placed on the council by the Virginia Company, was executed for mutiny in late November. He had been active in Europe before Jamestown, and reports indicated that he was a Roman Catholic and was attempting to smuggle out information on the colony's situation to Spain.[31]

George Percy recorded several plots. He sent Francis West, brother of future governor Sir Thomas West, Lord de la Warr, to the Potomac to get food for the starving colonists. Instead West absconded in his ship (he said at the insistence of his crew) for England. Later Percy learned that the colonists at Fort Algernon downriver had plenty of food but had concealed it from him and other leaders at Jamestown. So they were eating well while their fellows starved. Their plan was for the "better sort" to desert Virginia and return to England in the fort's two pinnaces.[32]

In 1610, the stories of malfeasance had reached such a height that the Virginia Company issued *A True Declaration of the Estate of the Colonie in Virginia, with a Confutation of Such Scandalous Reports as Have Tended to the Disgrace of So Worthy an Enterprise.* The *True Declaration* retold the story of the colony's desertion in the ships sent to help them and added that the deserters sailed as pirates in the Atlantic before returning to England. The company's statement included another kind of treachery: the sailors who brought supplies paid for by the Virginia Company and secretly traded part of their cargo to Native customers, thereby shortening colonists' provisions and lessening the value of English goods in trade.[33]

The *True Declaration* also condemned as traitors those who bad-mouthed Virginia. For this charge, the frame came from the Bible. Everyone knew the story in the book of Numbers in which Moses sent men to spy out the land of Canaan. They returned saying that the land flowed with milk and honey but that the people inhabiting there were strong. Caleb and Joshua were eager to move immediately and take the land from them, but the others were afraid: "for the people are stronger than we. So they brought up an evil report of the land which they searched for the children of Israel." Sir Thomas Dale wrote to Virginia Company head Sir Thomas Smyth in 1613, "be not gulled by the clamorous reports of base people: believe Caleb and Joshua." John Rolfe also praised those who, like Caleb and Joshua, "stood stoutly for the Lords Cause," in the face of others' "evil reports" and "slanders."[34]

Rev. Jonas Stockham put these critics close to the "turned Turk" category when he said, "there be many Italiannated and Spaniolized Englishmen envies our prosperities" and seek to "dishearten" the colony's supporters "by forging unjust tales to hinder our welfare." And John Rolfe wrote that during his time in Virginia, "I never amongst so few, have seen so many false-hearted, envious, and malicious people (yea amongst some who march in the better rank)."[35]

Atlantic enterprises brought all these complicated judgments about identity and integrity back to England. Londoners viewed the influx of foreign goods and people and the relationships that underlay it with a mixture of fear and fascination. The London apothecary Thomas Johnson claimed that England welcomed more "aliens from all parts of the world" than any other country, and offered shelter "to the distressed, to the persecuted, to the afflicted." But many English saw an invasion of foreigners with complicated motivations as the city continued to grow.[36]

The Portuguese merchant Pisaro in William Haughton's 1598 play *Englishmen for My Money* was the ideal inhabitant of this world because, as he says, "every soil to me is natural." Pisaro is loyal only to his own wealth, and he is at home in all countries as long as they are useful to him. Ambiguous identities are all around. Pisaro, who lives in London in the play, describes himself as "Judas-like" in his smiling demeanor, and this touched on a theme familiar to the English. Francis Limbreck's ambiguous identity was resolved when he was executed as the "English Judas." The Portuguese, especially, were thought to have been corrupted because they had offered refuge to many Sephardic Jews in the past. In 1578, Anthony Parkhurst wrote that he had not brought home a cargo of fish worth £600 because the Portuguese sailors who had promised to bring him salt had defaulted. He called them "vile Portingals, descending of the Jews and Judas kind." Treachery of any kind was associated with Jews, as when Capt. John Smith derided Iopassus as the "old Jew" for betraying Pocahontas.[37] Even Jews who had converted to Christianity were suspect, because everyone assumed they were still secretly Jews and "counterfeit Christians."[38] Because no one could discern their real identity for certain, most people just assumed that their hidden intentions were treacherous.

Fears also centered around secret Roman Catholics, who might be planning new treacheries like the Gunpowder Plot of 1605, or the Englishmen who were prepared to help the Spanish plant a spy in Jamestown. The Protestant establishment believed that many Roman Catholic recusants, who paid a fine for refusing to attend Church of England services, harbored Jesuits, who were secretly active in England, and some people thought that Jesuits had entered the kingdom disguised as Jews. *Jesuitical* meant twisting words and meanings to achieve one's own goals, and Protestants believed not only that Jesuits were specially trained in that skill but also that they had papal permission to lie in service of their greater truth. These categories had a wide reach. Just as Iopassus's betrayal of Pocahontas made him like a Jew, George Wyatt, in a letter to his son Gov. Sir Francis Wyatt in 1624, wrote of Jack of the Feathers's request to be buried secretly that it "smells of a Jesuit" because he wanted to hide the truth from his followers.[39]

What does conversion mean? That was the fundamental question. Renegades who returned to England argued that they had never really converted and claimed they had practiced what Nabil Matar calls "the distinction of inner faith and outer dissimulation."[40] But it was much more complicated than that. The life of Paquiquineo, the Paspahegh man who had spent ten years with the Spanish and had been baptized as Don Luis de Velasco, is a case in point. The Jesuits who brought him back to Virginia were so convinced of his complete and sincere conversion that they refused to bring any soldiers to protect them. And Jesuits were hard to fool. Paquiquineo may actually have been a sincere convert while he lived among the Spanish. But once he was back with his own people, he could not sustain his commitment to Christianity and try to convert the Paspaheghs.

England itself had required its subjects to be Roman Catholics, then Protestants, then Roman Catholics, and finally Protestants again in the sixteenth century. What went on in people's heads (or hearts) as they experienced these changes? No one could claim to know. As Jesus says in the Gospel of Luke, only "God knoweth your hearts." John Milton, citing scripture after scripture, wrote that no men can be "infallible judges . . . in matters of religion to any other men's consciences than their own."[41]

One example from the reign of Queen Mary I shows how weird the situation became. Henry VIII had been succeeded by his son Edward VI, who maintained the Protestant establishment that his father had begun. After Edward's early death, Henry's daughter Mary took the throne in 1553 and returned the country to her religion, Roman Catholicism, and church officials took steps to root out any lingering Protestant sentiments.

As part of the campaign, a young man known as Blind Tom was examined for heresy by Chancellor John Williams of Gloucester. The question was whether the actual body of Christ was offered at communion. Blind Tom said no. When Chancellor Williams demanded to know "who taught you this heresy?" Blind Tom replied, "You, Mister Chancellor," pointing to the pulpit where Williams had preached back when the Protestant Edward VI was on the throne and Williams, like everyone in England, was a Protestant. The chancellor then counseled Blind Tom to just go along as he himself had done, but Blind Tom refused and was sentenced to death by Williams for believing what Williams himself had preached.[42]

Many people, like Chancellor Williams, formed an allegiance to one version of Christianity and just went along when the other was in power. So were they like the Jewish conversos or the repentant returnees from Islam? Who knew?[43] Queen Elizabeth I ascended the throne at the death of Mary I in 1558, and England was returned to Protestantism. But English Protestants feared crypto-Catholics in their midst on both sides of the Atlantic. The Gunpowder Plot of 1605 showed just how real those fears were. And recent archaeology by the team headed by William Kelso at Jamestown has discovered a very large number of artifacts used in Roman Catholic worship, so many secret recusants may have been present in addition to Don Diego de Molina and Father Biard.[44]

And later in the sixteenth century, puritanism arose, arguing that the Church of England had lost its true spiritual mission and seeking a new revitalized Christian movement. Most puritans attended weekly worship in their local churches, because the law required it, but held their own opinions in their hearts and met for worship separately with like-minded people. Some, who could not conform, exiled themselves to the Netherlands and then to America; hundreds of puritans went to Virginia beginning in 1618.[45]

England itself was torn apart by continuing political and religious conflict in the middle decades of the seventeenth century. Puritans, following the lead of Continental Protestant leaders such as John Calvin, wanted to end the system of bishops and archbishops by which the Church of England was governed and revert to control by local congregations. James I, who came to the throne at the death of Elizabeth in 1603, responded, "No bishop, no king." Threatening hierarchy in one institution meant losing it everywhere. When Parliament refused requests for new taxes, James's son and successor, Charles I, ruled for years without calling Parliament into session.

The Roman Catholic Baron Arundell of Wardour may have been interested in helping the Spanish to plant a spy in Jamestown because, according to Pedro de Zúñiga, he had wanted to be Jamestown's founder and had been turned down because he was Roman Catholic. During Charles I's period of "personal rule," however, he authorized Cecilius Calvert, Lord Baltimore, to found the Roman Catholic colony of Maryland, named for Charles's queen, Henrietta Maria, on ten million acres of land taken from Virginia's original grant, so Virginians now had a Roman Catholic presence right on their border and on land they considered their own. Earlier colonies, such as Virginia, had been founded by joint stock companies; but Calvert and his heirs were "the true and absolute lords and Proprietaries" of Maryland, and Jesuits took charge of the religious foundation there. Henry Fleet interpreted for Leonard Calvert, who had gone over as governor, but many of Virginia's leaders did not trust him and feared he was manipulating their relationship with the Piscataways.[46]

In 1640, financial exigency forced Charles to call two Parliaments. The first one was sent home by the king after three weeks; but another was called late that year, and it came to be called the Long Parliament. Puritans within Parliament, many of whom were investors in the Virginia Company, mounted a firm opposition, and ultimately war broke out between king and Parliament in 1642. Robert Rich, the Earl of Warwick, the man who Henry Spelman had thought was coming to be governor of Virginia, was one of the leaders of the forces opposing the king. The victorious Parliament tried King Charles for making war on his own people, and he was executed in January 1649. An eleven-year interregnum, led by Lord Protector Oliver Cromwell, ensued, and the nation was officially Protestant and puritan.

The Protectorate collapsed after the death of Cromwell, and Charles II returned from his long exile in France to claim the throne in 1660. Charles and his brother James were thought to be crypto-Catholics after growing up in France. When James II became king in 1685 and declared his Catholicism openly, another rebellion ensued in 1688, and the Dutch William of Orange and his wife, Mary Stuart, James's daughter, were installed as monarchs. Only then was the hidden threat of Roman Catholicism considered finished in England.

Seventeenth-century fears about ambiguous identities and hidden motives evoke modern examples. In the 1930s, as Japanese forces became ever more aggressive in the Pacific, Americans increasingly feared treachery by U.S. citizens of Japanese descent. Fishermen operating on the West Coast were said to be using torpedo boats disguised as simple crafts, so they would be ready to assist Japanese invaders when the time came. Farmers, reporters said, were prepared to spray arsenic on their crops in order to poison consumers who were gullible enough to buy them. Despite these citizens' fervent proclamations of allegiance to the United States, their neighbors were convinced of Japanese Americans' potential for treason. By the end of the decade, even though President Franklin D. Roosevelt was determined to stay out of the war that began in Europe in 1939, plans were already being laid for internment camps for aliens.

Fears of sabotage by local people led to a disastrous mistake as planes on Hickam Field in Hawaii were grouped close together for easier guarding, rendering them much more vulnerable when Japanese planes attacked in December 1941. Despite resistance by many national leaders, including Eleanor Roosevelt, the president signed Executive Order 9066 less than two months after Pearl Harbor; the order called for removing all people of Japanese descent, aliens and citizens, from the West Coast and putting them into hastily built camps. As John DeWitt, the army general in command of the West Coast, said, "A Jap's a Jap. They are a dangerous element, whether loyal or not." They were dangerous because, like Thomas, Henry, and Robert, their true minds were unknowable.[47]

Ambiguity turned to certainty in the 1950s, when, to the nation's horror and disbelief, twenty-three Americans taken prisoner during the Korean War and confined in prison camps in China chose not to return home after the armistice was signed, although two soon changed their minds. It seemed impossible that red-blooded American boys would choose life in a still-developing Communist country over prosperous democratic America. One popular theory was that the men had been brainwashed using techniques that the Chinese were developing to enforce conformity among their own people. The *New York Times*, reporting on the former prisoners' appearance in a press conference, said that "the men were speaking like robots." They seemed to "have had their life memories wiped out and delusions put in their place"; in fact, they were victims of "an artificially imposed mental illness."[48]

As stories of returning prisoners began to come out, different interpretations developed. Many writers now alleged that the "turncoats" had actually collaborated with the enemy in the prison camps and had refused repatriation because they were afraid of prosecution when they came home. They were "rats" rather than victims. Chalmers M. Roberts wrote a group portrait for the *Washington Post*, arguing that they had grown up in impoverished families, had been habitual troublemakers, and were all "of extremely low mentality." They hoped for advancement under the Communists. Roberts also included rumors of homosexual activities among some of them, including letting their hair grow long and even wearing women's clothes.[49]

Military authorities saw all ex-POWs as potential fifth columnists, whose indoctrination had planted seeds that would sprout and grow when a new national crisis loomed. The two turncoats who repented and came home were court-martialed and sentenced to prison at hard labor. Other former prisoners were also tried, and suspicion dogged all of them. Senator Joseph McCarthy conducted a search for hidden agents more broadly, and he claimed that Communists had infiltrated the State Department. As the Cold War with the Soviet Union and its allies took center stage, fears initially sparked by the turncoats spread broadly.[50]

Other concerns about the stability of identity emerged in the 1970s. The scholar Helen Rountree uses Stockholm Syndrome as a way to think about Pocahontas's experience as she began to accept the religion and customs of her captors. The idea of Stockholm Syndrome emerged from an episode in August 1973, when a man armed with a submachine gun attempted to rob a Stockholm bank. A standoff ensued, and the robber took four hostages into a vault. He demanded that his friend be released from prison, so soon there were two gunmen in the vault. The captivity lasted six days. When the police finally released the hostages, they appeared to have formed bonds of affection with their captors, and they were immediately placed in a psychiatric hospital. The doctor overseeing their care said that they would require months of hospitalization to achieve their "reorientation." Later, as the hostages spoke about their experience, a clearer picture emerged: the key was initial terror followed by kind treatment. That was what led to the bonding.[51]

Stockholm Syndrome achieved a new currency six months later when the heiress Patty Hearst was captured by a radical group that called itself the Symbionese Liberation Army (SLA). After two months, Hearst, having taken the name Tania, announced that she was joining the SLA and participated with them in a bank robbery. When she was recaptured after a yearlong crime spree with the SLA, her lawyers called psychiatrists to testify about her mental state. They talked about research on American Korean War prisoners and compared her experience to theirs. The defense failed, and she was sentenced to seven years in prison.[52]

Stockholm Syndrome as a concept can help illuminate the experience of Thomas, Henry, and Robert as well as Pocahontas. All four were forced into terrifying situations in which they found kindness and good treatment and in which they formed affectionate ties. All these modern examples may enhance our understanding of the way they reacted to their different situations and of the way people in authority interpreted the actions of the three boys and thought about their true identity.

The seventeenth century did not have the word *brainwashing*, but philosophers such as John Locke were concerned about personal identity and how to assess whether a person in the present was actually identical to the being with the same name and shape in the past. As Locke wrote, English people described someone who was distracted or seemed radically different as someone who is "not himself or is besides himself," implying "that self was changed." And, he pointed out, laws did not punish "the Sober man for what the Mad Man did, thereby making them two persons."[53]

The English in charge in Jamestown were adamant in their belief that Pocahontas was not in fact the same person as she had been when living with her people, the Powhatans. But they were extremely disturbed as they considered whether Thomas, Henry, and Robert had been so radically changed by their experiences that continuity of personal identity had been lost for them.

The boys had been selected for service with the Chesapeake Algonquians because they were still malleable, unbaked dough, and could therefore adapt to life with the Powhatans and learn new languages more easily. In their new settings, they experienced initial terror followed by acceptance. They also saw a way of life well adapted to the environment. As the colonists raged and starved because they could not cope, the boys saw competence and a culture in which status was earned rather than acquired. They saw the reality behind the curtain of English claims of superiority, as the colonists began to thrive only after they adopted Native crops and techniques. They could see the value of both sides.

But for English leaders, the question remained: Who were they?

ACKNOWLEDGMENTS

MANY PEOPLE HAVE ASSISTED ME in the process of tracking down the story of these actors and framing it. Charlie Jane Anders and Annalee Newitz have commented on several drafts and made many important suggestions on framing and presentation. Numerous conversations with Bonnie Smith have been invaluable, because Bonnie asks the right questions. Martha McCartney and Helen Rountree have given me invaluable assistance, and the work of Emily Rose has contributed to my understanding of the issues, as has that of James Rice. Michael Braddick, Joyce Lorimer, and Gwenda Morgan helped me to understand the larger issues on the English side, and Samantha Bullat and Bly Straube of the Jamestown Yorktown Foundation tutored me on seventeenth-century English clothing.

NOTES

NOTES ON SOURCES AND ON TERMINOLOGY

1. See Henry Spelman, *Relation of Virginia*, ed. Karen Ordahl Kupperman (New York: NYU Press, forthcoming). Quotes from Spelman give the folio numbers of the manuscript, and these are included in the forthcoming edition.

2. Capt. John Smith, *The Generall Historie of Virginia, New-England, and the Summer Isles* (London, 1624), in *The Complete Works of Captain John Smith*, ed. Philip L. Barbour, 3 vols. (Chapel Hill: University of North Carolina Press, 1986), 2:41.

3. William M. Kelso, *Jamestown: The Truth Revealed* (Charlottesville: University of Virginia Press, 2017); Martin D. Gallivan, *The Powhatan Landscape: An Archaeological History of the Algonquian Chesapeake* (Gainesville: University Press of Florida, 2016). For Powhatan's statement, see Smith, *Generall Historie*, in Barbour, *Complete Works*, 2:196.

4. For more information on names, see the National Museum of the American Indian, "Did You Know?," www.nmai.si.edu; for Virginia tribes, see www. pamunkey.net; www.chickahominytribe.org; www.cied.org; http://patawomeck-indiantribeofvirginia.org; www.nansemond.org; www.uppermattaponi.org.

5. The Virginia Council on Indians can be contacted at vci@governor.virginia.gov.

INTRODUCTION

1. Helen C. Rountree, *Pocahontas, Powhatan, Opechancanough: Three Indian Lives Changed by Jamestown* (Charlottesville: University of Virginia Press, 2005), 101.

2. John Smith, *A True Relation of Such Occurrences and Accidents of Noate as Hath Hapned in Virginia*, 1608, in Barbour, *Complete Works*, 1:93.

3. See Juliana Barr, *Peace Came in the Form of a Woman: Indians and Spaniards in the Texas Borderlands* (Chapel Hill: University of North Carolina Press, 2007).

4. Martha W. McCartney has tracked down every European present in Virginia in the first twenty-eight years, in her collection, *Virginia Immigrants and Adventurers 1607–1635: A Biographical Dictionary* (Baltimore: Genealogical Publishing, 2007). Each entry contains information from all available records and directions on where to look in the sources.

5. Edward Maria Wingfield, "Discourse," 1608, in *The Jamestown Voyages under the First Charter, 1606–1609*, ed. Philip L. Barbour, 2 vols. (Cambridge, UK: Hakluyt Society, 1969), 1:216.

6. Smith, *Generall Historie*, in Barbour, *Complete Works*, 2:192–93.

7. Alexander Brown, *The First Republic in America* (Cambridge, MA: Riverside, 1898), 149.

8. Rachel Moss, "The Youth of Today," *History Today*, June 2018, 18–20; Paul Griffiths, *Youth and Authority: Formative Experiences in England, 1560–1640* (Oxford: Oxford University Press, 1996), chap. 1; Anthony Fletcher, *Growing Up in England: The Experience of Childhood, 1600–1914* (New Haven, CT: Yale University Press, 2008), chap. 2; Alexandra Shepard, *Meanings of Manhood in Early Modern England* (Oxford: Oxford University Press, 2002), 23–38, 93–126.

9. Lorena S. Walsh, *Motives of Honor, Pleasure, and Profit: Plantation Management in the Colonial Chesapeake, 1607–1763* (Chapel Hill: University of North Carolina Press for the Omohundro Institute, 2010), 106–7; Ann Kussmaul, *Servants in Husbandry in Early Modern England* (Cambridge: Cambridge University Press, 1981).

10. John Pory to Sir Dudley Carleton, 1619, *Massachusetts Historical Society Collections*, 4th ser., vol. 9 (1871): 283.

11. Spelman, *Relation of Virginia*, ed. Kupperman, 224v.

12. Helen C. Rountree, *The Powhatan Indians of Virginia: Their Traditional Culture* (Norman: University of Oklahoma Press, 1989), 80–82.

13. William Shakespeare, *Alls Well That Ends Well*, act 4, scene 5; William Vaughan, *The Golden Grove Moralized in Three Bookes* (London, 1600), book 3, chap. 32, "Of the Education of Gentlemen."

14. Charlotte Gradie, "The Powhatans in the Context of the Spanish Empire" in *Powhatan Foreign Relations, 1500–1722*, ed. Helen Rountree (Charlottesville: University of Virginia Press, 1993), 154–72; Gradie, "Spanish Jesuits in Virginia: The Mission That Failed," *Virginia Magazine of History and Biography* 96 (1988): 131–56; Paul E. Hoffman, *A New Andalucia and a Way to the Orient: The American Southeast during the Sixteenth Century* (Baton Rouge: University of Louisiana Press, 1990), 181–87, 261–66; Camilla Townsend, "Mutual Appraisals: The Shifting Paradigms of the English, Spanish, and Powhatans in Tsenacomoco, 1560–1622," in *Early Modern Virginia: Reconsidering the Old Dominion*, ed. Douglas Bradburn and John C. Coombs (Charlottesville: University of Virginia Press, 2011), 57–64; Anna Brickhouse, *The Unsettlement of America: Translation, Interpretation, and the Story of Don Luis de Velasco, 1560–1945* (Oxford: Oxford University Press, 2011).

15. Alida C. Metcalf, *Go-Betweens and the Colonization of Brazil, 1500–1600* (Austin: University of Texas Press, 2005).

16. James McDermott, *Martin Frobisher: Elizabethan Privateer* (New Haven, CT: Yale University Press, 2001), 28–47 and chaps. 8–12.

17. John T. McGrath, *The French in Early Florida: In the Eye of the Hurricane* (Gainesville: University Press of Florida, 2000), 67–74, 94; "Report of Manrique de Rojas," trans. Lucy L. Wenhold, in *Laudonnière and Fort Caroline: History and Documents*, by Charles E. Bennett (Tuscaloosa: University of Alabama Press, 2001), 107–24; Rouffin's testimony is on 116–22.

18. Derek Massarella, ed., *Japanese Travellers in Sixteenth-Century Europe: A Dialogue Concerning the Mission of the Japanese Ambassadors to the Roman Curia (1590)*, trans. J. F. Moran (London: Ashgate for the Hakluyt Society, 2012).

19. David Beers Quinn, *Set Fair for Roanoke: Voyages and Colonies, 1584–1606* (Chapel Hill: University of North Carolina Press, 1985); Karen Ordahl Kupperman, *Roanoke: The Abandoned Colony* (Lanham, MD: Rowman and Littlefield, 1984; 2nd ed., 2007).

20. David B. Quinn, "Turks, Moors, Blacks, and Others in Drake's West Indian Voyage," in *Explorers and Colonies: America, 1500–1625* (London: Hambledon, 1990), 197–204; Andrew Lawler, "Did Francis Drake Bring Enslaved Africans to North America Decades before Jamestown?," Smithsonian.com, August 20, 2018, www.smithsonianmag.com.

21. The First Colony Foundation, comprising archaeologists and historians, is conducting research on promising sites on the North Carolina mainland and has uncovered one with Elizabethan artifacts and signs of occupation by some of the English. See www.firstcolonyfoundation.org. On legends about the 1587 colonists' fates, see Andrew Lawler, *The Secret Token: Myth, Obsession, and the Search for the Lost Colony of Roanoke* (New York: Doubleday, 2018).

22. George Percy, *Observations Gathered out of a Discourse of the Plantation of the Southerne Colonie in Virginia by the English, 1606*, in Barbour, *Jamestown Voyages*, 1:140.

23. Sir Walter Ralegh, *Sir Walter Ralegh's Discoverie of Guiana*, ed. Joyce Lorimer (London: Ashgate for the Hakluyt Society, 2006), 176–77.

24. Percy, *Observations*, in Barbour, *Jamestown Voyages*, 1:145–46.

25. "Relation of what Francis Magnel, an Irishman, learned in the land of Virginia during the eight months he was there," 1610, in Barbour, *Jamestown Voyages*, 1:151–57; for the grant, see SP 94/17/170, National Archives, Kew, UK.

26. Capt. John Smith, *The True Travels, Adventures, and Observations of Captaine John Smith*, in Barbour, *Complete Works*, 3:137–243.

27. *Oxford English Dictionary*, s.v. "traduce."

28. Smith, *Generall Historie*, in Barbour, *Complete Works*, 2:193, 315.

CHAPTER 1. SETTLING IN

1. Gillian T. Cell, introduction to *Newfoundland Discovered: English Attempts at Colonisation, 1610–1630*, ed. Cell (London: Hakluyt Society, 1982), 1–59.

2. Kenneth R. Andrews, *Elizabethan Privateering: English Privateering during the Spanish War, 1585–1603* (Cambridge: Cambridge University Press, 1964); On Frobisher as a privateer, see McDermott, *Martin Frobisher*, 48–78.

3. Audrey Horning, *Ireland in the Virginian Sea: Colonialism in the British Atlantic* (Chapel Hill: University of North Carolina Press for the Omohundro Institute of Early American History and Culture, 2013); Nicholas Canny, *The Elizabethan Conquest of Ireland: A Pattern Established, 1565–76* (New York: Barnes and Noble

Books, 1976); Jane H. Ohlmeyer, "'Civilizinge of Those Rude Partes': Colonization within Britain and Ireland," in *The Oxford History of the British Empire*, vol. 1, *The Origins of Empire: British Overseas Enterprise to the Close of the Seventeenth Century*, ed. Nicholas Canny (Oxford: Oxford University Press, 1998), 124–47.

4. Dennis B. Blanton, "Drought as a Factor in the Jamestown Colony, 1607–1612," *Historical Archaeology* 34 (2000): 74–81.

5. Mark Nicholls, "George Percy's 'Trewe Relacyon': A Primary Source for the Jamestown Settlement," *Virginia Magazine of History and Biography* (*VMHB*) 113 (2005): 212–75, quote on 214.

6. Percy, *Observations*, in Barbour, *Jamestown Voyages*, 1:143–45.

7. The observations of plants and foods in this and the following paragraphs come from Smith, *Generall Historie*, in Barbour, *Complete Works*, 2:108–13; William Strachey, *The Historie of Travell into Virginia Britania* (1612), ed. Louis B. Wright and Virginia Freund (London: Hakluyt Society, 1953), 117–24; Percy, *Observations*, in Barbour, *Jamestown Voyages*, 1:139–42; Gabriel Archer, "A Relatyon of the Discovery of Our River" and "The Discription of the Now Discovered River and Country of Virginia," in Barbour, *Jamestown Voyages*, 1:80–87, 98–102; Spelman, *Relation of Virginia*, ed. Kupperman, 225. On digging and preparing tuckahoe, see Helen C. Rountree, "Powhatan Indian Women: The People Captain John Smith Barely Saw," *Ethnohistory* 45 (1998): 1–29.

8. Smith, *True Relation*, in Barbour, *Complete Works*, 1:43–61; and Smith, *Generall Historie*, ibid., 2:146–51.

9. Jean Howard, "Gender on the Periphery," in *Shakespeare and the Mediterranean*, ed. Tom Clayton, Susan Brock, and Vicente Forés (Newark: University of Delaware Press, 2004), 344–63.

10. Capt. John Smith, *A Map of Virginia* (1612), in Barbour, *Complete Works*, 1:136–39.

11. Strachey, *Historie of Travell*, 72.

12. The passenger list is in Smith, *Generall Historie*, in Barbour, *Complete Works*, 2:160–62.

13. *The Bible, That Is, the Holy Scriptures, Contained in the Old and New Testament* (London: Robert Barker, printer to the Queen's most Excellent Maiestie, 1603), 194.

14. Percy, *Observations*, in Barbour, *Jamestown Voyages*, 1:129; J. J. Roche, "Thomas Harriot's Observations of Halley's Comet in 1607," in *The Light of Nature: Essays in the History and Philosophy of Science Presented to A. C. Crombie*, ed. J. D. North and J. J. Roche, International Archives of the History of Ideas 110 (Dordrecht: Martinus Nijhoff, 1985), 175–92.

15. Peter Heylyn passed on this story in his *Cosmographie in Four Bookes: Containing the Chorographie and Historie of the Whole World* (London, 1652), bk. 1, 262.

16. On early descriptions of the Caribbean and Virginia environments, see Percy, "Observations," in Barbour, *Jamestown Voyages*, 1:129–46; Archer, "Relatyon of the Discovery" and "Discription of the Now Discovered River," ibid., 1:80–87, 98–102; William Brewster to the Earl of Salisbury, between May 27 and June 22, 1607, ibid., 1:107; Virginia Company, *A True Declaration of the Estate of the Colonie in*

Virginia, with a Confutation of Such Scandalous Reports as Have Tended to the Disgrace of So Worthy an Enterprise (London, 1610).

17. Smith, *Generall Historie*, in Barbour, *Complete Works*, 1:108.

18. Smith, *True Relation*, ibid., 1:63–77; Capt. John Smith, *Proceedings of the English Colonie in Virginia*, ibid., 1:216–18.

19. Pedro de Zúñiga to Philip III, February 23, 1609, in Barbour, *Jamestown Voyages*, 2:257.

20. Ralph Hamor, *A True Discourse of the Present Estate of Virginia* (1615; repr., Richmond: Virginia State Library, 1957), 38.

21. The list for Mace is printed in David Beers Quinn, "Thomas Harriot and the Virginia Voyages of 1602," in *England and the Discovery of America, 1481–1620* (London: George Allen and Unwin, 1974), 110–12; Quinn, "Thomas Harriot and the New World," in *Thomas Harriot: Renaissance Scientist*, ed. John W. Shirley (Oxford, UK: Clarendon, 1974), 50.

22. Smith, *Proceedings of the English Colonie in Virginia*, in Barbour, *Complete Works*, 1:216; Ben Jonson, *Epicoene; or, The Silent Woman* (London, 1620), act 5, scene 1; Alden T. Vaughan, "Powhatans Abroad: Virginia Indians in England," in *Envisioning an English Empire: Jamestown and the Making of the North Atlantic World*, ed. Robert Appelbaum and John Wood Sweet (Philadelphia: University of Pennsylvania Press, 2005), 49–67.

23. Spelman, *Relation of Virginia*, ed. Kupperman, 225.

24. A. H. Dodd, *Life in Elizabethan England* (London: B. T. Batsford; New York: G. P. Putnam's Sons, 1961), chap. 4.

25. Spelman, *Relation of Virginia*, ed. Kupperman, 233.

26. Michael A. LaCombe, *Political Gastronomy: Food and Authority in the English Atlantic World* (Philadelphia: University of Pennsylvania Press, 2012), chap. 6.

27. Wingfield, "Discourse," in Barbour, *Jamestown Voyages*, 1:216.

28. Anna Reynolds, *In Fine Style: The Art of Tudor and Stuart Clothing* (London: Royal Collection Trust, 2013); Ann Rosalind Jones and Peter Stallybrass, *Renaissance Clothing and the Materials of Memory* (Cambridge: Cambridge University Press, 2000); Janet Arnold, *Patterns of Fashion: The Cut and Construction of Clothes for Men and Women, c. 1560–1620* (London: Macmillan, 1985).

29. William Byrd I to John Clayton, May 25, 1686, in *The Correspondence of the Three William Byrds of Westover, Virginia, 1684–1776*, ed. Marion Tinling, 2 vols. (Charlottesville: University of Virginia Press for the Virginia Historical Society, 1977), 1:61.

30. Spelman, *Relation of Virginia*, ed. Kupperman, 234.

31. Smith, *True Relation*, in Barbour, *Complete Works*, 1:91–93.

32. Strachey, *Historie of Travell*, 113.

33. Sir Thomas Dale to Virginia Council, June 10, 1613, in *Virginia Company Archives: The Ferrar Papers FP 1–FP 2314, Ferrar Print 1-562, 1590–1790*, ed. David Ransome, www.amdigital.co.uk, doc. 40. On colonists' view of Native child-rearing practices, see Anna Mae Duane, "Casualties of the Rod: Rebelling Children, Disciplining

Indians, and the Critique of Colonial Authority in Puritan New England," in *Messy Beginnings: Postcoloniality and Early American Studies*, ed. Malini Johan Schueller and Edward Watts (New Brunswick, NJ: Rutgers University Press, 2003), 63–79; and Duane, *Suffering Childhood in Early America: Violence, Race, and the Making of the Child Victim* (Athens: University of Georgia Press, 2010).

34. Smith, *Generall Historie*, in Barbour, *Complete Works*, 2:181, 191–93. On Mistress Forrest and Anne Burras, see Virginia Bernhard, "'Men, Women and Children' at Jamestown: Population and Gender in Early Virginia, 1607–1610," *Journal of Southern History* 58 (1992): 599–618, esp. 616; on the Germans, see Gary C. Grassl, "First Germans at Jamestown, Virginia," 1997, www.germanheritage.com; on the Poles, see Philip L. Barbour, "The Identity of the First Poles in America," *William and Mary Quarterly* 21 (1964): 77–92.

35. Smith, *True Relation*, in Barbour, *Complete Works*, 1:3.

36. Smith, *Generall Historie*, ibid., 2:182–83; Samuel Purchas, *Purchas His Pilgrimage*, 2nd ed. (London, 1614), 764–65. On Diana and Actaeon in Elizabethan masque, see W. R. Streitberger, *The Masters of the Revels and Elizabeth I's Court Theatre* (Oxford: Oxford University Press, 2016), 74.

37. Smith, *Generall Historie*, in Barbour, *Complete Works*, 2:182–84.

38. Ibid., 2:205.

39. Ibid., 2:192–93; see Rountree, *Pocahontas, Powhatan, Opechancanough*, 117.

40. Smith, *Generall Historie*, in Barbour, *Complete Works*, 2:195–99.

41. Ibid., 199–200, 209, 217.

42. Martin D. Gallivan, *The Powhatan Landscape: An Archaeological History of the Algonquian Chesapeake* (Gainesville: University Press of Florida, 2016).

43. Strachey, *Historie of Travell*, 57.

CHAPTER 2. NEW REALITIES

1. William Crashaw, *A Sermon Preached in London before the Right Honourable the Lord Lawarre* (London, 1610), sig. E4v–F1; Virginia Company, "Instructions, Orders, and Constitutions by Way of Advice . . . to Sir Thomas Gates, Knight, Governor of Virginia, 1609," in *Records of the Virginia Company of London*, ed. Susan Myra Kingsbury, 4 vols. (Washington, DC: U.S. Government Printing Office, 1906–35), 3:12–24, quote on 19; Thomas Harriot on Carolina Algonquian talk of metalworking, 1609, in *The Roanoke Voyages, 1584–1590*, ed. David Beers Quinn, 2 vols. (London: Hakluyt Society, 1955), 1:388.

2. Spelman, *Relation of Virginia*, ed. Kupperman, 220.

3. On how children's crimes were evaluated and punished, and the role of status in determining punishment, in early seventeenth-century England, see Holly Brewer, *By Birth or Consent: Children, Law, and the Anglo-American Revolution in Authority* (Chapel Hill: University of North Carolina Press for the Omohundro Institute of Early American History and Culture, 2005), chap. 6. I thank Michael Braddick, Joyce Lorimer, and Gwenda Morgan for help with this issue.

4. Will of Francis Saunder, Ewell, Surrey, gent., August 1613, in "Virginia Gleanings in England," *Virginia Magazine of History and Biography* 15 (1908): 305.

5. Margaret Spufford, *Small Books and Pleasant Histories* (London: Methuen, 1981), 30–31; on the Spelman family, see William Harvey, *The Visitation of Norfolk in 1563*, 2 vols. (Norwich, UK: Miller and Leavins, 1878), 1:249–60, esp. 253, 256. On the pain of separation from parents, see Ilana Krausman Ben-Amos, *Adolescence and Youth in Early Modern England* (New Haven, CT: Yale University Press, 1994), chap. 2.

6. Spelman, *Relation of Virginia*, ed. Kupperman, 220.

7. David Cressy, *Coming Over: Migration and Communication between England and New England in the Seventeenth Century* (Cambridge: Cambridge University Press, 1987), chap. 6.

8. William Strachey, "A True Reportory of the Wreck and Redemption of Sir Thomas Gates, Knight" (1610), in *A Voyage to Virginia in 1609: Two Narratives*, 2nd ed., ed. Louis B. Wright (Charlottesville: University of Virginia Press, 2013), 1–101, "winds and seas" on 7, "Truth is the daughter of Time" on 16; Michael J. Jarvis, *In the Eye of All Trade: Bermuda, Bermudians, and the Maritime Atlantic World, 1680–1783* (Chapel Hill: University of North Carolina Press for the Omohundro Institute, 2010), chap. 1; Ivor Noël Hume, *The Virginia Adventure: Roanoke to James Towne: An Archaeological and Historical Odyssey* (New York: Knopf, 1994), 240–44, 262, 266.

9. Kelso, *Jamestown: The Truth Revealed*, chap. 6.

10. Nicholls, "George Percy's 'Trewe Relacyon,'" *VMHB*, 113 (2005): 244–47; J. Frederick Fausz, "'Abundance of Blood Shed on Both Sides': England's First Indian War, 1609–1614," *Virginia Magazine of History and Biography* 98 (1990): 3–56.

11. Spelman, *Relation of Virginia*, ed. Kupperman, 221.

12. Ibid.

13. Nicholls, "George Percy's 'Trewe Relacyon,'" *VMHB*, 113 (2005): 246; Smith, *Generall Historie*, in Barbour, *Complete Works*, 2:220–24.

14. Spelman, *Relation of Virginia*, ed. Kupperman, 221; Smith, *Generall Historie*, in Barbour, *Complete Works*, 2:220–22.

15. Spelman, *Relation of Virginia*, ed. Kupperman, 221v–22.

16. Ibid. On gender roles among the Powhatans, see Rountree, *Powhatan Indians of Virginia*, chaps. 4 and 5.

17. Joan Thirsk, *Food in Early Modern England: Phases, Fads, Fashions 1500–1760* (London: Hambledon Continuum, 2007), 23; Paul S. Lloyd, *Food and Identity in England, 1540–1640: Eating to Impress* (London: Bloomsbury, 2016), 114–17.

18. Spelman, *Relation of Virginia*, ed. Kupperman, 225; Strachey, *Historie of Travell*, 75; Percy, *Observations*, in Barbour, *Jamestown Voyages*, 1:141; Archer, "Discription of the Now Discovered River," ibid. 99.

19. Spelman, *Relation of Virginia*, ed. Kupperman, 213v–32v.

20. Ibid.

21. Cornelia Hughes Dayton, *Women before the Bar: Gender, Law, and Society in Connecticut, 1639–1789* (Chapel Hill: University of North Carolina Press for the

Omohundro Institute of Early American History and Culture, 1995), 19–21; Daniel K. Richter, *Before the Revolution: America's Ancient Pasts* (Cambridge, MA: Harvard University Press, 2011), 46.

22. Spelman, *Relation of Virginia*, ed. Kupperman, 232v–33.

23. Nicholls, "George Percy's 'Trewe Relacyon,'" *VMHB*, 113 (2005): 159, 261; Alexander Whitaker to Mr. Crashaw, August 9, 1611, in *The Genesis of the United States*, ed. Alexander Brown, 2 vols. (Boston: Houghton, Mifflin, 1899), 1:497–99.

24. Henry told two versions of this episode in his *Relation of Virginia*: Spelman, *Relation of Virginia*, ed. Kupperman, 221v–22v, 238–38v.

25. Ibid., 222–22v.

26. Nicholls, "George Percy's 'Trewe Relacyon,'" *VMHB*, 113 (2005): 248–51; Strachey, "True Reportory," in Wright, *Voyage to Virginia* 63–64.

27. Virginia Company, *True Declaration of Estate*, 26.

28. Strachey, *Historie of Travell*, 131–32; Smith, *Generall Historie*, in Barbour, *Complete Works*, 2:215–17; Sir Thomas Dale to the Virginia Company, May 25, 1611, in Brown, *Genesis of the United States*, 1:490.

29. Spelman, *Relation of Virginia*, ed. Kupperman, 222v–23.

30. Smith, *Generall Historie*, in Barbour, *Complete Works*, 2:232.

31. Pocahontas's marriage to Kocoum is mentioned in Strachey, *Historie of Travell*, 62. On the significance of this marriage, see Rountree, *Pocahontas, Powhatan, Opechancanough*, 142–43.

32. Hamor, *True Discourse*, 37.

33. Strachey, *Historie of Travell*, 85–86; Sir Thomas Dale, "To the R. and my most esteemed friend Mr. D. M. at his house at F. Ch. in London," June 18, 1614, in Hamor, *True Discourse*, 53–54.

34. This story and the accompanying quotes in this and the following paragraphs are from Spelman, *Relation of Virginia*, ed. Kupperman, 227–28.

35. William Strachey, *For the Colony in Virginea Britannia: Lawes Divine, Morall and Martiall, etc.* (London, 1612), 7, 14, 18–19, 42–43; David Thomas Konig, "'Dale's Laws' and the Non-Common Law Origins of Criminal Justice in Virginia," *American Journal of Legal History* 26 (1982): 354–75.

36. Strachey, "True Reportory," in Wright, *Voyage to Virginia* 89; Fausz, "Abundance of Blood Shed," 32.

37. Nicholls, "George Percy's 'Trewe Relacyon,'" *VMHB*, 113 (2005): 252–55.

38. This story and the accompanying quotes in this and the following paragraphs come from Spelman, *Relation of Virginia*, ed. Kupperman, 228: Strachey, *Historie of Travell*, 101–3; Purchas, *Purchas His Pilgrimage*, 2nd ed., 767; and Smith, *Generall Historie*, in Barbour, *Complete Works*, 2:236.

CHAPTER 3. KNOWLEDGE SOUGHT AND GAINED

1. The "True Reportory" was published in Samuel Purchas, *Hakluytus Posthumus or Purchas His Pilgrimes* (1625), 20 vols. (Glasgow: J. MacLehose and Sons, 1906),

19:5–72, and is reprinted in Wright, *Voyage to Virginia in 1609*, 1–101. Many accounts circulated in manuscript before they were printed. See Alden T. Vaughan, "William Strachey's 'True Reportory' and Shakespeare: A Closer Look at the Evidence," *Shakespeare Quarterly* 59 (2008): 245–73. Hobson Woodward speculates on how Strachey would have experienced the play in his *A Brave Vessel: The True Tale of the Castaways Who Rescued Jamestown and Inspired Shakespeare's "The Tempest"* (New York: Viking Penguin, 2009), chaps. 15, 16, 17.

2. Strachey identified Blackfriars as his lodgings in the dedication of his edition of the *Laws Divine, Morall and Martiall*, sig. A4v. On his investment and previous presence at the Blackfriars Theatre, see S. G. Culliford, *William Strachey, 1572–1621* (Charlottesville: University of Virginia Press, 1965), xix, 53–55. On Blackfriars, see Janette Dillon, "Clerkenwell and Smithfield as a Neglected Home of London Theater," *Huntington Library Quarterly* 71 (2008): 115–35. On Jonson's residence there, see Martin Butler, "Jonson's London and Its Theatres," in *The Cambridge Companion to Ben Jonson*, ed. Richard Harp and Stanley Stewart (Cambridge: Cambridge University Press, 2000), 16.

3. Gordon McMullan, "The First Night of *The Tempest*," British Library, March 15, 2016, www.bl.uk.

4. This and following quotations are from William Shakespeare, *The Tempest*, first published in 1623.

5. Ralph Lane, *An Account of the Particularities of the Imployments of the English Men Left in Virginia* (1586), in Quinn, *Roanoke Voyages*, 1:276.

6. G[eorge] S[andys], *Ovid's Metamorphoses Englished, Mythologiz'd, and Represented in Figures* (Oxford, 1632), 224; Spelman, *Relation of Virginia*, ed. Kupperman, 235v, 238v.

7. Edmund Howes, *Annales; or, A Generall Chronicle of England* (London: Thomas Adams, 1615), 917.

8. Spelman, *Relation of Virginia*, ed. Kupperman, 220.

9. Ibid., 224–24v.

10. Ibid., 226v–27.

11. Ibid., 228v–29.

12. Alexander Whitaker to Mr. Crashaw, August 9, 1611, in Brown, *Genesis of the United States*, 1:498–99.

13. William M. Kelso, J. Eric Deetz, Seth W. Mallios, and Beverly A. Straube, *Jamestown Rediscovery VII* (Richmond: Association for the Preservation of Virginia Antiquities, 2001), 19–20; Keith Thomas, *Religion and the Decline of Magic: Studies in Popular Beliefs in Sixteenth- and Seventeenth-Century England* (Harmondsworth, UK: Penguin Books, 1973), 115–18, 328–30, 543–44; Rebecca Anne Goetz, *The Baptism of Early Virginia: How Christianity Created Race* (Baltimore: Johns Hopkins University Press, 2012), 45.

14. Marc Bloch, *The Royal Touch: Sacred Monarchy and Scrofula in England and France*, trans. J. E. Anderson (1973; repr., London: Routledge and Kegan Paul, 2015), esp. 191–92; Gallivan, *Powhatan Landscape*, 186.

15. Spelman, *Relation of Virginia*, ed. Kupperman, 229v–30.

16. Ibid., 230v–31.

17. Ibid., 235–36.

18. Ibid., 237.

19. Strachey, *Historie of Travell*, 46–47, 74, 101–3; Purchas, *Purchas His Pilgrimage*, 2nd ed., 767. The excerpts on Patawomeck religious life are included in Spelman, *Relation of Virginia*, ed. Kupperman,.

20. Strachey, *Historie of Travell*. For the date of its composition, see xv–xvii. The word list is at 174–207, and the reference to Harriot is on 21–22. On Harriot's syllabary, see Vivian Salmon, "Thomas Harriot (1560–1621) and the English Origins of Algonkian Linguistics," *Historiographia Linguistica* 19 (1992): 25–56.

21. Strachey, *Historie of Travell*, 39–40, 121–22, 131–32; Governor and Council in Virginia to the Virginia Company in London, July 7, 1610, in Brown, *Genesis of the United States*, 1:102–13, quote on 112; Harold B. Gill, *The Apothecary in Colonial Virginia* (Charlottesville: University Press of Virginia for the Colonial Williamsburg Foundation, 1972); Horning, *Ireland in the Virginian Sea*, 293–94. Wighsacan is milkweed, pocoones is today called hoary pucoon, and pellitory of Spain is similar to chamomile.

22. John Tradescant, *Museum Tradescantianum; or, A Collection of Rarities* (London, 1656); *Virginia Company Archives: The Ferrar Papers FP 1–FP 2314, Ferrar Print 1-562, 1590–1790*, ed. David Ransome, www.amdigital.co.uk, doc. 482; Jennifer Potter, *Strange Blooms: The Curious Lives and Adventures of the John Tradescants* (London: Atlantic Books, 2006); Penelope Leith-Ross, *The Tradescants: Gardeners to the Rose and Lily Queen* (London: P. Owen, 1998); Mea Allan, *The Tradescants: Their Plants, Gardens, and Museum, 1570–1662* (London: Michael Joseph, 1964). For John Smith's will see Barbour, *Complete Works*, 3:382–83.

23. Purchas, *Purchas His Pilgrimage*, 2nd ed., 732.

24. Alexander Whitaker, *Good Newes from Virginia* (London, 1613), 41; Susan Scott Parrish, "The Female Opossum and the Nature of the New World," *William and Mary Quarterly*, 3rd ser., 54 (1997): 475–514. See also Charles R. Eastman, "Early Portrayals of the Opossum," *American Naturalist* 49, no. 586 (1915): 585–94.

25. Zvi Ben-Dor Benite, *The Ten Lost Tribes: A World History* (Oxford: Oxford University Press, 2009); Strachey, *Historie of Travell*, 74; Purchas, *Purchas His Pilgrimage*, 2nd ed., 767.

26. Whitaker, *Good Newes from Virginia*, 27.

27. Morris dancing is a folk dance that dates from the fifteenth century in England. It was sometimes referred to as "Moorish" dance in early records. Michael Heaney and John Forrest, "An Antedating for the 'Morris Dance,'" *Notes & Queries* 247 (2002): 190–93; Michael Heaney, "The Earliest Reference to the Morris Dance?," *Folk Music Journal* 8 (2004): 513–15.

28. Alexander Whitaker to Mr. Crashaw, August 9, 1611, in Brown, *Genesis of the United States*, 1:497–500.

29. David J. Silverman, *Thundersticks: Firearms and the Violent Transformation of Native America* (Cambridge, MA: Harvard University Press, 2016), 25–26.

30. Whitaker to Crashaw, August 9, 1611, in Brown, *Genesis of the United States*, I: 497–500.

31. John Rolfe, *A True Relation of the State of Virginia Lefte by Sir Thomas Dale Knight in May Last 1616*, ed. Henry C. Taylor (Charlottesville: University of Virginia Press, 1971), 12–13.

32. Whitaker to Crashaw, August 9, 1611, in Brown, *Genesis of the United States*, I: 497–500. Whitaker reiterated his comparison of Powhatan priests and English witches and asked his readers to consider England's state before they had the Gospel in his *Good Newes from Virginia*, 24–26. The following year, he renewed his call for dedicated young ministers to come to Virginia; Alexander Whitaker, "To my verie deere and loving Cosen M. G. Minister of the B. F. in London," in Hamor, *True Discourse*, 59–61.

33. Pedro de Zúñiga to Philip III, September 22, 1607, in Barbour, *Jamestown Voyages*, 1:114–23; Don Zúñiga to His Majesty, June 26, 1608, ibid., 163.

34. "Relation of What Francis Magnel, an Irishman, Learned in the Land of Virginia during the Eight Months He Was There" (1610), ibid., 1:151–57.

35. Pedro de Zúñiga to Philip III, February 23 and July 5, 1609, ibid., 1:254–58, 269. On Arundell's efforts to create a refuge for English Catholics in America, see David Beers Quinn, "The English Catholics and America, 1581–1633," in *England and the Discovery of America*, 364–97.

36. Irene A. Wright, "Spanish Policy toward Virginia, 1606–1612," *American Historical Review* 25 (1920): 448–79; William S. Goldman, "Spain and the Founding of Jamestown," *William and Mary Quarterly* 68 (2011): 427–50.

37. Philip III to Don Alonso de Velasco, November 15, 1611, in Brown, *Genesis of the United States*, 2:525–26.

38. Nicholls, "George Percy's 'Trewe Relacyon,'" *VMHB*, 113 (2005): 260.

39. Sir John Digby to William Trumbull, June 20, 1612, in *Report on the Manuscripts of the Marquess of Downshire*, ed. Allen Banks Hinds, 4 vols. (London: H.M. Stationery Office, 1938), 1:318–19.

40. Don Diego de Molina to Don Diego de Velasco, May 28, 1613, in Brown, *Genesis of the United States*, 2:646–52.

41. Don Diego de Molina to Don Diego Sarmiento de Acuña, Count Gondomar, April 30, 1614, ibid., 2:740–44.

CHAPTER 4. POCAHONTAS BECOMES REBECCA ROLFE

1. Evidence of these promises is in a letter that Henry sent to Sir Henry three years later complaining that neither of them had been kept and asking Sir Henry to intervene; Henry Spelman, "To my honored and most esteemed uncle Sir Henry Spelman Kt: at his house in Cow Lane near Smiths Field in London," Bodleian Library, Tanner Manuscripts, Volume 74, folio 49, Oxford University, Oxford, UK.

2. Samuel Argall, "A Letter of Sir Samuell Argoll Touching His Voyage to Virginia, and Actions There, 1613," in Purchas, *Purchas His Pilgrimes*, 19:91–92.

3. The story and accompanying quotes in this and the following paragraphs are from Hamor, *True Discourse*, 4–10; Smith, *Generall Historie*, in Barbour, *Complete Works*, 2:243–44.

4. Argall, "Letter of Sir Samuell Argoll," in Purchas, *Purchas His Pilgrimes*, 19:92–93.

5. Hamor, *True Discourse*, 6; Rountree, *Pocahontas, Powhatan, Opechancanough*, chaps. 11–12.

6. See Historic Jamestowne, Jamestown Rediscovery, http://historicjamestowne.org; Kelso, *Jamestown: The Truth Revealed*, 111–14.

7. "Fr. Biard to Very Rev. Christopher Balthazar, Provincial of France, in Paris, May 1611," in Brown, *Genesis of the United States*, 1:475–76.

8. N. E. S. Griffiths, *From Migrant to Acadian: A North American Border People, 1604–1755* (Montreal: McGill-Queen's University Press, 2005), 23–24.

9. Allison Margaret Bigelow, "Gendered Language and the Science of Colonial Silk," *Early American Literature* 49 (2014): 271–325; Charles E. Hatch Jr., "Mulberry Trees and Silkworms: Sericulture in Early Virginia," *Virginia Magazine of History and Biography* 65 (1957): 3–61.

10. Charles M. Holloway, "Romancing the Vine in Virginia," *Colonial Williamsburg Journal*, Summer 2002, www.history.org.

11. Whitaker, *Good Newes from Virginia*, 25–26; Harry Culverwell Porter, "Alexander Whitaker: Cambridge Apostle to Virginia," *William and Mary Quarterly* 14 (1957): 317–43.

12. William Symonds, *Virginia: A Sermon Preached at White-Chappell, in the Presence of the Adventurers and Planters for Virginia* (London, 1609), 35.

13. John Rolfe, "The coppie of the Gentle-mans letters to sir Thomas Dale, that after maried Powhatans daughter, containing the reasons moving him thereunto," in Hamor, *True Discourse*, 61–68. The Virginia Company edited the letter for publication, leaving out parts that might be thought controversial, especially a passage in which Rolfe cited John Calvin for his argument that the child of a Christian and an unbeliever was "holy seed." For the full text from the surviving manuscript, which is in the Bodleian Library, MS Ashmole 830, fols. 118–19, see Edward Wright Haile, ed., *Jamestown Narratives: Eyewitness Accounts of the Virginia Colony* (Champlain, VA: Roundhouse, 1998), 850–56.

14. Spelman, *Relation of Virginia*, ed. Kupperman, 227.

15. The story and accompanying quotes in this and the following paragraphs are from Dale, "To the R. and my most esteemed friend Mr. D. M.," Hamor, *True Discourse*, 52–54; Hamor's own account is ibid., 6–11.

16. This story is in *The Bible and Holy Scriptures conteyned in the Olde and Newe Testament* (Geneva, 1562), Genesis 24, 12–14, quote at top of 13.

17. Whitaker, "To my verie deere and loving Cosen M. G.," in Hamor, *True Discourse*, 59–60; Dale, "To the R. and my most esteemed friend Mr. D. M.," ibid., 55–56; Spelman, *Relation of Virginia*, ed. Kupperman, 227.

18. The story and accompanying quotes in this and the following paragraphs are from Hamor, *True Discourse*, 37–46.
19. Alden T. Vaughan has examined all the existing evidence on Namontack's transatlantic journeys and his death in "Namontack's Itinerant Life and Mysterious Death: Sources and Speculations," *Virginia Magazine of History and Biography* 126 (2018): 170–209.
20. Smith, *Generall Historie*, in Barbour, *Complete Works*, 2:198, 205.
21. Melissa N. Morris, "Tobacco and Indigenous Agricultural Knowledge," paper presented at the Pocahontas and After Conference, London, Institute of Historical Research, March 17, 2016; Jean B. Russo and J. Elliott Russo, *Planting an Empire: The Early Chesapeake in British North America* (Baltimore: Johns Hopkins University Press, 2012), 55–58; James D. Rice, *Nature and History in the Potomac Country: From Hunter-Gatherers to the Age of Jefferson* (Baltimore: Johns Hopkins University Press, 2009), 110–13; T. H. Breen, *Tobacco Culture: The Mentality of the Great Tidewater Planters on the Eve of Revolution* (Princeton, NJ: Princeton University Press, 2001), chap. 2; Rountree, *Powhatan Indians of Virginia*, 44, 47.
22. Spelman, "To my honored and most esteemed uncle." Bodleian Library, Tanner Manuscripts, Volume 74, folio 49, Quotations from the letter in the following paragraphs also refer to this source.
23. Nicholls, "George Percy's 'Trewe Relacyon,'" *VMHB*, 113 (2005): 260; Purchas, *Purchas His Pilgrimes*, 19:117.

CHAPTER 5. ENGLISH EXPERIENCES

1. John Chamberlain to Sir Dudley Carleton, June 22, 1616, in *The Letters of John Chamberlain*, ed. Norman Egbert McClure, 2 vols. (Philadelphia: American Philosophical Society, 1939), 2:12.
2. On English life in this period, see Ian Mortimer, *The Time Traveler's Guide to Elizabethan England* (New York: Penguin Books, 2012); Ruth Goodman, *How to Be a Tudor: A Dawn-to-Dusk Guide to Tudor Life* (New York: Liveright, 2016); A. H. Dodd, *Life in Elizabethan England* (London: B. T. Batsford; New York: G. P. Putnam's Sons, 1961).
3. Samantha Bullat gave me invaluable advice on the clothing that Pocahontas wore. See Reynolds, *In Fine Style*; Susan North and Jenny Tiramani, eds., *Seventeenth-Century Women's Dress Patterns*, 2 bks. (London: V&A Publishing, 2011–12); Jones and Stallybrass, *Renaissance Clothing*; Janet Arnold, *Patterns of Fashion: The Cut and Construction of Clothes for Men and Women c. 1560–1620* (London: Macmillan, 1985); Denis Bruna, ed., *Fashioning the Body: An Intimate History of the Silhouette* (New York: Bard Graduate Center, 2015); Rebecca Quinton, *Glasgow Museums: Seventeenth-Century Costume* (London: Unicorn, 2013); C. Willett and Phillis Cunnington, *Handbook of English Costume in the Seventeenth Century* (London: Faber and Faber, 1967): M. Channing Linthicum, *Costume in the Drama of Shakespeare and His Contemporaries* (New York: Russell and Russell, 1963).

4. George Percy, in Purchas, *Purchas His Pilgrimage*, 2nd ed., 768, reprinted in Barbour, *Jamestown Voyages*, 1:146–47; William M. S. Rasmussen and Robert S Tilton, *Pocahontas: Her Life and Legend* (Richmond: Virginia Historical Society, 1994), 32.

5. Martha Carlin, "'What Say You to a Piece of Beef and Mustard?': The Evolution of Public Dining in Medieval and Tudor London," *Huntington Library Quarterly* 71 (2008): 213–15.

6. William Shakespeare, *The Tragedy of Julius Caesar*, act 1, scene 2, line 245. On the English diet, see Joan Thirsk, *Food in Early Modern England: Phases, Fads, Fashions 1500–1760* (London: Hambledon Continuum, 2007); Paul S. Lloyd, *Food and Identity in England, 1540–1640: Eating to Impress* (London: Bloomsbury, 2015); Annette Hope, *Londoners' Larder: English Cuisine from Chaucer to the Present* (Edinburgh: Mainstream, 2005.

7. Lena Cowen Orlin, "Temporary Lives in London Lodgings," *Huntington Library Quarterly* 71 (2008): 219–42, see 219.

8. Henry C. Shelley, *Inns and Taverns of Old London* (Boston: L. C. Page, 1909), 73–77; Duncan Salkeld, "The Bell and the Bel Savage Inns, 1576–1577," *Notes and Queries* 51 (2004): 242–43; Lawrence Manley, "Why Did London Inns Function as Theaters?," *Huntington Library Quarterly* 71 (2008): 181–97.

9. Ben Jonson, *The Staple of News* (1626), act 2, scene 5. See Philip L. Barbour, "Captain John Smith and the London Theater," *Virginia Magazine of History and Biography* 83 (1975): 277–79.

10. H. S. Bennet, *English Books and Readers, 1603–1640* (Cambridge: Cambridge University Press, 1970), 1; Howes, *Annales*, 1002.

11. Jonathan Gil Harris, "Ludgate Time," *Huntington Library Quarterly* 71 (2008): 11–32, quote on 17.

12. On the produce market near St. Paul's, see C. Anne Wilson, *Food and Drink in Britain: From the Stone Age to the 19th Century* (Chicago: Academy Chicago, 1991), 140–41. On Covent Garden's redesign, see Chris R. Kyle, "Remapping London," *Huntington Library Quarterly* 71 (2008): 245–53, esp. 245.

13. Karen Newman, "'Goldsmith's Ware': Equivalence in *A Chaste Maid in Cheapside*," *Huntington Library Quarterly* 71 (2008): 97–113, esp. 103; Dillon, "Clerkenwell and Smithfield"; Butler, "Jonson's London and Its Theatres," 16; Michelle O'Callaghan, "Patrons of the Mermaid Tavern," *Oxford Dictionary of National Biography*, www.oxforddnb.com.

14. Emily Cockayne, *Hubbub: Filth, Noise, and Stench in England, 1600–1740* (New Haven, CT: Yale University Press, 2007).

15. Sarah Fraser, *The Prince Who Would Be King: The Life and Death of Henry Stuart* (London: William Collins, 2017), chaps. 34–35.

16. Alden Vaughan, *Transatlantic Encounters: American Indians in Britain, 1500–1776* (Cambridge: Cambridge University Press, 2006); Coll Thrush, *Indigenous London: Native Travellers at the Heart of Empire* (New Haven, CT: Yale University Press, 2016).

17. Purchas, *Purchas His Pilgrimage*, 2nd ed., 767; Whitaker, "To my verie deere and loving Cosen M. G.," in Hamor, *True Discourse*, 59.

18. Samuel Purchas, *Purchas His Pilgrimage*, 3rd ed. (London, 1617), 954–57; Purchas, *Purchas His Pilgrimes*, 19:117–18.

19. Deborah E. Harkness, *John Dee's Conversations with Angels: Cabala, Alchemy, and the End of Nature* (Cambridge: Cambridge University Press, 1999); David B. Quinn, ed., *The Voyages and Colonising Enterprises of Sir Humphrey Gilbert*, 2 vols. (London: Hakluyt Society, 1940), 1:96–100, 116–17, 167–70, 280; 2:313, 329, 341–46, 483–88; William H. Sherman, "John Dee's Role in Martin Frobisher's Northwest Enterprise," in *Meta Incognita: A Discourse of Discovery*, ed. Thomas H. B. Symons, 2 vols. (Hull, QC: Canadian Museum of Civilization, 1999), 1:283–95.

20. Purchas, *Purchas His Pilgrimes*, 19:118.

21. John Chamberlain to Sir Dudley Carleton, January 18, 1617, in McClure, *Letters of John Chamberlain*, 2:50; Karen Robertson, "Pocahontas at the Masque," *Signs* 21 (1996): 551–83.

22. The description of the masque and accompanying quotes in this and the following paragraphs come from Ben Jonson, *Ben Jonson: The Complete Masques*, ed. Stephen Orgel (New Haven, CT: Yale University Press, 1969), 245–55.

23. Chamberlain to Carleton, January 18, 1617, in McClure, *Letters of John Chamberlain*, 2:49–50.

24. Smith, *Generall Historie*, in Barbour, *Complete Works*, 2:261.

25. Spelman, *Relation of Virginia*, ed. Kupperman, 234; Ian W. Archer, "City and Court Connected: The Material Dimensions of Royal Ceremonial, ca. 1480–1625," *Huntington Library Quarterly* 71 (2008): 157–79, esp. 160–61.

26. John Oglander, *A Royalist's Notebook: The Commonplace Book of Sir John Oglander Kt. of Nunwell*, ed. Francis Bamford (London: Constable, 1936), 193–98.

27. Smith, *Generall Historie*, in Barbour, *Complete Works*, 2:127; Duke of Buckingham to King James I, in *Letters of the Kings of England, Now First Collected from Royal Archives: And Other Authentic Sources, Private as Well as Public*, ed. James Orchard Halliwell-Phillipps (London: Henry Colburn, 1848), 2:254.

28. Smith, *Generall Historie*, in Barbour, *Complete Works*, 2:261.

29. John Smith, *A Description of New England* (London, 1616). See Karen Ordahl Kupperman, "Fear of Hot Climates in the Anglo-American Colonial Experience," *William and Mary Quarterly* 41 (1984): 213–40.

30. Smith, *Description of New England*, in Barbour, *Complete Works*, 1:352; James Phinney Baxter, ed., *Sir Ferdinando Gorges and His Province of Maine*, 3 vols. (Boston: Prince Society, 1890), 1:209.

31. Ralph Davis, *The Rise of the English Shipping Industry in the Seventeenth and Eighteenth Centuries* (New York: St. Martin's, 1962), 228, 230, 235–39; Gillian Cell, *English Enterprise in Newfoundland, 1577–1660* (Toronto: University of Toronto Press, 1969), 53–76, 105, Slany on 54, 60, 71–72, 77–78.

32. I thank Neal Salisbury for sharing his manuscript, "Tisquantum, the Atlantic-Mediterranean, and the Colonization of New England." See Alden T. Vaughan, "Norumbega's Reluctant Guides," in *Transatlantic Encounters*, 57–76.

33. See Emily Rose, "Guest Post: Did Squanto Meet Pocahontas, and What Might They Have Discussed?," *The Junto* (blog), November 21, 2017, http://earlyamericanists.com.

34. I thank Emily Rose for sharing her unpublished article, "The First Advertisement for Virginia"; Virginia Company vs. William Leveson: The Answer of William Leveson to the Bill of Complaint, November 30, 1613, in Kingsbury, *Virginia Company Records*, 3:54–55.

35. Samuel Pepys, *Pepys Ballads*, ed. Hyder Edward Rollins, 8 vols. (Cambridge, MA: Harvard University Press, 1929), 1:24–31; for an image of the ballad as printed and a recording of it, see English Broadside Ballad Archive, University of California at Santa Barbara, http://ebba.english.ucsb.edu.

36. Vaughan, "Powhatans Abroad," 57–59.

37. E. M. Rose, "'Bewitching Lotteries for Virginia,' 1616–21: A List of Sites and Charitable Donations," *Huntington Library Quarterly* 81 (2018): 107–19; Robert C. Johnson, "The Lotteries of the Virginia Company," *Virginia Magazine of History and Biography* 74 (1966): 259–92; Johnson, "The 'Running Lotteries' of the Virginia Company," *Virginia Magazine of History and Biography* 69 (1960): 156–65; Peter Walne, "The 'Running Lottery' of the Virginia Company: In Reading, 1619 and in Chester, 1616," *Virginia Magazine of History and Biography* 70 (1962): 30–34.

38. V. T. Harlow, *Ralegh's Last Voyage* (London: Argonaut, 1932), 24; Philip Edwards, ed., *Last Voyages: Cavendish, Hudson, Ralegh* (Oxford, UK: Clarendon, 1988). On the Virginia Company's funding, see Robert Brenner, *Merchants and Revolution: Commercial Change, Political Conflict, and London's Overseas Traders, 1550–1653* (Princeton, NJ: Princeton University Press, 2003), 97. The Virginia Company's investors and their contributions are in Kingsbury, *Virginia Company Records*, 3:79–90.

39. "The Description of the Ile of Trinidad, the Rich Country of Guiana, and the Mightie River of Orenoco Written by Francis Sparrey Left There by Sir Walter Raleigh, 1595. and in the End Taken by the Spaniards and Sent Prisoner into Spaine, and after long Captivitie Got into England by Great Sute. 1602," in Purchas, *Purchas His Pilgrimes*, 4:1247–50; Joyce Lorimer, introduction to *Sir Walter Ralegh's "Discoverie of Guiana,"* lxxii, Ralegh's mention of Sparry's interrogation in Spain on 268–73; Alden T. Vaughan, "Raleigh's American Interpreters," in *Transatlantic Encounters*, 21–41.

40. John Chamberlain to Sir Dudley Carleton, November 21, 1618, in McClure, *Letters of John Chamberlain*, 2:184–86.

41. Thomas Harriot, *A Briefe and True Report of the Newfound Land of Virginia* (Frankfort: Theodor de Bry, 1590), 16. The English called the entire east coast of North America Virginia, and the Spanish called it La Florida. Ironically, Harriot was said to have died of a cancer on his nose, possibly a result of his smoking. The notes of his doctor, Theodore Mayerne, who was the personal physician to

the king, are reproduced in John W. Shirley, *Thomas Harriot: A Biography* (Oxford, UK: Clarendon, 1983), 433–34.

42. Peter C. Mancall, "Tales Tobacco Told in Sixteenth-Century Europe," *Environmental History* 9 (2004): 648–78; David Harley, "The Beginnings of the Tobacco Controversy: Puritanism, James I, and the Royal Physicians," *Bulletin of the History of Medicine* 67 (1993): 28–50; Jeffrey Knapp, "Elizabethan Tobacco," *Representations* 21 (1988): 26–66; Nicholas Zwager, *Glimpses of Ben Jonson's London* (Amsterdam: Swets and Zeitlinger, 1926), chap. 3.

43. Shepard, *Meanings of Manhood*, 104–5.

44. Thomas Deacon, *Tobacco Tortured; or, The Filthy Fume of Tobacco Refined* (London, 1616); T.W., *The Arraignement and Execution of the Late Traytors* (London, 1606), sig. B2v–B3.

45. John Winthrop, *The Journal of John Winthrop, 1630–1649*, ed. Richard S. Dunn, James Savage, and Laetitia Yeandle (Cambridge, MA: Harvard University Press, 1996), 263.

46. G. R. Batho, "Thomas Harriot and the Northumberland Household" (The Durham Thomas Harriot Seminar Occasional Paper No. 1, 1983), citing Syon House MSS. at Alnwick Castle, X.II.12 (6); Shirley, *Thomas Harriot: A Biography*, 209; John Aubrey, *"Brief Lives," Chiefly of Contemporaries, Set Down by John Aubrey between the Years 1669 and 1696*, ed. Andrew Clark, 2 vols. (Oxford, UK: Clarendon, 1898), 2:181; *The Honesty of Our Age* (London), 25 (1614 edition), 21 (1616 edition); Russell R. Menard, "A Note on Chesapeake Tobacco Prices, 1618–1660," *Virginia Magazine of History and Biography* 84 (1976): 401–10; John Pory to Sir Dudley Carleton, September 30, 1619, *Massachusetts Historical Society Collections*, 4th ser., vol. 9 (1871): 284.

47. Court held February 14, 1625, in *Minutes of the Council and General Court of Colonial Virginia, 1622–1632, 1670–1676*, ed. H. R. McIlwaine (Richmond: Virginia State Library, 1924), 94. See the biography of Thomas Spelman in McCartney, *Virginia Immigrants and Adventurers*, 660.

48. Shirley, *Thomas Harriot: A Biography*, 365.

49. Matthias Schemmel, *The English Galileo: Thomas Harriot's Work on Motion as an Example of Preclassical Mechanics* (New York: Springer, 2008), 15–24. See also the essays in Robert Fox, ed., *Thomas Harriot and His World* (Farnham, UK: Ashgate, 2012); and Shirley, *Thomas Harriot: Renaissance Scientist*.

50. Harriot, *Briefe and True Report*, 25–26.

51. John Smith, "To the Most High and Vertuous Princesse Anne Queene of Great Brittanie," in *Generall Historie*, in Barbour, *Complete Works*, 2:258–60.

52. Smith's account of the meeting and the accompanying quotes in this and the following paragraphs are ibid., 260–62.

53. John Chamberlain to Sir Dudley Carleton, February 22, 1617, in McClure, *Letters of John Chamberlain*, 2:56–57.

54. David R. Ransome, "Pocahontas and the Mission to the Indians," *Virginia Magazine of History and Biography* 99 (1991): 81–94; Peter Walne, "The

Collections for Henrico College," *Virginia Magazine of History and Biography* 80 (1972): 259–66.

55. Robert Heath Hiscock, *A History of the Parish Churches of Gravesend and the Burial Place of Pocahontas* (Gloucester, UK: British Publications, 1961), 22–28.

56. Purchas, *Purchas His Pilgrimes*, 19:118; John Chamberlain to Sir Dudley Carleton, January 18, 1617, in McClure, *Letters of John Chamberlain*, 2:50.

57. Eric Gethyn-Jones, *George Thorpe and the Berkeley Company* (Gloucester, UK: Alan Dutton, 1982), 55–58.

58. Minutes of Virginia Court Meeting, May 11, 1620, in Kingsbury, *Virginia Company Records*, 1:338–39; Whitaker, "To my verie deere and loving Cosen M.G.," in Hamor, *True Discourse*, 59–61. On Gough, see Ransome, "Pocahontas and the Mission to the Indians," *VMHB*, 99 (1991): 88.

59. Minutes of Virginia Court Meeting, June 13, 1621, in Kingsbury, *Virginia Company Records*, 1:496; Ransome, "Pocahontas and the Mission to the Indians," 88–90.

60. Smith, *Generall Historie*, in Barbour, *Complete Works*, 2:384, 386.

CHAPTER 6. VIRGINIA'S TRANSFORMATION

1. John Rolfe to Sir Edwin Sandys, June 8, 1617, in Haile, *Jamestown Narratives*, 887–90.

2. Virginia Company, instructions to George Yeardley, November 18, 1618, in Kingsbury, *Virginia Company Records*, 3:98–104.

3. David R. Ransome, "Wives for Virginia, 1621," *William and Mary Quarterly*, 3rd ser., 48 (1991): 3–18.

4. "The Companies Declaration to the Lord Mayor and Court of Aldermen, Nov. 17, 1619," in Kingsbury, *Virginia Company Records*, 1:21–22; Sir Edwin Sandys to Sir Robert Naunton, January 28, 1620, ibid., 3:259; Great Britain, Privy Council, *Acts of the Privy Council of England, 1619–1621* (London: H.M. Stationery Office, 1930), 118. See Gwenda Morgan and Peter Rushton, *Banishment in the Early Atlantic World: Convicts, Rebels and Slaves* (London: Bloomsbury, 2013), chap. 1; Robert C. Johnson, "The Transportation of Vagrant Children from London to Virginia, 1618–1622," in *Early Stuart Studies*, ed. Howard S. Reinmuth Jr. (Minneapolis: University of Minnesota Press, 1970), 137–51; A. L. Beier, "Social Problems in Elizabethan London," *Journal of Interdisciplinary History* 9 (1978): 203–21.

5. John Donne, *A Sermon upon the VIII Verse of the I Chapter of the Acts of the Apostles Preached to the Honourable Company of the Virginia Plantation 13 Novemb. 1622*, in *Three Sermons upon Special Occasions* (London, 1623), 21–22; John Chamberlain to Sir Dudley Carleton, October 14, 1618, in McClure, *Letters of John Chamberlain*, 2:170.

6. "A Relation from Master John Rolfe, June 15, 1619," in Smith, *Generall Historie*, in Barbour, *Complete Works*, 2:268. There are two versions of this letter with some of the same and some different content. The other is John Rolfe to Sir Edwin Sandys, January 1620, in Kingsbury, *Virginia Company Records*, 3:241–48. The passage about selling men and boys does not appear in the letter to Sandys.

7. Rolfe to Sandys, January 1620, in Kingsbury, *Virginia Company Records*, 243; Engel Sluiter, "New Light on the '20. and Odd Negroes' Arriving in Virginia, August 1619," *William and Mary Quarterly* 54 (1997): 395–98.

8. Brown, *First Republic in America*, 288.

9. Capt. John Martin, "The Manner Howe to Bringe the Indians into Subjection," December 15, 1622, in Kingsbury, *Virginia Company Records*, 3:705; "The Answer of Sir George Yeardly Knight Defendant to the Demands of Capt. John Martin Esquire Complaynant Whereby He Requireth Recompence of Wrongs Donn Him," February 4, 1625, ibid., 4:514; On Martin, see James P. C. Southall, "Captain John Martin of Brandon on the James," *Virginia Magazine of History and Biography* 54 (1946): 21–67.

10. The story of the assembly proceedings and accompanying quotes in this and the following paragraphs come from John Pory, who as colony secretary wrote the official report of the assembly meeting, in Kingsbury, *Virginia Company Records*, 3:153–77. Robert's testimony is on 174–75; John Rolfe's description of it is on 242, and John Pory's letter to Sir Edwin Sandys, January 13, 1620, is on 249–53, quote on 253. The London Company's record of the sentence is ibid., 1:310. Robert Poole's deposition, taken July 13, 1619, is in *Virginia Company Archives: The Ferrar Papers FP 1–FP 2314, Ferrar Print 1–562, 1590–1790*, ed. David Ransome, www.amdigital.co.uk, doc. 113.

11. Rolfe to Sandys, January 1620, in Kingsbury, *Virginia Company Records*, 3:242; Smith, *Generall Historie*, in Barbour, *Complete Works*, 2:304–5. See Greg Koabel, "Youth, Manhood, Political Authority and the Impeachment of the Duke of Buckingham," *Historical Journal* 57 (2014): 595–615.

12. Rolfe to Sandys, January 1620, in Kingsbury, *Virginia Company Records*, 242, 244–45.

13. John Pory to Sir Edwin Sandys, January 13, 1620, in Kingsbury, *Virginia Company Records*, 3:249–53, quote on 253; Rolfe to Sandys, January 1620, ibid., 242, 244–45.

14. "Master Stockam's Relation," in Smith, *Generall Historie*, in Barbour, *Complete Works*, 2:285–86.

15. Rolfe to Sandys, January 1620, in Kingsbury, *Virginia Company Records*, 247.

16. John Pory, *A Geographical Historie of Africa, Written in Arabicke and Italian by John Leo a More, Borne in Granada and Brought Up in Barbarie* (London, 1600). See Natalie Zemon Davis, *Trickster Travels: A Sixteenth-Century Muslim between Worlds* (New York: Hill and Wang, 2006). On Pory's biography, see William S. Powell, *John Pory, 1572–1636* (Chapel Hill: University of North Carolina Press, 1977); for his reputed fondness for alcohol, see 60–61.

17. "Occurrents in Virginia," May 1622, in Kingsbury, *Virginia Company Records*, 3:641–62; and in Purchas, *Purchas His Pilgrimes*, 19:246.

18. "The Observations of Master John Pory, Secretarie of Virginia, in His Travels," in Smith, *Generall Historie*, in Barbour, *Complete Works*, 2:288–89; Virginia General Court meeting, July 10, 1621, in Kingsbury, *Virginia Company Records*, 1:504.

19. "Observations of Master John Pory," in Smith *Generall Historie*, Barbour, *Complete Works*, 2:288–89.

20. Ibid.

21. Ibid. Archer, "Relatyon of the Discovery," in Barbour, *Jamestown Voyages*, 1:80–98. Markham's name is on 81.

22. The story and accompanying quotes in this and the following paragraphs come from "Observations of Master John Pory," in Smith *Generall Historie*, Barbour, *Complete Works*, 2:289–91. On Pory's tenants, see Virginia Council to Virginia Company, January 1622, in Kingsbury, *Virginia Company Records*, 3:585.

23. Helen C. Rountree and Thomas E. Davidson, *Eastern Shore Indians of Virginia and Maryland* (Charlottesville: University of Virginia Press, 1997), 52.

24. Council in Virginia to the Virginia Company in London, January 20, 1623, in Kingsbury, *Virginia Company Records*, 4:10; Stillman Drake and Charles Donald O'Malley, trans., *The Controversy on the Comets of 1618* (Philadelphia: University of Pennsylvania Press, 1960).

25. Virginia Council to Virginia Company, January 1622, Kingsbury, *Virginia Company Records*, 3:584; "Occurrents in Virginia," in Purchas, *Purchas His Pilgrimes*, 19:158.

26. Nicholls, "George Percy's 'Trewe Relacyon,'" *VMHB*, 113 (2005): 261; Council in Virginia, November 11, 1619, in Kingsbury, *Virginia Company Records*, 3:228; Virginia Council to the Virginia Company, January 20, 1623, in Kingsbury, *Virginia Company Records*, 4:10–11; "Voyage of Anthony Chester to Virginia, Made in the Year 1620" (Leiden, 1707), printed in "Two Tragical Events," *William and Mary Quarterly* 9 (1901): 213.

27. Council in Virginia to the Virginia Company in London, January 20, 1623, in Kingsbury, *Virginia Company Records*, 4:11.

28. The Council in Virginia admitted that it had ignored Thomas's warning in a letter sent months after the great attack: Virginia Council to the Virginia Company, January 20, 1623, in Kingsbury, *Virginia Company Records*, 4:10–11.

29. Smith, *Generall Historie*, in Barbour, *Complete Works*, 2:304–5, 308.

30. Virginia Company Preparative Court, April 26, 1623, in Kingsbury, *Virginia Company Records*, 2:532.

31. Smith, *Generall Historie*, in Barbour, *Complete Works*, 2:293–305; "Two Tragical Events," *William and Mary Quarterly* 9 (901): 209–13; Virginia Company, "A Declaration of the State of the Colonie and Affairs in Virginia," 1622, in Kingsbury, *Virginia Company Records*, 3:555. On the attack and its context, see J. Frederick Fausz, "George Thorpe, Nemattanew, and the Powhatan Uprising of 1622," *Virginia Cavalcade*, Winter 1979, 111–17.

32. Smith, *Generall Historie*, in Barbour, *Complete Works*, 2:318.

33. The story and accompanying quotes in this and the following paragraphs come from ibid., 2:309, 312–14, 320–21.

34. Peter Arundel to William Caninge, April 1623, in Kingsbury, *Virginia Company Records*, 4:89; George Sandys to John Ferrar, April 8, 1623, ibid., 4:108.

35. Arundel to Caninge, April 1623, ibid., 4:89.

36. See Fleet's narrative with an introduction in Edward D. Neill, *The Founders of Maryland as Portrayed in Manuscripts, Provincial Records, and Early Documents* (Albany, NY: Joel Munsell, 1876), 9–37.

37. Council in Virginia to the Virginia Company in London, April 4, 1623, in Kingsbury, *Virginia Company Records*, 4:98–99.

38. J. Frederick Fausz, "The Missing Women of Martin's Hundred," *American History* 33 (1998): 56–62.

39. John Chamberlain to Sir Dudley Carleton, July 13, 1622, in McClure, *Letters of John Chamberlain*, 2:445–47; Christopher Brooke, *A Poem on the Late Massacre in Virginia* (London, 1622). On *A Tragedy of the Plantation in Virginia* and *Mourning Virginia*, see The Lost Plays Database: www.lostplays.org.

40. Richard Frethorne to his mother and father, March 20, April 2 and 3, 1623, in Kingsbury, *Virginia Company Records*, 4:58–62. Sandra L. Dahlberg puts his age at twelve: "'Doe Not Forget Me': Richard Frethorne, Indentured Servitude and the English Poor Law of 1601," *Early American Literature* 47 (2012): 1–31; see also Emily Rose, "The Politics of Pathos: Richard Frethorne's Letters Home," in Appelbaum and Sweet, *Envisioning an English Empire*, 92–108.

41. Capt. Nathaniel Butler, "The Unmasked Face of Our Colony in Virginia," in Kingsbury, *Virginia Company Records*, 2:374–76; replies from the colony are in *Journals of the House of Burgesses of Virginia, 1619–1658/59*, ed. H. R. McIlwaine (Richmond: Virginia State Library, 1915), 21–37; Butler's arrival in Virginia was noted by Capt. John Smith, *Generall Historie*, in Barbour, *Complete Works*, 2:318.

42. Virginia General Court meeting, December 8, 1624, in McIlwaine, *Minutes of the Council and General Court of Colonial Virginia*, 29–30.

43. Capt. John Martin, "Howe Virginia May Be Made a Royal Plantation," in Kingsbury, *Virginia Company Records*, 3:707–10.

44. Emily Rose, "The End of the Gamble: The Termination of the Virginia Lotteries in March 1621," *Parliamentary History* 27 (2008): 175–97.

45. Smith, *Generall Historie*, in Barbour, *Complete Works*, 2:327–33.

46. The classic history of these developments is W. F. Craven, *The Dissolution of the Virginia Company: The Failure of a Colonial Experiment* (New York: Oxford University Press, 1932). See also Powell, *John Pory*, 110–23; Brenner, *Merchants and Revolution*, chap. 3. On charges and countercharges within the company, see Extraordinary Court, April 12, 1623, and "The Humble Petition of Sundry the Adventurers and Planters of the Virginia and Summer Ilands Plantations," in Kingsbury, *Virginia Company Records*, 2:346–62, 370–72.

CHAPTER 7. ATLANTIC IDENTITIES

1. Susie M. Ames, *Studies of the Virginia Eastern Shore in the Seventeenth Century* (Richmond, VA: Dietz, 1940), 20–23, 59.

2. Governor Yeardley to Sir Edwin Sandys, 1619, in Kingsbury, *Virginia Company Records*, 3:121; John Rolfe to Sir Edwin Sandys, January 1620, ibid., 3:242. On Grainger, see Johnson, "Transportation of Vagrant Children," in Reinmuth, *Early Stuart Studies*, 148.

3. Virginia General Court, March 7, 1624, in McIlwaine, *Minutes of the Council and General Court of Colonial Virginia*, 48; Virginia General Court, February 5, 1626, ibid., 138; extremely graphic testimony about the adultery was presented by several eyewitnesses, February 19, 1626, ibid., 139–40. On Eppes's reputation and influential friends, see Felix Hull, ed., "The Tufton Manuscripts and the Virginia Connection," *Virginia Magazine of History and Biography* 65 (1957): 313–27, esp. 316.

4. Ames, *Studies of the Virginia Eastern Shore*, chap. 3.

5. Smith, *Generall Historie*, in Barbour, *Complete Works*, 2:290.

6. Nell Marion Nugent, *Cavaliers and Pioneers: Abstracts of Virginia Land Patents and Grants, 1623–1800*, 5 vols. (Richmond, VA: Dietz, 1934), 1:524. On Thomas Savage's descendants, see Martha Bennett Stiles, "Hostage to the Indians," *Virginia Cavalcade* 12 (1962): 5–11.

7. Robert Poole, petition to Gov. Sir Francis Wyatt, February 1624, in Kingsbury, *Virginia Company Records*, 4:457–58.

8. Virginia General Court meeting, December 8, 1624, in McIlwaine, *Minutes of the Council and General Court of Colonial Virginia*, 29–30.

9. J. Frederick Fausz, "Merging and Emerging Worlds: Anglo-Indian Interest Groups and the Development of the Seventeenth-Century Chesapeake," in *Colonial Chesapeake Society*, ed. Lois Green Carr, Philip D. Morgan, and Jean B. Russo (Chapel Hill: University of North Carolina Press, 1988), 63.

10. Capt. Henry Fleet, "A Brief Journal of a Voyage in the Bark Virginia," in Neill, *Founders of Maryland*, 37.

11. Virginia General Court meeting, May 2, 1625, in McIlwaine, *Minutes of the Council and General Court of Colonial Virginia*, 57.

12. Virginia General Court meeting, December 8, 1624, ibid., 30.

13. Virginia General Assembly, October 16, 1629, in McIlwaine, *Journals of the House of Burgesses of Virginia*, 53.

14. Conway Robinson, "Notes from the Council and General Court Records, 1641–1659," *Virginia Magazine of History and Biography* 13 (1906): 394–95; Rountree, *Pocahontas, Powhatan, Opechancanough*, 186, 226.

15. Robert Beverley, *The History and Present State of Virginia*, 1705, ed. Susan Scott Parrish (Chapel Hill: University of North Carolina Press for the Omohundro Institute, 2013), 46–48.

16. G. B. Harrison, ed., *Advice to His Son by Henry Percy, Ninth Earl of Northumberland* (1609; repr., London: E. Benn, 1930), 53; Smith, *Generall Historie*, in Barbour, *Complete Works*, 2:215. On these issues, see Judith Weil, *Service and Dependency in Shakespeare's Plays* (Cambridge: Cambridge University Press, 2005).

17. On John Clark's voyage with the Pilgrims, see William Bradford, *Of Plymouth Plantation, 1620–1647*, ed. Samuel Eliot Morison (New York: Knopf, 1953), 366.

18. Ibid., 80–89, 98–99, 114; Edward Winslow, *"Good News from New England": A Scholarly Edition*, ed. Kelly Wisecup (Amherst: University of Massachusetts Press, 2014), 59–66.

19. Paul E. J. Hammer, "An Elizabethan Spy Who Came In from the Cold: The Return of Anthony Standen to England in 1593," *Historical Research* 65 (1992): 277–95.

20. Smith, *Generall Historie*, in Barbour, *Complete Works*, 2:226.

21. On numbers, see J. B. Gramaye, "Relations of the Christianitie of Africa, and Especially of Barbarie, and Algier," in Purchas, *Purchas His Pilgrimes*, 19:267, 281–82. For a modern discussion of numbers, see Robert C. Davis, *Christian Slaves, Muslim Masters: White Slavery in the Mediterranean, the Barbary Coast, and Italy, 1500–1800* (New York: Palgrave Macmillan, 2003).

22. John Rawlins, *The Famous and Wonderfull Recoverie of a Ship of Bristoll, Called the Exchange, from the Turkish Pirates of Argier* (London, 1622). See Mary C. Fuller, "English Turks and Resistant Travelers: Conversion to Islam and Homosocial Courtship," in *Travel Knowledge: European "Discoveries" in the Early Modern Period*, ed. Ivo Kamps and Jyotsna G. Singh (New York: Palgrave, 2001), 66–73. On the numbers of renegade captains, see Peter Earle, *Corsairs of Malta and Barbary* (Annapolis, MD: United States Naval Institute, 1970), 35.

23. William Shakespeare, *The Tragedy of Hamlet, Prince of Denmark*, act 3, scene 2, lines 253–54.

24. Daniel J. Vitkus presents the plays and the ballads and royal proclamation in *Three Turk Plays from Early Modern England* (New York: Columbia University Press, 2000). On these themes, see the work of Nabil Matar, especially *Islam in Britain, 1668–1685* (Cambridge: Cambridge University Press, 1998) and *Turks, Moors, and Englishmen in the Age of Discovery* (New York: Columbia University Press, 1999); Howard, "Gender on the Periphery," in Clayton Brock, and Forés, *Shakespeare and the Mediterranean*.

25. Adam Knobler, "'Christianized' Muslims in the Middle East (1400–1635)," chap. 6 in *Mythology and Diplomacy in the Age of Exploration* (Leiden: Brill, 2016).

26. Pory, *Geographical Historie of Africa*. On al-Hasan al-Wazzan / Leo Africanus, see N. Davis, *Trickster Travels*; and Oumelbanine Zhiri, "Leo Africanus's *Description of Africa*," in Kamps and Singh, *Travel Knowledge*, 250–66. On Pory's shaping of the *Historie*, see Emily C. Bartels, *Speaking of the Moor: From Alcazar to Othello* (Philadelphia: University of Pennsylvania Press, 2008), chap. 6.

27. María Antonia Garcés, *Cervantes in Algiers: A Captive's Tale* (Nashville, TN: Vanderbilt University Press, 2002).

28. Philip L. Barbour, "Captain John Smith's Route through Turkey and Russia," *William and Mary Quarterly* 14 (1957): 358–69.

29. Smith, *True Travels*, in Barbour, *Complete Works*, 3:141–42, 146–47, 153–213; Philip L. Barbour, "Captain John Smith and the London Stage," *Virginia Magazine of History and Biography* 83 (1975): 277–79. For *The Hungarian Lion*, see The Lost Plays Database: www.lostplays.org.

30. Wingfield, "Discourse," 1:216; White's testimony is in Barbour, *Jamestown Voyages*, 1:145–50; Dale, "To the R. and my most esteemed friend Mr. D. M.," in Hamor, *True Discourse*, 53; Rolfe to Sandys, January 1620, in Kingsbury, *Virginia Company Records*, 245.

31. Philip L. Barbour, "Captain George Kendall: Mutineer or Intelligencer?," *Virginia Magazine of History and Biography* 70 (1962): 297–313. For evidence of other Roman Catholics among the colonists, see Kelso, *Jamestown: The Truth Revealed*, chap. 5.

32. Smith, *Generall Historie*, in Barbour, *Complete Works*, 2:143–45; Nicholls, "George Percy's 'Trewe Relacyon,'" *VMHB*, 113 (2005): 248–50.

33. Virginia Company, *True Declaration*, 36–38, 42.

34. Numbers 13:18–21, 31–33, in *Geneva Bible* (1562); Virginia Company, *True Declaration*, 38; fragment of letter from Sir Thomas Dale to Sir Thomas Smyth, June 1613, in Kingsbury, *Virginia Company Records*, 2:399–400; Rolfe, *True Relation*, 13.

35. "Master Stockams Relation," in Smith, *Generall Historie*, in Barbour, *Complete Works*, 2:285–86; Rolfe to Sandys, January 1620, in Kingsbury, *Virginia Company Records*, 247.

36. Thomas Johnson, *Cornucopiae, or Divers Secrets* (London, 1596), F2.

37. William Haughton, *Englishmen for My Money* (1598), in Lloyd Edward Kermode, *Three Renaissance Usury Plays* (Manchester: Manchester University Press, 2009), act 1, scene 1, lines 6, 28; Lloyd Edward Kermode, *Aliens and Englishmen in Elizabethan Drama* (Cambridge: Cambridge University Press, 2009), 2–3, chap. 5; Crystal Bartolovich, "London's the Thing: Alienation, the Market, and *Englishmen for My Money*," *Huntington Library Quarterly* 71 (2008): 137–56, esp. 145; Anthony Parkhurst, "A letter written to M. Richard Hakluyt of the middle Temple, conteining a report of the true state and commodities of Newfoundland, 1578," in *The Original Writings and Correspondence of the Two Richard Hakluyts*, ed. E. G. R. Taylor (London: Hakluyt Society, 1935), 1:127–34, quote on 133; Smith, *Generall Historie*, in Barbour, *Complete Works*, 2:243–44.

38. James S. Shapiro, *Shakespeare and the Jews* (New York: Columbia University Press, 1996), chap. 1; Stephen Orgel, "Shylock's Tribe," in Clayton, Brock, and Forés, *Shakespeare and the Mediterranean*, 38–53; Ariel Hessayon, "Jews and Crypto-Jews in Sixteenth and Seventeenth Century England," *Cromohs* 16 (2011), www.fupress. net; E. M. Rose, *The Murder of William of Norwich: The Origins of the Blood Libel in Medieval Europe* (Oxford: Oxford University Press, 2015).

39. J. Frederick Fausz and John Kukla, eds., "A Letter of Advice to the Governor of Virginia, 1624," *William and Mary Quarterly* 34 (1977): 104–29, quote on 117.

40. On all these issues, see Matar, *Islam in Britain*, chaps. 1–2, quote on 68; and the essays by Jonathan Bate, Jean Howard, and Gary Taylor in Clayton, Brock, and Forés, *Shakespeare and the Mediterranean*.

41. Luke 16:25, in *Geneva Bible* (1562); John Milton, *A Treatise of Civil Power in Ecclesiastical Causes* (London, 1659), 6.

42. "The Examination of the Blind Boy of Gloucester," in "The Reminiscences of John Louth, Archdeacon of Northamptonshire, Written in the Year 1579," in *Narratives of the Days of the Reformation*, ed. John Gough Nichols (London: Camden Society, 1859), 18–20. See also Barbara Rosen, *Witchcraft in England, 1558–1618* (1969; repr., Amherst: University of Massachusetts Press, 1991), 36–37.

43. See Jeffrey S. Shoulson, *Fictions of Conversion: Jews, Christians, and Cultures of Change in Early Modern England* (Philadelphia: University of Pennsylvania Press, 2013).

44. William M. Kelso, *Jamestown: The Buried Truth* (Charlottesville: University of Virginia Press, 2006), 187–88.

45. Babette M. Levy, "Early Puritanism in the Southern and Island Colonies," *Proceedings of the American Antiquarian Society* 70 (1960): 69–348; John Bennet Boddie, *Seventeenth-Century Isle of Wight County Virginia* (Chicago: Chicago Law Press, 1938), chaps. 2–5; James Horn, "To Parts beyond the Seas," in *"To Make America": European Emigration in the Early Modern Period*, ed. Ida Altman and James Horn (Berkeley: University of California Press, 1991), 86–87, 106–7; Horn, *Adapting to a New World: English Society in the Seventeenth-Century Chesapeake* (Chapel Hill: University of North Carolina Press, 1994), 55–57, 388–94.

46. David Beers Quinn, "Introduction: Prelude to Maryland," in *Early Maryland in a Wider World*, ed. David Beers Quinn (Detroit: Wayne State University Press, 1982), 11–29, quote on 26; Russell R. Menard and Lois Green Carr, "The Lords Baltimore and the Colonization of Maryland," ibid., 167–215, Fleet on 171.

47. Allen Walker, "A Slap's a Slap: General John L. DeWitt and Four Little Words," *The Text Message Blog*, National Archives, November 23, 2013, https://text-message.blogs.archives.gov; Jeremy Treglown, "Sweet Land of Liberty—Lessons from Japanese Internment in the Second World War," *Times Literary Supplement*, April 14, 2017, 16–17; Greg Robinson, *A Tragedy of Democracy: Japanese Confinement in North America* (New York: Columbia University Press, 2009), chaps. 1–2; T. A. Frail, "American Incarceration: The Injustice of Japanese-American Internment Camps Resonates Strongly to This Day," *Smithsonian Magazine*, January 2017, www.smithsonianmag.com.

48. "Fruits of Brainwashing," *New York Times*, January 28, 1954.

49. Chalmers M. Roberts, "The GIs Who Went Red: A Portrait of Poverty, Ignorance, Strife," *Washington Post*, December 29, 1953.

50. Susan L. Carruthers, *Cold War Captives: Imprisonment, Escape, and Brainwashing* (Berkeley: University of California Press, 2009), chap. 5, epilogue.

51. Rountree, *Pocahontas, Powhatan, Opechancanough*, 162; Henry Kamm, "Four Held in Stockholm Reported in Shock," *New York Times*, August 29, 1973;

Kathryn Westcott, "What Is Stockholm Syndrome?," *BBC News Magazine*, August 23, 2013.

52. Jeffrey Toobin, *American Heiress: The Wild Saga of the Kidnapping, Crimes and Trial of Patty Hearst* (New York: Doubleday, 2016), chap. 25.

53. John Locke, *An Essay Concerning Humane Understanding: In Four Books, With Large Additions*, 2nd ed. (London, 1694), chap. 27 ("Of Identity and Diversity"), quotes on 186.

INDEX

Newfoundland, fishing in, 15–16, 127
Newfoundland Company, 128
Newport, Capt. Christopher, 15, 18; arrives with supplies, 33–34; bravado,
 27; crowns Powhatan, 34; fooled by
 Powhatan, 27; gives Thomas Savage to
 Powhatan, 1–3, 26; takes Namontack
 to England, 27
nonage, youth, 4–5, 140, 151

Oglander, Sir John, 126
Opechancanough
 (a.k.a.Mangopeesomon), 21; accepts
 Robert Poole, 3; attack on English
 in Virginia, 157–159; attacks English
 second time, 171; brought to Jamestown as a prisoner, 171; captures Capt.
 John Smith, 21–22; changes name, 158;
 distressed by conflict between Poole
 and Henry Spelman, 145–150; enlists
 Patuxents in plan to kill Thomas
 Savage, 154–157; invites visit by Gov.
 Yeardley, 148; killed by guard, 172;
 returns captive Sara Boyce, 162; sends
 Chauco to Jamestown with peace
 proposal, 162; shows Poole evidence
 that Capt. John Smith's taught
 Powhatans to shoot, 165; stands in for
 Powhatan at meeting, 100; strategy
 toward English, 147, 156–157; takes
 over from Powhatan, 108–109, 141;
 tries to expand influence to the
 Potomac, 153, 159; turns against Poole,
 152; visited by Thomas Rolfe, 171
Orapax, Powhatan's second capital, 37–38,
 100

Pace, Richard, 159
Pacific Ocean, access to, 11, 17, 45, 86–87, 90
Pasptanzie (Patawomeck town): 59, 92–93
Paquiquineo (Don Luís de Velasco), 6–7,
 34, 128, 139, 183–184

Parahunt: attacks settlers, 47; Henry
 Spelman left with, 3, 46–47
Parker, William, 107–108
Parkhurst, Anthony, 183
Patuxets, 173
Peirce, Joan, third wife of John Rolfe, 170
Peirce, Capt. William, paid for Thomas
 Rolfe's passage back to Virginia, 170
Percy, George, 10–11, 18, 21, 25, 28; aids
 in moving party of Pocahontas to
 Brentford, 135; becomes acting gov-
 ernor in Jamestown, 47; description
 of Nemattanew, 158; hesitates to kill
 Paspahegh queen, 61; records deaths
 in first year, 18; on Powhatan tattooing,
 114; on plots to desert Jamestown, 181;
 receives beads and copper on advice
 of Harriot, 28; settlement attempt
 near Nansemonds fails, 45
Percy, Henry, Earl of Northumberland,
 18, 28; consults Harriot on gifts for
 Namontack, 28; on lower orders, 172;
 imprisoned in Tower of London, 135;
 scientific experiments facilitated by
 Harriot, 135
Perkins, Francis, letter intercepted, 87
Perry, William, 159–160
"Perry's Indian": Jamestown spared from
 attack because of, 159; taken to England, 160
Philip II, of Spain, 8
Philip III, of Spain, 11; receives reports
 from inside Jamestown, 87–92
Pocahontas, vii–viii, 1, 6, 13–14; arrives in
 London with Uttamattomakin and
 Mattachanna, 112–113; baptized Rebecca, 102–104; brought to Matchut
 by Dale, 100–102; calls the English
 liars, 137, 175; captured on the Potomac, 93–96; comes to Jamestown
 for Thomas Savage, 34; conversion
 to Christianity, 98–104, 112;

ABOUT THE AUTHOR

KAREN ORDAHL KUPPERMAN specializes in sixteenth- and seventeenth-century Atlantic history. Like this book, much of her work focuses on the very early trial-and-error period of English engagement with America, and it examines the responses and strategies of America's Native people as well as those of European newcomers.